The Chartered
Institute of Mar

# CIM Companion:

# integrated marketing communications

CIM Publishing

**CIM Publishing**

The Chartered Institute of Marketing
Moor Hall
Cookham
Berkshire
SL6 9QH

www.cim.co.uk

First published 2002
© CIM Publishing 2002

Series editors Mark Stuart and John Ling.
Editorial assistant Hannah Williams.

Applications for the copyright holder's written permission to reproduce any part of this publication should be addressed to the Editors at the publisher's address.

The publishers believe that the contents of this book contribute to debate and offer practical advice. No responsibility will be taken by the publishers for any damage or loss arising from following or interpreting the advice given in this publication.

It is the publisher's policy to use paper manufactured from sustainable forests.

**British Library Cataloguing in Publication Data**
A CIP catalogue record for this book can be obtained from the British Library.

ISBN 0 902130 90 0

Printed and bound by The Cromwell Press, Trowbridge, Wiltshire.
Cover design by Marie-Claire Bonhommet.

# contents

# Study guide

This Companion is written to complement the recommended core text by Chris Fill: *Marketing Communications – Contexts, Strategies and Applications, 3rd Edition*, FT Prentice Hall. It aims to offer you support as either an individual or group learner as you move along the road to becoming a competent and proficient marketer. This is a process of learning that has two important elements:

## Understanding marketing concepts and their application

The study text in the following Sessions has been written to highlight the concepts that you will need to grasp as you start to understand the principles of strategic marketing communications, what strategic marketing communications can achieve, and how they are implemented. The material is described briefly and concisely, to enable you to cover a range of key material at the entry point to strategic marketing communications. It does not attempt to be fully comprehensive and you should read widely from other sources. To develop your understanding of the concepts introduced here, your reading should include:

■ Recommended course texts (readings are shown in Table 2 for each of the Sessions in this book).
■ Marketing press and quality national newspapers.
■ More comprehensive marketing textbooks detailed on the module reading list in the syllabus, which provide a wider context for the concepts explained in this Companion and more case studies and examples to illustrate integrated communications in practice.

## Developing the skills to implement marketing activity

Equally important in the journey towards marketing excellence is the acquisition, development and refining of a range of skills that are required by marketers across all industries and sectors. These transferable skills hold the key to the effective implementation of the marketing techniques explored in the study text.

## Using the Companion

You should familiarise yourself with the syllabus for this module, which is shown in Appendix 2. For this Companion, it has been broken down into fifteen Sessions, each of which covers approximately the same proportion of the content. Every student brings with them to their studies different levels of experience – as a customer, from previous studies, and from working in marketing or sales. You should therefore be aware that, whilst you may need to spend considerable time on an unfamiliar area of the syllabus, you may make up this time when studying another area with which you are more familiar.

Each Session has a series of short Activities, which you should try to complete as you work your way through the text. These will help you to check your understanding of the material, and brief feedback is provided at the end of each Session, so that you can compare your answers. Some of these are exam questions from past papers, so you can use them to practise your exam technique.

Each Session also contains a Case Study and a series of related questions. Many of these have been taken from past examination papers, so you can use them to help prepare you for the mini-case within your exam. Try to complete these without reference to your notes, or the Session text, and then compare your answers with some key points that are given at the end of the Companion, in Appendix 1.

At the end of each Session you will also find a number of Projects. These are designed to help you to extend and apply your understanding of the subject covered in the Session. These often take the form of practical activities undertaken in your own organisation or an organisation of your choice. Although not all participants in CIM programmes are working in an organisation, these Projects can still provide valuable learning if interpreted rather than followed to the letter, or if they are applied to organisations that you are aware of.

Finally, you will see that there is a past Examination paper in Appendix 3. This can help you with your revision, examination technique, and preparation. Nearer to your actual examination, allow time to complete the paper under examination conditions – that is, allow three hours of uninterrupted time, and complete the paper without reference to your notes or the study material. When you have completed the exercise, you can compare your answers to the notes in Appendix 4. If either your approach to the exercise or the comparison of your answers highlight areas of particular weakness, you should refer back to the text and re-read the relevant Session, together with the chapters of the supporting textbook.

This Companion's structure and content follows the syllabus order, as this module follows a standard 'process' which in itself is logical in its 'flow'.

# Table 1 – Web sites

| | |
|---|---|
| www.connectedinmarketing.com | |
| www.connectedinmarketing.com/cim/index.cfm | |
| www.adslogans.co.uk | Online database of advertising slogans enabling marketers to check whether a slogan is already in use. |
| www.ipa.co.uk | Institute of Practitioners in Advertising. |
| www.asa.org.uk | Advertising Standards Agency. |
| www.spca.org.uk | The Marketing Communications Consultants Association. |
| www.isp.org.uk | The Institute of Sales Promotion. |
| www.ppa.co.uk | Periodical Publishers Association. |
| www.adassoc.org.uk | Advertising Association. |
| www.new-marketing.org | Research updates into new marketing issues, customer segmentation and repercussions for marketing practitioners. |
| www.e-bulletin.com | Guide to exhibitions, events and resources. |
| www.venuefinder.com | International venue and event suppliers directory. |
| www.europa.eu.int | European Union online. |
| www.wapforum.org | Industry Association responsible for creating the standards for WAP (Wireless Application Protocol). |
| www.prnewswire.co.uk | UK media monitoring service – reviews mentions in all media types (print, online publications and broadcast). |
| www.keynote.co.uk | Market research reports. |
| www.verdict.co.uk | Retail research reports. |
| www.datamonitor.com | Market analysis providing global data collection and in-depth analysis across any industry. |
| www.store.eiu.com | Economist Intelligence Unit, providing country-specific global business analysis. |
| www.mintel.com | Consumer market research. |
| www.royalmail.co.uk | General marketing advice and information. |
| www.ft.com | Financial Times online newspaper and archives (subscription based). |
| www.afxpress.com | Business news plus industry trends. |
| www.statistics.gov.uk | Detailed information on a variety of consumer demographics from the UK Government Statistics Office. |
| www.worldmarketing.org | World Marketing Association. |
| www.accountingweb.co.uk | Provides the latest financial news, company information, taxation guides and other financial matters. |

| www.financewise.com | Specialist index of web sites providing links to information on all aspects of finance (registration required). |
|---|---|
| http://web.utk.edu/~jwachowi/wacho_world.html | Exhaustive listing of web financial resources presented with a student perspective. |
| www.bized.ac.uk | Contains a complete example of a company called Cameron Balloons complete with finances. Can be used to illustrate all the basic principles of financial decisions made in this Companion. |
| www.amazon.co.uk | Classic example of groundbreaking online customer service and marketing orientation in practice. |
| www.johnsonandjohnson.com | An example of a 'credo' and its documented influence on the activities of this global corporation. |
| www.mckinseyquarterly.com | Free full text articles on strategy issues from one of the world's premier business journals. |
| www.strategy-business.com | Online journal on the topic of business strategy, with good search facilities. |
| www.virgin.com | A well-known successful example of unrelated diversification. |
| www.cbi.org.uk/innovation/index.html | Information on innovation in industry. |
| www.marketing.haynet.com | Useful notes on the preparation of marketing plans, and access to research data. |
| www.hbsp.harvard.edu | Free abstracts from Harvard Business Review articles. |
| http://wps.prenhall.com/ema_uk_he_fill_markcomm_3/0,4005,129377-,00.html | Student Resource site for main text – Chris Fill: *Marketing Communications – Contexts, Strategies and Applications.* |

# Table 2 – Background reading

The following references are suggested background readings for each Session. It is suggested that the student undertake this reading before studying the relevant Companion Session.

| Session | Reading from Core Text: Chris Fill: Marketing Communications – Contexts, Strategies and Applications, 3rd Edition, FT Prentice Hall. |
|---|---|
| Session 1 | Chapter 1 – An introduction to marketing communication. |
| Session 2 | Chapter 6 – Ethics in marketing communications. |
| Session 3 | Chapter 2 – Communication theory. |
| Session 4 | Chapter 7 – Internal marketing communications.<br>Chapter 8 – Financial resources.<br>Chapter 9 – Environmental influences on marketing communications.<br>Chapter 10 – Stakeholders, supply chains, and inter-organisational relationships.<br>Chapter 11 – The communications industry. |
| Session 5 | Chapter 12 – Marketing communications strategies and planning.<br>Chapter 19 – Integrated marketing communication. |
| Session 6 | Chapter 3 – Understanding how customers process information.<br>Chapter 4 – Customer decision-making. |
| Session 7 | Chapter 5 – Purpose and audiences.<br>Chapter 13 – Promotional objectives and positioning. |
| Session 8 | Chapter 12 – Marketing communications strategies and planning.<br>Chapter 15 – Business-to-business marketing communications.<br>Chapter 16 – Corporate identity and reputation.<br>Chapter 18 – Interactive communication strategy. |
| Session 9 | Chapter 19 – Integrated marketing communication.<br>Chapter 20 – Advertising – how it might work.<br>Chapter 21 – Advertising messages and creative approaches.<br>Chapter 22 – Media and media planning – delivering the message. |
| Session 10 | Chapter 23 – Sales promotion.<br>Chapter 24 – Sales promotion techniques.<br>Chapter 25 – Online marketing communications.<br>Chapter 26 – Public relations.<br>Chapter 27 – Sponsorship.<br>Chapter 28 – Direct marketing.<br>Chapter 29 – Personal selling.<br>Chapter 30 – Exhibitions, packaging and field marketing. |
| Session 11 | Chapter 8 – Financial resources. |
| Session 12 | Chapter 14 – Branding and the role of marketing communications. |
| Session 13 | Chapter 31 – Evaluating marketing communications. |
| Session 14 | Chapter 31 – Evaluating marketing communications. |
| Session 15 | Chapter 17 – Marketing communication across borders. |

# Table 3 – Marketing models

The text in the Companion Sessions refer to appropriate models but does not reproduce these as they can be seen in the core textbooks. The references for these are supplied in the following table. Please note that this does not necessarily represent the full range of models that you will need to study for your exam or assessment.

| Session | Marketing Model | Reference |
|---|---|---|
| Session 1 | ■ The marketing communications mix<br>■ Above- and below-the-line communications | ■ Page 11<br>■ Page 15 |
| Session 2 | ■ No specific models. | |
| Session 3 | ■ Linear model of communication<br>■ Source characteristics<br>■ Innovation decision process of adoption | ■ Page 32<br>■ Page 36<br>■ Page 44 |
| Session 4 | ■ Impact of advertising on employees<br>■ Example stakeholder map<br>■ Example marketing channel | ■ Page 181<br>■ Page 239<br>■ Page 245 |
| Session 5 | ■ Model of integrated marketing communications | ■ Page 477 |
| Session 6 | ■ Elements of information processing<br>■ Three component attitude model<br>■ Buyer decision process<br>■ Three phases of individual involvement and attitude development<br>■ Promotional strategies for different levels of involvement | ■ Page 59<br>■ Page 76<br>■ Page 91<br>■ Page 97<br><br>■ Page 105 |

| Session | Marketing Model | Reference |
|---|---|---|
| **Session 7** | ■ Traditional activities associated with the PLC<br>■ Awareness Grid<br>■ Perceptual Map | ■ Page 138<br><br>■ Page 315<br>■ Page 326 |
| **Session 8** | ■ FCB Grid<br>■ Rossiter Percy Grid<br>■ Direction of communication of a profile strategy<br>■ Marketing Communications Planning framework<br>■ Corporate perception gap<br>■ Corporate identity management process | ■ Page 289<br>■ Page 290<br>■ Page 294<br><br>■ Page 300<br><br>■ Page 387<br>■ Page 398 |
| **Session 9** | ■ Cognitive processing model<br>■ Message Tactics<br>■ Media scheduling | ■ Page 495<br>■ Pages 525 & 526<br>■ Page 551 |
| **Session 10** | ■ No specific models. | |
| **Session 11** | ■ Gaining market share by<br>■ increasing adspend | ■ Page 206 |
| **Session 12** | ■ No specific models. | |
| **Session 13** | ■ No specific models. | |
| **Session 14** | ■ No specific models. | |
| **Session 15** | ■ No specific models. | |

# Session 1

# Strategic marketing communications – marketing and corporate communications

## Introduction

This Session introduces marketing communications at a strategic level, and looks at the tools that contribute to its success or failure. We consider the overall role of promotion in helping to build relationships with all stakeholders, and also take a look at each element of the promotional mix in terms of its effectiveness in various situations.

---

### LEARNING OUTCOMES

At the end of this Session you will be able to:

■ Explain promotion's role in the marketing mix.

■ Consider the scope and potential impact of marketing communications.

■ Identify the key characteristics of each communication tool.

■ Examine the effectiveness of each communication tool.

■ Explore communication's role in developing and maintaining relationships with stakeholders of the organisation.

---

## The role of promotion in the marketing mix

Marketing promotion is the process through which we communicate the rest of the marketing mix. Having made the strategic decisions about product, price and distribution, promotion is used to attract the customers and keep them loyal to the brand.

The term promotion has misled many professionals and is now referred to as 'marketing communications' so as not to get mixed up with sales promotion, one medium used for encouraging consumer purchase.

Promotional plans (marketing communication plans) are designed to fulfil certain objectives such as re-positioning the brand or launching a new product. The plans are developed using a number of media in an integrated way, so that the whole is greater than the sum of the parts.

Marketing Communications media may be clustered around an event, such as an exhibition or seasonal occasions like Christmas or Valentine's Day. There needs to be one central idea or theme to the promotional campaign, giving it a competitive advantage.

Visit the Pizza Express web site: pizzaexpress.co.uk. The site clusters a number of different promotional opportunities on the home page creating immediate involvement. Once a customer becomes a member, it makes it easier to attract them to other products and services. With this as a central theme, all promotional media can reinforce the same messages; in the restaurant, promotional material can encourage you to use the web site, attend jazz events and become a member or even buy the membership as a present for a friend. Each idea builds on the next and creates a 'whole brand experience' for the consumer.

The different elements of marketing communications include:

- Personal selling.
- Advertising.
- Sales promotion.
- Sponsorship.
- Publicity.
- Point of purchase.
- Direct mail.
- Exhibitions.
- Events.
- E-Marketing.

Other elements of the marketing mix, such as packaging, also communicate with the customer; however, the primary tools are shown above.

Each promotional tool has different capacities to communicate and to achieve different objectives. Using the buying process, purchase decisions can be tracked. For example, advertising is more effective at creating awareness and sales promotion in encouraging trial purchase.

---

**Activity 1.1**

Using the AIDA model (Attention Interest Desire Action), describe the effectiveness of the promotional tools at achieving different objectives throughout the communication process.

---

## Marketing tools and their potential impact

Traditionally the main marketing tools were advertising, sales promotion, public relations and personal selling and were referred to as the promotional mix. Major changes have occurred over the last 10 years; new media has proliferated and competition has increased, so organisations are constantly looking for new fresh mixes to attract customers.

Originally communications were split into above the line – paid-for advertising, and below the line, such as publicity and PR. These terms are rarely used these days as most media has a cost; with the proliferation of agencies offering a 'one-stop-shop' for all types of media, the more common terms are media campaigns including a whole spectrum of different tools.

### Advertising

This is a non-personal communication; it is often hard to target to specific segments except in the case of special interest groups, such as geographical or sporting magazines. Advertising can create awareness; however, it falls short of encouraging immediate action and is unable to carry the detailed information needed for immediate purchase.

Advertising can be international, national or local and placed in newspapers, magazines, cinemas, TV and radio. All of these different media offer different opportunities and access to target audiences, and a mix of advertising across a number of media is often more successful due to the repetitive messages received by the consumer, building customer confidence.

11

## Sales promotion

This tool is often used to encourage trial of a new product or stimulate usage during a seasonal low. Its philosophy is to provide value added, such as buy one get one free, competitions and prizes and free gifts.

It is generally cheaper than advertising and much more targeted at the consumer.

## Personal selling

Most often used in retail or business-to-business marketing, face-to-face selling or telephone marketing creates a short- or long-term relationship with the customer in order to accomplish a sale or achieve a sales lead to be followed up by a more experienced salesperson. This direct form of communication can use demonstration of the product, persuasion and negotiating techniques to sell the product.

## Public relations

Public relations use the press to raise the profile and instil third party credibility in the public; this method is used to great effect by the government to change attitudes and win favour through news programmes and newspapers. The media is not paid for; however, the agencies are costly, and media attention is not always forthcoming and may need to be carefully planned.

Other tools used by public relations are events such as press conferences, sponsorship and lobbying.

## Direct marketing

Direct marketing has become popular because of its ability to deliver personalised messages to specific groups of individuals. Direct marketing tries to build a direct relationship with the customer and requires a high cost in researching an up-to-date database of named contacts. These contacts can be accrued from other marketing communication activities such as promotional prizes where customers have to submit personal details.

Promotional tools need to be selected dependent on the industry sector, the degree of control needed over the delivery of the message and the financial resources available to achieve the objectives.

---

### Activity 1.2

Taking a current campaign from the media, collect data on the different promotional tools to see how the campaign is integrated and try to determine the likely objectives.

How effective do you think the campaign will be?

---

# Characteristics of the elements of the communications mix

The characteristics of the various elements of the communications mix give us valuable information about the appropriateness of mixing different activities to achieve specific, measurable marketing communications objectives.

## Personal selling

Organisations differ as to the types of personal selling employed, depending on the complexity of the products and services. In the retail business the trend has been for goods to sell themselves through high brand visibility and for retail staff to support the process, whilst not being experts.

The skill of the salesperson changes when we look at the business-to-business market, where sales can either be the job of an 'order taker' or an 'order getter' – someone who demonstrates the product and persuades the customer to buy. In some markets, such as the travel business, 'order collectors' gather orders over the phone, supported by sales personnel who process the information.

The skills required vary with the value and complexity of the product and the culture of the industry sector.

## Sponsorship

Sponsorship can be beneficial if the organisations want to communicate with a number of different stakeholder groups. The brand association helps organisations re-position themselves and requires the brand values to reinforce one another to be successful.

There are a number of different types of sponsorship:

- Arts
- Sport
- Heritage
- Charity
- Conservation

Sport has historically attracted large audiences and major TV coverage. Tag Heuer, the Swiss watch company, have positioned their brand as a sports watch and therefore 'timed' events such as Formula 1 racing, the America's Cup yachting event and skiing events provide the perfect opportunity to align the brand with their major target audience.

## Advertising

There are six main categories of advertising:

- Broadcast
- Print
- Outdoor
- In-store
- E-marketing
- Product placement

There are a huge number of media vehicles, which can be used in an integrated way to gain the best coverage. For example, a campaign to create awareness of a new exhibition at a museum can use a mixture of posters, adverts, print media, e-marketing and broadcasting opportunities. Advertising can be expensive because of the design and production costs, while the ability to convey information is limited.

## Public relations

Organisations use public relations to raise their profile and instil confidence. This tool can be used to communicate with a number of different stakeholders to achieve various objectives. For example, press campaigns can be used to lobby the government to change attitudes towards issues of public interest, whereas consumer organisations use the press to launch new products and gain third party endorsement for their goods.

Public relations should be a planned activity although often it's difficult to control the messages that the press choose to transmit. The cost of using an external agency is high, although they usually have the skills and the relationships to create greater coverage than internal PR personnel.

## Sales promotion

Sales promotion is used to encourage trial of a new product and increase usage. One of the main objectives is also to create brand loyalty so that the sales do not diminish after the promotion has ended. Sales promotions can be directed at dealers to encourage sales and stimulate activity.

Methods of sales promotion include:

- Coupons
- Competitions

- Buy one get one free
- Samples
- Refunds
- Free gifts

Sales promotion is often used at the introductory stage of the product life cycle and to stimulate further usage at the mature stage. The major objectives of advertising are to inform, differentiate, remind and persuade the target audience. The tool gives marketers control over the message and the environment in which it is transmitted.

### Direct marketing

Direct marketing is used to create relationships with the target audience. This is not a mass audience tool and requires organisations to develop customer profiles so that targeted media can be addressed to individuals, building a two-way communication.

For example, a sales promotion such as a competition seeks to collect profiling information for a database that can then be used to contact targets directly through a mailing campaign. The Internet has also created a greater opportunity for interactive communications and direct marketing through the collection of personal information.

---

**Activity 1.3**

Develop a mini campaign to promote a new product that waters your garden while you are away. It's a reasonably priced product available through mail order or over the web.

Who are the target audience and how can you communicate with them directly?

---

## The purpose and effectiveness of each communication tool

The effectiveness of marketing communication tools to achieve given objectives depends on the type of product, the industry sector and whether it is consumer or business-to-business marketing.

The following objectives and the likely match with communication tools are described overleaf:

## Product launches

Launching a new FMCG (Fast Moving Consumer Goods) product, such as a new chocolate bar, is often achieved through TV and point of sale advertising. This links with the spontaneous purchase of confectionary products. Shelf space is vital in newsagents, confectioners and supermarkets, preferably near the till where impulse purchase is predominant.

In the business-to-business market, launching a new product is often achieved by winning trust through credibility; therefore, an emphasis on press relations and launch events may be essential. Often companies have a direct sales force that also needs to be briefed internally, and this requires extensive briefings and internal launches to take place. In the case of the pharmaceutical industry, to launch a new medical product requires an even greater emphasis on research and development results, often launched at a congress sponsored by the company brand. This ensures that opinion formers are the first to know about the product so that they can directly influence the achievement of market share.

## Re-positioning

The re-positioning of a brand often coincides with a re-branding exercise to change attitudes towards the organisation in the marketplace. This may be driven by loss of market share or the launch of a new range of products and services. Strategically re-positioning is a response to competition and the need to find a gap in the market where the organisation can gain competitive advantage.

Depending on the type of product re-packaging is essential alongside a complete revamp of all visual materials, including the organisational environment. BT undertook a major overhaul of their brand in the 1980s – it was a drive to revitalise the brand in advance of the telecommunications explosion. This included new products and a complete re-branding and re-structuring of the business.

Kellogg's, however, re-positioned Cornflakes as a late night snack without re-branding; this is an example of creating further usage of an existing product.

## Niche marketing

New market segments tend to be homogeneous groups that usually have dedicated magazines and events that marketers can use to create direct relationships. Take for example the motorbike market. There are a number of national events organised by associations and bike clubs, in addition to regional events hosted by sub-divisions of the clubs. All the clubs have events and regional magazines, and as a small market they all know one another.

The events give companies opportunities to set up small exhibition stands, give out leaflets, sponsor events and promotional materials and advertise in the national and regional magazines. Local bike shops are usually happy to co-operate with joint marketing and within a short space of time direct relationships can be achieved with the target audience.

Web sites can also be a useful tool, especially if they are linked directly to all the clubs and regional bike shops.

**Achieving market share**

Selling more products to your existing market is linked to gaining further distribution and influencing other buying segments. In the business-to-business market, this objective requires a combination of motivating the sales channels to sell one product, whether that be direct sales or through an intermediary and influencing new buying groups through direct marketing.

Sales incentives, corporate hospitality and promotions are often used to motivate additional sales. Direct marketing can support this process by gaining sales leads to be followed up by sales staff.

To sell more products in the FMCG market, sales promotions can be used to stimulate purchase, such as 'buy one get one free', competitions and prizes.

There are various ways of integrating communications to achieve given objectives, and the effectiveness will also rely on the timing of the execution and the quality of the communication, plus the skill of determining the customer profile. It is complex to design effective communications, and often organisations have to risk trying different mixes to ascertain which tools gain the most attention in a busy marketplace.

---

**Activity 1.4**

Develop a number of SWOT (Strengths, Weaknesses, Opportunities and Threats) analyses highlighting the Strengths and Weaknesses of using advertising and events as communication tools for the launch of new high performance car.

---

## Communicating with customers, channel members and other stakeholders

Strategically the decisions concerning the combination of marketing communications for a given campaign are centred on the target audience. Depending on the objectives of the campaign and whether the organisation is trying to reach consumers, business-to-business or other stakeholders is key to the appropriate communications mix.

Stakeholders have very different interests and therefore require different messages and forms of communication. The added complexity is dependent on the type of product or service and the need to deliver more or less information. The level of involvement of the purchase and whether risks are high or low also plays a role in the decision-making process.

## Push v pull strategies

This means promoting the product or service to the next link in the distribution chain, selling hard to the resellers and incentivising them to sell your product in preference to the competition, hence pushing the product through to the customer. Pull strategies involve focusing the marketing communications on the consumer and creating greater demand through the distribution chain. In fact most organisations need to communicate to all members of the sales channel, and distributors will be heavily influenced to stock a product if they think there is a major advertising campaign that will create demand.

## Stakeholders

Stakeholders are anyone who has an interest in the way an organisation provides products and services and their success and failures.

Analysing the stakeholders' needs is a complex job. Mapping stakeholders and identifying key relationships is an important piece of research for marketers. Take for example an organisation that provides road maintenance. They will be contracted through a tendering process to the local authority's traffic department. Once the bid has been won, a number of different stakeholders have expectations that need to be met:

- Central government road safety standards and material specifications.
- General public who are using the roads whilst they are being maintained and want minimum congestion.
- The local authority for reliability and delivery within budget.
- The supply organisation to work within the tender specifications and provide a reliable, safe service.
- The shareholders and investors to gain a return on their investment.
- Suppliers of raw materials and payment terms.

All these stakeholders have interests that need to be satisfied, and all require different forms of communications. The shareholders will get an annual report giving an overview of achievements, central government will receive proposals and presentations for approval of specifications, suppliers may use the web site to gain confidence about likely payment of bills, and of course the tender document and associated promotional materials wins the contract. In this example we can see that various needs are identified and appropriate levels of communication are designed to satisfy all interested parties.

In the above example, communication is explained as any form of communication that is directed at a target audience and not just the traditional promotional tools. All communications need to be consistent and support the corporate brand, giving the same messages about brand values and corporate culture.

---

**Activity 1.5**

Design a presentation to your manager detailing the various stakeholders interested in your business and how you currently communicate with them.

Make recommendations for improvement.

---

# Case Study – Dutton Engineering

During the 1990s Dutton Engineering's impressive growth was based on a strategy that was focused on the development and maintenance of strong customer relationships. Rather than spend money speculating about the generation of new customers, Dutton's policy has been to invest and build relationships with current customers.

Dutton manufacture steel and aluminium components, and in order to help realise their strategy they removed their middle management and devolved responsibility to teams of production oriented personnel, who focus upon their clients' total requirements. Clients talk directly to these 'Production Cells' who are empowered to make decisions and manage all aspects of their clients' requirements. There are no appointed cell leaders, managers or even secretaries, as each cell manages itself organically and recruits its own new staff.

The role of senior management has been to manage time and resources through the use of management information systems. They are able to identify areas across and within Production Cells where productivity might be improved, and help ensure that 85% of the man hours in each Production Cell are used to generate revenue. As a result of this approach, revenue has doubled to £2.3m, profits are stable at 6.5% and sales per worker are double that of the national average in the sector, yet staff numbers have remained relatively stable.

Not surprisingly, Dutton has become the centre of attention for its innovative and seemingly successful approach.

The company's success has been built around 42 client companies, some of whom are very loyal. Part of the company's philosophy has been 'to meet and beat customers' expectations', and the attitude of staff in each Production Cell reflects this perspective. Through high levels of quality production and customer involvement, new orders have been won. However, the growth experienced to date has been based on new orders from existing clients and very little new business has been acquired. Senior management are regarded (by the Production Cells) as responsible for generating new customers, yet they see their role as managing and teaching the 'Dutton Way'.

Little effort appears to have been made to attract new customers and there is no Marketing Department or sales force. These are costs that do not fit the current culture and are regarded as activities that would add little value and merely create high overheads. The company currently outsources transport, cleaning and payroll, so outsourcing a sales operation would be a compatible activity.

There has been little planned use of marketing and/or corporate communications, and the primary emphasis has been on strong word-of-mouth communications, supported by some limited public relations activities. However, a rudimentary web site, some use of telemarketing, the unplanned use of some out-of-date sales literature and attendance at exhibitions constitutes the main thrust of the communications to date. Therefore, the organisation needs to address the balance of its current customer portfolio and attract new clients if it is to achieve ambitious growth targets, which it aims to accomplish in the first few years of the new millennium.

**Source:** *Integrated Marketing Communications Examination Paper*, December 1999.

---

**Questions**

1. Summarise Dutton Engineering's current situation from a communications perspective.

2. Identify the communications tools currently used by the company, and suggest how these might be changed to communicate with all audiences.

## SUMMARY OF KEY POINTS

In this Session, we have introduced the communications mix, and covered the following key points:

- Marketing communications play a key role in the marketing mix, attracting customers and keeping them loyal to the brand.

- The different elements of the marketing communications mix include:
  - Personal selling
  - Advertising
  - Sales promotion
  - Sponsorship
  - Publicity
  - Point of purchase
  - Direct mail
  - Exhibitions
  - Events
  - E-Marketing

- Each tool plays a different role, and is used under different circumstances.

## Improving and developing own learning

The following projects are designed to help you develop your knowledge and skills further by carrying out some research yourself. Feedback is not provided for this type of learning because there are no 'answers' to be found, but you may wish to discuss your findings with colleagues and fellow students.

### Project A

Talk to your colleagues in the marketing department and analyse the promotional mix currently used for one of your products or services.

How might this be improved?

---

**Project B**

Identify and examine one of your organisation's recent promotional campaigns.

Compare its objective with the mix of promotional tools used.

How appropriate were these tools for the purpose?

Did the campaign achieve its objectives?

---

**Project C**

Identify the key stakeholders of your organisation.

How does your organisation communicate with them at the moment?

---

## Feedback to activities

### Activity 1.1

| | |
|---|---|
| Personal selling | Action, purchase, negotiation. |
| Sales promotion | Trial purchase, encourage usage. |
| Sponsorship | Align with other brands, hospitality. |
| Publicity | Create third part credibility. |
| Point of purchase | Information. |
| Direct mail | Creating sales leads. |
| Exhibitions | Face to face relationships. |
| Events | Rewards, motivation, publicity. |
| E-Marketing | E-commerce, advertising, relationship building. |

### Activity 1.2

Campaigns are often created to launch new products or the re-positioning of a mature brand. The choice of tools depends on whether the brand is already established in the marketplace, the complexity of sale and the value and market sector of the goods.

### Activity 1.3

Special interest groups are easy to target through recognised media. The national press on a Sunday often have inserts in their magazines, and in the spring there is often a gardening supplement. National databases exist that can be purchased or used to target gardeners and other interest groups. Joint promotions with other garden suppliers may also be a possibility.

**Activity 1.4**

| Advertising | |
|---|---|
| **Strengths**<br>Advertising gains immediate awareness. | **Weaknesses**<br>Aimed at a mass market, little possibility of relationship building. |
| **Opportunities**<br>Innovative ads can create immediate positioning in a busy market and highlight competitive advantage. | **Threats**<br>Advertising is a high cost activity and relies on the creative designers to come up with an innovative concept. |

| Events | |
|---|---|
| **Strengths**<br>Creates interest with specific target audience. | **Weaknesses**<br>High cost activity. |
| **Opportunities**<br>Attracts PR and third party credibility. | **Threats**<br>Highly visible to the competition. |

**Activity 1.5**

For each business sector the needs vary; however, here is a generic list of stakeholders for the telecommunications industry and possible communication options:

| Stakeholders | Communications |
|---|---|
| Consumers | Advertising, PR, Sales Promotions, Direct Marketing |
| Oftel | Lobbying, PR, presentations, papers |
| Suppliers | Web site, PR |
| Competitors | Exhibitions, PR, web site |
| Media | Press releases, press launches, TV appearances |
| Business | Personal selling, promotional materials, web site |
| Investors | PR, annual report, AGM |

# Session 2

# Ethical influences on communications and the role of social responsibility

## Introduction

This Session considers the main ethical issues surrounding marketing communications activity, and looks at frameworks organisations can use to help think through ethical considerations when planning their communications activities. It also looks at the role of social responsibility in communications.

---

### LEARNING OUTCOMES

At the end of this Session you will be able to:

- Understand how ethical issues impact on marketing communications.

- Use various models to help assess ethical issues when planning marketing communications.

- Explain social responsibility and its role in marketing communications.

---

## The impact of ethical considerations on marketing communications

Ethics is about what is right or wrong. Where should the line be drawn between them? How should these judgements be made? Whose values should be applied?

Views on business ethics are as diverse as people's views on any other moral issues. At one extreme there is the free-market view which says that everybody benefits if businesses are successful (through employment, taxes etc.) and that consumers force self-regulation on business by 'voting' with their wallets and purses. At the other extreme is the interventionist, regulatory approach which says that state controls must be in place to stop businesses abusing their power. A middle ground suggests that there should be controls, but these should be through voluntary, self-regulating codes of conduct rather than state-imposed. The 1998 Ethical Trade Initiative, which was a response to accusations of exploitation of workers from less developed countries, attempts to implement voluntary codes of labour practice for producers. However many major UK companies have refused to join it, for various reasons.

Thinking about these issues in relation to communications forces marketers to address some challenging questions:

25

- Are marketing communications in themselves unethical?
- What are the ethical aspects of employing various promotional techniques?
- Should there be restrictions on the way that communications are used to promote certain products or to target certain market segments?
- What is the role of communications when organisations are accused of using unethical business practices?

We will consider these issues in this and the following section.

## Are marketing communications unethical?

Marketing communications have sometimes been accused of being intrinsically 'bad'. From a societal point of view they are alleged to encourage materialism, greed, selfishness and aspirations beyond the reach of many people. Crime may be one result. A different view is that these communications are beneficial and a requirement of a healthy market economy. They promote choice and underpin the concept of satisfying customer needs. Consumer sovereignty – the power of the consumer in the marketplace – is preferable to an interventionist approach. You must form your own opinion, but if you agree with the first view you may be in the wrong business!

A different criticism is that communications are one-sided, giving at best a biased view, and often a misleading one. Marketers are out to manipulate a gullible public's view and obfuscate the arguments through the use of 'spin' and deception.

The argument that marketing communications are one-sided is generally a true one, but is this not, again, an outcome of the consumer-led approach? Marketers will put forward one view of a product or service, and potential customers must weigh this up against alternative offerings. The consumer, of course, has the ultimate power – buying or not buying, recommending or not recommending etc. To some extent *caveat emptor* – let the buyer beware – still applies. But the rise of **consumerism** over the past few decades has tipped the scale far more in favour of the buyer. A huge body of rules and regulations, emanating from diverse sources and with varying degrees of weight, now exists to protect the consumer one way or another. For example:

- Trade Descriptions Act (1968)
- Data Protection Act (1984)
- European Data Protection Act (1999)
- The British Code of Advertising Practice

■ Control of Misleading Advertisements Regulations 1988

■ The ITC Code of Advertising Standards and Practice

■ The Code of Sale Promotion Practice

and many more.

Despite all this, ethical boundaries are constantly pushed against, and sometimes transgressed. The 1980s 'pensions mis-selling' debacle left many people with inappropriate products, despite the high level of regulation of the financial services industry, as a result of dubious personal selling practices. Some utility regulators have been accused of using unethical doorstep, telephone and written means to persuade consumers to change suppliers, while some communications are launched with an apparent intention to shock and thus gain attention. For example the 'fcuk' branding and associated campaigns, and Yves Saint Laurent's 2001 Opium perfume advertisements. Concern has also often been expressed about how particular products are targeted at certain groups. 'Alcopops' came under heavy attack from the public and pressure groups in the 90s when their names, labelling and other communications were considered as being used to target underage drinkers. The drinks industry was forced to review its position and a code of conduct was drawn up for the alcopops sector.

The challenge for the marketing communicator in all this is to find the line between ethical practice and using communications as a legitimate means to gain competitive advantage.

---

**Activity 2.1**

You work for a UK-based charity, operating internationally, which supports civilian individuals and their families affected by death and injuries arising from wars and terrorism. A proposal has been put forward for a fund-raising campaign using posters and press advertising depicting explicit and graphic real images of war dead, and individuals as they lie maimed following a violent event.

a. What would be the pros and cons of running such a campaign?

b. What further information might you seek before deciding whether or not to run the campaign?

---

## The role of communications in taking a socially responsible stance

Businesses are under increasing scrutiny to persuade them to act with 'corporate social responsibility'. This concerns the 'duty' of an organisation to conduct its business activities in a responsible way with a view towards the interests of society generally.

This responsibility is partly driven by a recognition of the increasing power of businesses. 51 of the largest economies in the world are companies, not countries (comparing turnover against GDP)[1]. But with power comes responsibility, and businesses that fail to act responsibly risk incurring the wrath of governments and citizens generally.

Social responsibility is wide-ranging: it may involve employment issues, such as the use of slave or child labour as part of the supply chain; it may be about environmental concerns – rainforest destruction or CFC emissions; or it may involve refusal to use certain practices, such as animal testing. From a communications perspective, responsibility might be about exercising care about which groups promotional efforts are directed towards. Nestlé endured years of opprobrium for targeting powdered milk at mothers of infants in less developed countries, using a variety of tools in the promotional mix. But even when social responsibility is not directly about communications, communications still play a crucial role. Interest in social responsibility comes from stakeholders, and communication forms the bridge between the organisation and those stake-holding groups.

Some groups have an obvious interest – employees, customers, shareholders and so on – but it could be argued that we are all stakeholders. We all have a personal interest, for example, in protecting the environment, and most of us would be concerned to know that labourers are being exploited and work in dreadful conditions. Several clothing brand names have come in for much criticism following media reporting of the conditions in less developed countries in which producers of their goods work, while in 2002 children's clothes retailers have had to withdraw ranges aimed at "tweenies" (children aged about 9-13) which included padded bras and G-strings, following public outrage. Businesses are having to learn that they are part of a much bigger community – local, national and global – and, as such, need to act like citizens within that community.

It is unsurprising, therefore, that organisations are putting increased emphasis on communicating about how responsible they are. Visit almost any corporate web site, or read public company's Annual Reports and you will see plenty of space given over to detailing claims to Corporate Citizenship. Not only do these paint the

  [1] Financial Times, 20th April 2002

company in a good light to stakeholders, but some schemes also give opportunities for stakeholders actually to participate. NatWest has launched a Community Bond which allows its customers, as 'social investors', to forego interest on their investments which then passes to charitable projects. Royal & Sun Alliance, the insurer, sponsored environmental projects in Antarctica and gave some staff the opportunity to visit and help.

Some businesses choose to use their socially responsible stance as a differentiator. The Body Shop, the Co-Operative Group and Traidcraft are examples, ensuring that this point comes across through a variety of communications, such as advertising, packaging, press announcements and so on. Even if social responsibility is not a specific differentiator it does help to reinforce corporate brand values. Consumers may equate social responsibility with trustworthiness, potentially improving the organisation's image, reputation and customer loyalty.

**Activity 2.2**

Explore the web site or other communications of a multi-national brand.

What efforts does the company make to project its credentials of corporate social responsibility?

## Models and frameworks to aid an ethical approach to planning marketing communications

Several factors contribute to decision-making about ethical issues. A framework might look like this:

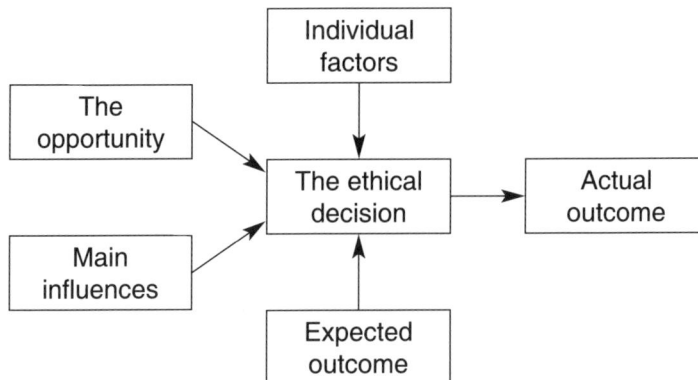

**Figure 2.1: Factors influencing ethical decision-making.**

**Individual factors** relate to the characteristics of the decision-maker himself or herself. Each of us has different ethical viewpoints that we may choose to use, or deliberately exclude, when making business decisions. Different motivations might apply such as the need for career progression, or to 'fit' with the organisation, and our knowledge and experience will affect our judgements.

**The opportunity** relates to the prevailing conditions of the situation. What are the factors that apply here; e.g. is there competitor weakness? Is the opportunity a one-off? What happened when we encountered this situation before?

Thirdly we need to consider the main **influences** on and within the organisation. What is the prevailing organisational culture? What are the legal issues involved? What perceptions do the business's publics have?

The expected **outcome** is a key influence on the decision – maybe financial rewards or altruistic satisfaction, or risk of press opprobrium and lost sales. Whatever decision is made will translate into an actual outcome, which may then influence future behaviour.

Businesses can use this framework to ensure key factors are considered in ethical decision-making. It also recognises and reminds them about significant influences on decision-making, such as the value judgements of the individual in making the decision.

N.C. Smith[2] suggested three tests that can be applied by businesses targeting consumers to assess whether they are behaving ethically:

■ **Consumer capability:** how vulnerable is the target market, to the extent that their decision-making capabilities may be limited? For example, could the business be seen as exploiting the young, the poor or the distressed?

■ **Information:** are consumers given enough information to make a judgement about the product/service? Will what they have been told by the organisation meet their expectations?

■ **Choice:** to what extent is this limited? Would significant costs or inconvenience be imposed on consumers if they used an alternative supplier?

These tests have significant implications for marketing communicators. They beg questions about where communications are placed and which audiences should see them: how much should organisations tell would-be consumers? What is the balance between promotion and information in communications? How up-front is the business about the cost of peripherals, spare parts, and so on?

[2] Smith, N.C. (1995), *Marketing strategies for the ethics era*, Sloan Management Review, Summer, pp. 85-97.

Other tests have been suggested by various writers. Laczniak and Murphy suggest some pragmatic rules of thumb for marketers to consider when facing ethical options:

■ The golden rule – act how you would expect others to act towards you.

■ The professional ethic – only act in a way that a panel of objective, professional colleagues would think appropriate. There is already assistance here: most fields of marketing have one or more professional bodies which will have produced guidelines, codes, statements of ethical practice or similar. Find examples relating to your own discipline.

■ The TV test – would you be comfortable explaining your actions to the general public on television? Bear in mind that this theoretical question might just translate into a real-life situation!

■ Kant's categorical imperative – act in a way that would be deemed to be universally appropriate for anyone facing the same situation.

■ Think about what the outcomes of the decision would be, e.g. the implications for, and reactions of, those affected by the decision.

Perhaps the biggest problem with ethical dilemmas is that there are few absolutes. What is right for one business may be completely inappropriate for another. Even 'we will not break the law' may be subject to legal debate about whether an action is allowable or not, or whether it contravenes the spirit if not the letter of the law. Ultimately, like many marketing decisions, context really matters and this means that marketers, and particularly marketing communicators, have to have an acute sense of what is happening around them, both inside and outside the organisation.

---

**Activity 2.3**

Some food manufacturers have been criticised by the Food Standards Agency for using the word 'Farmhouse' on product labelling, e.g. 'Farmhouse cheese' or 'Farmhouse Vegetable Soup', when the products have emanated from a factory, not a farmhouse kitchen.

Make notes on why you think manufacturers do this. Are consumers misled by it? How does this affect the decision whether to call produce 'Farmhouse'?

---

## Case Study – Café Direct

Café Direct holds approximately three percent of the UK fresh ground and freeze-dried coffee markets, despite very little marketing spend. The company began trading in 1991 as a non-profit joint venture involving the following ethical trading organisations: Equal Exchange, Oxfam Trading, Traidcraft and Twin Trade.

Cutting out the middlemen is key to the organisation's success. The company buys coffee beans directly from small co-operatives in Latin and Central America and Africa. Café Direct guarantees an agreed trade price for the coffee beans which means they have occasionally paid suppliers more than twice the normal market rate. If the international coffee price rises above the agreed trade price, they pay the international price plus a ten percent 'social premium' which the co-operatives distribute as they see fit. Café Direct also provides an upfront subsidy of up to sixty per cent of the value of one contract. It also provides regular updates on world coffee prices. This is important because the fourteen co-operatives who supply the company only sell a quarter to one half of their beans to Café Direct.

What does all this ethical trading mean for the consumer? The recommended retail price for a 227 gram jar of roast or ground Café Direct is £2.09. A jar of the leading brand, Kenco, costs £1.99. Café Direct's 100 gram freeze-dried product retails at £2.39; Nestlé Gold Blend sells for £2.19. The UK supermarkets have maintained their profit margins and have passed on the cost of ethical business practices to the consumers, a number of whom are clearly willing to pay a slight premium if they believe the company behind the brand is operating ethically.

The issue of ethical trading has been driven by publicity about poor working conditions in factories and plantations in some less developed countries. A recent documentary focused on the relationship between a major supermarket chain and one of its larger suppliers of peas in Zimbabwe, where it revealed that out of the retail price of a 99p pack of peas, the pickers got less than 1p. Supermarkets have been prompted to initiate audits of their supply and production lines and make public statements about their commitment to ethical trading. For example, Tesco recently set up a team of ethical advisors to help monitor the goods it sells in its stores and develop an ethical trading policy. Other major chains, such as the Co-operative, have signed up to participate in a project with the Fair Trade Foundation to investigate the mechanics of implementing independent auditing procedures to meet international ethical trading standards. These include agreements to negotiate with independent worker organisations and to honour or better any locally agreed minimum wage.

As the profile of ethical trading increases, the retailers' position that consumers will have to pay a premium may become untenable, especially if one of the supermarket chains takes a more definite ethical stance to distinguish itself from the other companies.

**Source:** *Marketing Operations Examination Paper*, December 1998.

---

**Questions**

1.  Explain what supermarkets hope to gain by stocking Fair Trade products.

2.  Recommend an appropriate communications mix for a supermarket deciding to communicate their stance on ethical trading.

3.  Explain why marketing communications in themselves are sometimes considered unethical. How can organisations measure whether they are acting unethically through their communications?

---

**SUMMARY OF KEY POINTS**

In this Session, we have introduced issues of ethics and social responsibility in marketing communications, and covered the following key points:

■ Marketing ethics are moral principles that define right and wrong behaviour in marketing.

■ Social responsibility refers to an organisation's obligation to minimise its negative impact and maximise its positive impact on society as a whole.

■ Marketing communications needs to balance the need to use communications to achieve competitive advantage with ethical practice.

■ There are several frameworks which organisations can use to check the ethics of their communications.

## Improving and developing own learning

The following projects are designed to help you develop your knowledge and skills further by carrying out some research yourself. Feedback is not provided for this type of learning because there are no 'answers' to be found, but you may wish to discuss your findings with colleagues and fellow students.

**Project A**

Talk to your colleagues in the marketing department about the audiences you target with your communications.

Could any of these audiences be considered vulnerable?

If so, how is your communication adapted to deal with this audience?

**Project B**

Does your organisation have a policy on social responsibility?

How does it communicate its stance to its publics?

**Project C**

Apply Smith's framework to your organisation's activities.

How ethical do you consider its actions to be?

What recommendations would you make for the future?

## Feedback to activities

### Activity 2.1

**a.**

**Pros**

- Grabs attention of viewer/reader: likely to boost awareness of your charity and its cause.
- Likely to generate word-of-mouth comment and media attention.
- Reflects realities of your charity's work.

**Cons**

- May distress some viewers/readers: likely to occasion many complaints.
- Selected media may be too indiscriminate, particularly posters which may be seen by anybody, e.g. young children.
- Is graphic content likely to make people turn away and ignore the message? Will it just solicit 'compassion fatigue'?

## b.

Will the campaign be effective in its fund-raising objectives? Might it be beneficial in the short-term, i.e. give an immediate revenue increase, but have a long-term detrimental effect, generating an organisational reputation for being offensive and distressing? Research is needed (within the constraints of the charity's limited budget) to test out its proposition.

The hard-hitting content may ramp up attention on using funds for advertising rather than other fund-raising efforts, or spending directly on the cause. Care is needed in justifying the campaign. Opinions of major donors should be sought.

The charity should consult guidelines in the British Code of Advertising Practice and talk to the Copy Advice Team of the Committee for Advertising Practice (CAP). They can give guidance on what may be acceptable, and can draw on experience of any similar proposals or campaigns in the past.

## Activity 2.2

As an example, McDonald's is often targeted by campaigners against global capitalism who believe its multinational operations exemplify all that is bad about modern economies.

But the company's web sites (www.mcdonalds.com and www.mcdonalds.co.uk) stress the organisation's social responsibility, with headings about the Community, the Environment, and the Marketplace (food sourcing, toy safety, supplier relationships). It discusses its People Promise and includes an extended Social Responsibility report.

Literature in restaurants reinforces these themes, including detailed ingredient sourcing information and details of community links.

## Activity 2.3

The word 'farmhouse' has associations of freshness and wholesomeness. Manufacturer might argue that it suggests the style of the soup rather than the origin. The general effect is to make it sound more attractive, compared to reducing the name to its basic contents.

Are consumers misled? Well, are buyers likely to believe that a product filling a substantial portion of the supermarket shelf (and presumably the shelves of hundreds of other supermarkets) was actually made in a farmhouse kitchen? Do they not realise these products are mass-produced and that the labelling is not literal? Are we crediting the buyer with too little intelligence? In any event, the original ingredients would largely have derived from a farm, presumably near a farmhouse, so is the labelling incorrect? If we restrict this, how far does it go? Is the retail chain's name 'Farm Foods' misleading, as the majority of their produce is, presumably, not processed and packaged on a farm?

On the other hand, where does that leave producers who do make their products in a farmhouse? Small-scale production using local expertise and 'original' recipes is popular: the rapid rise of farmers' markets across the country has shown there is a demand for these authentic products, but how do you distinguish them if everything is 'farmhouse'? And if 'farmhouse' is OK for factory produce, what about 'barn-fresh', or 'country', or 'natural'? Do these words have any meaning, or can anyone use them, however the goods are produced?

How does your view affect the outcome? This is the ethical decision. The choices are:

■ It's misleading, but we'll do it anyway.

■ It's misleading, so we won't do it.

■ It's not misleading so we'll do it.

■ It's not misleading but we'll still call it something else.

You will have to choose and live with your decision. But beware that consumers are increasingly willing to complain, and that the food labelling regulatory regime is becoming more demanding!

# Session 3

# A theoretical background to marketing communications

## Introduction

In this Session we look at the background to communications theory and how it shapes marketing communication. We will look at personal influences on the consumer, as well as perception, personality and attitude as they impact on the buying process. Finally, we look at the importance to the marketer of understanding the need to influence the customer's intention to act.

---

**LEARNING OUTCOMES**

At the end of this Session you will be able to:

■ Explain how communication theory helps to shape marketing communications.

■ Examine the impact of the following on the communications process:

■ Personal influences.

■ Personality.

■ Perception.

■ Explain how learning processes influence communications.

■ Understand why it is important to understand an individual's intention to act in a particular way when designing communications activities.

■ Explain other environmental influences which affect the consumer buying process.

---

## Theoretical models of communication

Many mistakes are made in marketing and other business communications in assuming that communication is simply 'A tells B what A wants B to know', or, in diagrammatic form:

| A | | B |
|---|---|---|
| *(the source)* | → *Message* → | *(the receiver)* |

The reality of any communication is more complex in practice, and good communication is often more demanding.

A more realistic model of communication is as follows:

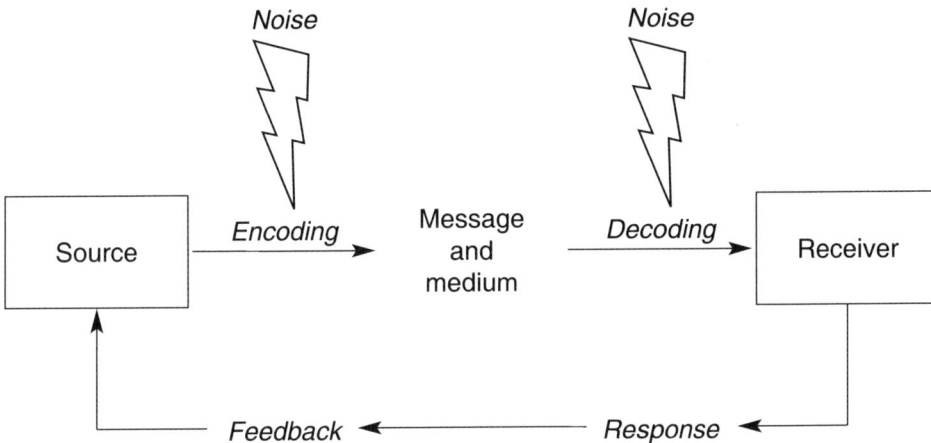

The **source** is the individual or organisation sending the message.

**Encoding** is the process of turning the message into written or spoken words, pictures, symbols or whatever other mechanism is used. This creates a **message** which is sent via a selected **medium**. Though the sender knows what he wants to say, the **receiver** – the person or organisation receiving the message – will interpret it using their own frames of reference; in other words, they will **decode** it in a way that makes sense to them. We have probably all said something in a well-meaning way that was misunderstood by the person we said it to who thought, for example, that we were being sarcastic or rude. We encoded it in the way we thought best, but the receiver decoded it differently. Successful communications require the sender to encode their message in a way that ensures the receiver interprets it in the same way. Clearly this requires a thorough understanding by the source of the receiver and the ways in which he or she is likely to interpret the message.

**Noise** relates to the factors that interfere with the message between sending and receipt, and it can take many forms. They might be uncontrollable factors such as reception problems while viewing a TV channel or sending a text message. Inappropriate encoding, such as using jargon which the target audience will not understand, is an illustration of noise which is controllable. The mass of competing advertisements, for example in a trade telephone directory, also creates noise.

The receiver will have a **response** to the message and the part of the response that gets back to the sender is **feedback**. Feedback is valuable because it allows the source to check that the message got through and elicit how the receiver reacted. The source may want to know whether the message was decoded in the way that was intended, how the receiver reacted having decoded the message and whether further communications might be needed to clarify or develop the message. Feedback may come in many different ways, such as counting coupons returned from a direct marketing promotion, doing research to identify consumer awareness and attitudes following an advertising campaign, or monitoring complaint letters received from the public following adverse media coverage of a press release.

The model above suggests that communication is a straightforward linear process between two parties, sometimes generating feedback. One can relate this quite easily to a TV advertising campaign targeted at a mass market, or to an internal Team Briefing to the Marketing Department. But modern communications allow far more scope for interactivity, and communications between different parties in the process. Whereas marketing communication traditionally has been mainly about business-to-customer (B2C) or business-to-business (B2B) communication, **e-marketing** has facilitated customer-to-business (C2B) communication, where the individual seeks information via the Internet from the business, and customer-to-customer communication (C2C) where individuals share information.

Thus, while the fundamentals of the previous model, such as encoding, decoding and feedback still apply, a complex set of relationships develops. A model might look like this, with the Internet acting as a hub through which two-way communications can be undertaken via personalised messages (m) and general content (c):

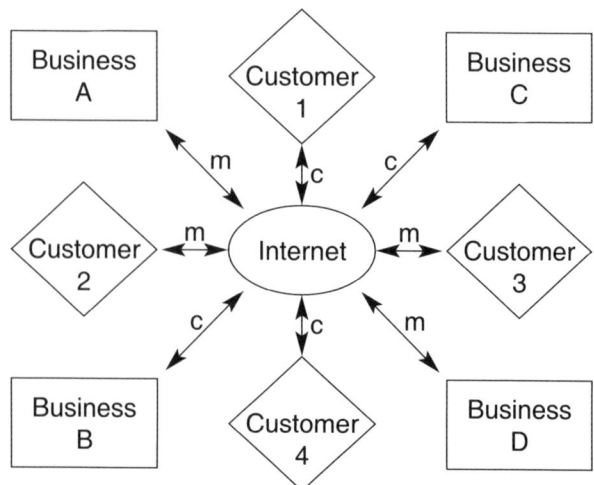

**Figure 3.1: Model of Internet marketing communications.**

**Activity 3.1**

Use the elements of the communication model to describe a likely cause of each of the following problems. How could these problems be dealt with?

■ Post-campaign research shows that a large proportion of your target audience had failed to see advertisements you had placed in magazines.

■ Staff complain that they do not understand the strategic messages written by the Managing Director in the company news-sheet.

■ Business is good, but you don't know whether it's coming because of the newspaper advert you ran, the door-drop leaflets you distributed or the positive mention you have received on your trade body's web site.

■ Certain overseas staff (whose English is good) have not responded to a memo you asked a junior colleague to send in your absence, instigating new procedures for processing invoices.

■ A direct marketing campaign has a much lower than expected response rate, using material that has proved effective elsewhere.

## The impact of personal influences, personality and perception on the communication process

Each of us will respond to marketing communications in different ways. We all have different **frames of reference** – the sum of our experiences, attitudes, personal circumstances and so on – that distinguish our own perspective from someone else's. The marketer's skill lies in constructing his or her communications so that they relate to the frames of reference of as many people as possible within his target audience. This requires an understanding of different customer **contexts**, as in the varying background circumstances that influence how existing or potential customers will process and respond to the information that marketers want to communicate.

### Personal influences

These influences are often demographic, and their importance lies in the way they shape our attitudes. The marketer cannot directly change these factors; indeed they are often outside any individual's immediate control, but the marketer must be aware how they will affect people's perspective. The main factors are:

■ **Personal factors:** age, sex, race, religion, income and wealth, life cycle stage, lifestyle.
■ **Social factors:** reference groups, role, family.
■ **Cultural:** nationality, race; religion, social class.

## Personality

Personality is the series of traits and characteristics, in total unique to each one of us, which consistently influences our behaviour. We may describe people, for example, as self-confident or studious or sociable. Communications may be framed with particular personalities in mind. For many years Volvo car's communications were primarily built on an appeal to those who were risk-averse; their more recent communications appeal to more adventurous and sporty personalities.

## Perception

This is a key influence in the way we process communications, and the marketer can make a direct impact here.

Perception relates to the way we mentally process the various stimuli that we receive. We are each bombarded with hundreds of advertisements every day in one form or another, yet most of these fail to register in our consciousness. We go through a process of **selecting** messages, and then **organising** and **interpreting** the information within them.

**Selection:** to get us to pay attention to their communication, amongst so many others, marketers may use one or more devices to prompt us to pick it out. The visual image in an advertisement may be unexpected, the packaging of a product may be distinctive or the music in a TV commercial may quickly create a particular atmosphere.

Sometimes communications will challenge us, enticing us to study them further or interact with them, or they may appeal to sensations like fear, sex or humour. Dulux paints ran an award-winning campaign aimed at "adventurous" under-35s. It ran bold, bright and quirky advertisements and used naked body-painted models to successfully generate PR coverage.

Our interest may also be aroused through heightened awareness. If we are considering booking a holiday we will be more alert to communications about holidays. Once our booking has been made these messages will be less potent, though we may still register some as we subconsciously seek to confirm we made the right choice.

The way that a communication is put together will help us to organise it in our own minds. The marketer aims to help the receiver by creating links he or she can make sense of easily. A radio commercial may lead us through a short, logical story. An advertising leaflet may aim to balance important text, less important text and images so that we can grasp the message without confusion. **Grouping** is a common tactic, creating associations between images in a communication.

For example, Sunny Delight, the citrus-flavoured soft drink, grouped a blazing sun and the bold words 'California Style' on the label. Together with the brightly coloured liquid visible in the transparent plastic bottle, the product had a vibrant, outdoor feel bursting with energy and Baywatch-style sunshine. This contributed to creating one of the most successful ever UK product launches although, ultimately, widespread concerns about the product's real attributes led to a re-launch.

Finally we **interpret** the information we have received. The communication cues we have received will be shaped in the light of our backgrounds, personalities and experiences to give our own meaning to the received message(s).

## The difference between conditioning and cognitive learning processes

Learning concerns the way that an individual's behaviour changes as a result of his/her experience. Marketers seek to influence people's learning using associations between **stimuli** – the product they are interested in – and **cues** – lesser stimuli that prompt mental reactions, or **responses**. The object is to solicit changes in behaviour. That behaviour itself will result in learning, which hopefully, from the marketer's view, leads to **reinforcement** of responses, so that the process is partly cyclical.

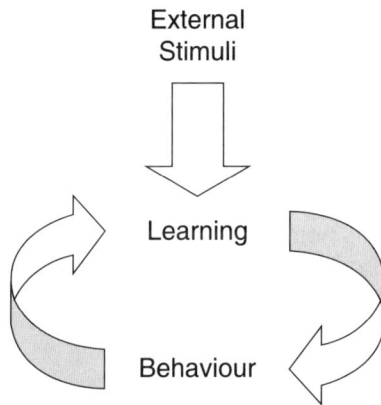

**Figure 3.2: The learning process.**

There are two types of learning: **behavioural learning**, also known as **conditioning**, and **cognitive learning**.

## Behavioural learning or conditioning

The best known (non-marketing) example of this resulted from an experiment by Russian psychologist Ivan Pavlov. He noted that a dog salivated when it saw food; in other words there was a stimulus – the food – and a response – salivation. He then rang a bell each time food was brought. After a while the dog began to salivate when the bell was rung, even when no food was brought. It had become **conditioned** to respond to a new stimulus – the bell – in a particular way.

Humans, too, can learn to respond to stimuli so that these responses become habitual. You may choose to use a particular product because it has been endorsed by a personality you admire. You may then continue to use that product long after the personality has ceased to be associated with it: you have become conditioned to using it.

## Cognitive learning

With this, individuals take a more active approach to learning. They draw on information, and process it to solve a problem or make choices. The information may be stored in one's memory or it may be from a new source such as a product brochure.

As an example of cognitive learning, let's say you are buying a washing machine for your first home. Your mother has used a WonderWash model for years and swears by it (of course, you have no personal experience of actually using it!). Thus you have become conditioned to respond positively to the WonderWash name but, as machines are costly, you plan to 'shop around'. You find a consumer magazine survey that says WonderWash is reliable and eco-friendly, factors that are important to you. But then you come across competitor literature which explains how their own model is cheaper to run and fits in smaller spaces than Wonderwash's. You use **discrimination** – recognising differences and adjusting your response – so that now both WonderWash and the competitor's product may be on your shortlist. You then use **reasoning** to weigh the products' relative merits and make your decision.

## Marketing's use of learning

Marketers seek to influence individuals' learning in many ways. Personal selling, recipe leaflets and **Infomercials** all contribute to cognitive learning, by creating or extending understanding of products' uses and applications. In-store DIY demonstrations and free samples, such as the 2 million biscuits recently sent out by McVities for women to enjoy in the relaxed setting of hairdressing salons, encourage trial and reduce the consumer's perception of risks associated with purchase. Viral e-mails may provoke comment and suggest endorsement by people whose opinions we value.

Marketers may also aim to develop conditioned associations between consumers and products through cues. A particular font and colour may make you think of Cadbury's chocolate, or BBC1, even if the context is not explicit. For example, BBC1 launched its 2002 re-branding with a poster that simply said 'The One' in their new signature red, and distinctive boxed lettering; there was no name on it but the source was clear. A product may be shown in a context that automatically evokes feelings of pleasure, such as Häagen-Dazs's sensual 1990s black and white ads. Learning may also help with brand extension: for example, if a consumer has learned to like a brand through use of a particular product, then when the brand launches a new line, short-cut thinking translates past learning about the brand into reflex buying behaviour.

---

**Activity 3.2**

You have responsibility for marketing a new wine brand. Suggest six ways you could generate learning in your target market.

---

## How attitudes are thought to develop, and their relevance to communications

The outcome of our information processing, through perception and learning, is to form an attitude. Our attitude reflects how we view the particular product or brand. The attitude we form may be completely new – perhaps after using a service for the first time – or it may reinforce or even contradict a previous attitude. On the whole, though, attitudes tend to remain fairly consistent. It may take a lot of prompting to change an attitude, and to do so may also require shifting of other views too.

Attitudes are important to marketers because they provide a string link between individuals' thought processes; what they have perceived and learned so far and their subsequent behaviours, and what they are going to do now they have this knowledge.

There are three components of attitude – the cognitive, affective and connotative, which can be summarised as 'learn, feel, do'.

**Cognitive** ('learn') – what we have learnt about the product's features and benefits;
**Affective** ('feel') – our feelings, emotions and sentiments towards it;
**Connotative** ('do'): what we do about it.

For example, marketing communications about a breakfast cereal may have left us believing it is high in fibre, low in sugar and salts, and will be filling enough to see us through to lunch – all **cognitive** elements of attitude. We therefore feel favourably towards the product, and towards its associations with the healthy lifestyle that we are seeking – the **affective** element. We resolve that next time we shop we'll buy it, and if we like it we'll mention it to our friends down at the gym – examples of the **connotative** element.

### Attitudes and marketing communications

Marketing communications aim to create, change or reinforce attitudes. The communications may focus on any one or more of the cognitive, affective or connotative elements of attitude.

From a cognitive perspective, communications may aim to build up our understanding of the product's attributes and performance. Sometimes this may involve changing beliefs that have become entrenched in consumers' minds. Skoda's multi-disciplinary (and relatively low-budget) 2000 campaign for the Fabia was a great success. Its appeal came from tackling people's negative attitudes head-on, rather than pretending that they weren't there. Another approach is to persuade the consumer to review the priorities he or she attaches to the product's attributes. Sometimes this can be done by comparison with competitors' products.

Affective approaches will aim to influence how we feel about the product. Associations may be created between, say, the feeling of pleasure and consuming a particular bar of chocolate. Using a 'personality' to endorse the product may have a similar effect, while branding can also play a part. If research shows that consumers feel well-disposed towards a particular brand, then marketers may stress that brand name when introducing a new product from the same stable.

A connotative approach aims to make us willing to take action. For example, different stages of a successful direct marketing campaign by Saab persuaded their targets to put Saab on their shortlist when considering quality cars, enter a free prize draw via the Internet and take up the offer of a day's free test drive.

As attitudes are important in influencing purchasing behaviour, it is vital that marketers understand consumers' attitudes to the product through research. Much effort is directed into attitudinal research, which may measure actual or potential users' attitudes before and after promotional activity, in order to identify changes.

### The importance of understanding an individual's intention to act, and its part in the decision process

In the previous section we mentioned that attitudes are important because they link thought processes and subsequent behaviour. But does that mean that a positive attitude is the best indicator that someone will actually act in a particular way?

Research suggests that two other components are very influential in disposing individuals to behave in a particular way.

First there is the **subjective norm**. This concerns what others might think about what we are planning to do. Take the example of the successful 2000 Skoda campaign mentioned previously. Many people may have become convinced by the messages from the various campaign communications and have developed a positive attitude to the new Fabia. But some of those may still have held back from buying the car, not because of their doubts about the product, but because of the fear of ridicule from others – friends, neighbours, relations, even the man-in-the-street – who had not yet learned that the new Skoda was very different from the old image. Thus, fear of others' judgement may inhibit the intention to act. (Interestingly, a 2002 Skoda campaign tackles this issue: it recognises that some people will never change their mind about Skodas – it doesn't matter, they are the mad ones, the ads imply).

The second component that will influence intention to act is the belief that our actions will end in certain outcomes, good or bad. A buyer may feel positively disposed towards buying particular brand of car: there is a positive expected outcome to acquiring it. But the buyer cannot face the process of negotiating finance to get it – he expects forms, hassle and maybe even rejection. This inhibits the intentions to buy, even though a positive attitude has been formed to the car.

From a marketer's view, then, it is not sufficient on its own to develop a positive attitude to a product in buyers' minds. We also need to consider how disposed they are to actually act in a particular way. Marketers need to recognise and overcome barriers to desired behaviours; they also need to focus on measuring not just attitudes to products, but also attitudes to the intentions to act, if they wish to have the most accurate assessment of people's likelihood of making a purchase.

---

**Activity 3.3**

A 2002 TV advertisement for AA car loans explains that borrowers will get a free check of their intended second-hand purchase. It compares this to getting loans from elsewhere and asks, "What does your bank manager know about cars?"

How does this ad relate to the intention to act, as discussed above?

---

# Case Study – Dutton Engineering

*The following Case Study was used in Session 1, but is used again here with different questions.*

During the 1990s Dutton Engineering's impressive growth was based on a strategy that was focused on the development and maintenance of strong customer relationships. Rather than spend money speculating about the generation of new customers, Dutton's policy has been to invest and build relationships with current customers.

Dutton manufacture steel and aluminium components, and in order to help realise their strategy they removed their middle management and devolved responsibility to teams of production-orientated personnel, who focus upon their clients' total requirements. Clients talk directly to these 'Production Cells' who are empowered to make decisions and manage all aspects of their clients' requirements. There are no appointed cell leaders, managers or even secretaries, as each cell manages itself organically and recruits its own new staff.

The role of senior management has been to manage time and resources through the use of management information systems. They are able to identify areas across and within Production Cells where productivity might be improved, and help ensure that 85% of the man hours in each Production Cell are used to generate revenue. As a result of this approach, revenue has doubled to £2.3m, profits are stable at 6.5%, sales per worker are double that of the national average in the sector, yet staff numbers have remained relatively stable. Not surprisingly, Dutton has become the centre of attention for its innovative and seemingly successful approach.

The company's success has been built around 42 client companies, some of whom are very loyal. Part of the company's philosophy has been to 'meet and beat customers' expectations', and the attitude of staff in each Production Cell reflects this perspective. Through high levels of quality production and customer involvement, new orders have been won. However, the growth experienced to date has been based on new orders from existing clients and very little new business has been acquired. Senior management are regarded (by the Production Cells) as responsible for generating new customers, yet they see their role as managing and teaching the 'Dutton Way'.

Little effort appears to have been made to attract new customers and there is no Marketing Department or sales force. These are costs that do not fit the current culture and are regarded as activities that would add little value and merely create high overheads. The company currently outsources transport, cleaning and payroll, so outsourcing a sales operation would be a compatible activity.

There has been little planned use of marketing and/or corporate communications, and the primary emphasis has been on strong word of mouth communications, supported by some limited public relations activities. However, a rudimentary web site, some use of telemarketing, the unplanned use of some out-of-date sales literature and attendance at exhibitions constitutes the main thrust of the communications to date. Therefore, the organisation needs to address the balance of its current customer portfolio and attract new clients if it is to achieve ambitious growth targets, which it aims to accomplish in the first few years of the new millennium.

**Source:** *Integrated Marketing Communications Examination Paper*, December 1999.

---

**Questions**

1.  Dutton Engineering is now trying to attract new customers rather than merely maintain relationships with existing clients. How might their communications need to be adapted to handle these differences?

2.  The Managing Director is concerned that, if an expensive communications campaign is launched to attract new customers, you may not be able to establish where any new business is coming from. What element of the communication model might cause this problem?

3   The Case Study mentions that much of Dutton's existing communication is via 'word-of-mouth'. How might this element be used to attract new customers? Use the communication theory in this Session to explain.

## SUMMARY OF KEY POINTS

In this Session, we have considered the theoretical background to marketing communications, and covered the following key points:

■ Good communication is a complex issue, and there are many factors that influence its effectiveness.

■ Individuals are influenced by previous experiences, their personality, their family and other influential groups, their culture, and many personal factors when they are making a buying decision.

■ Marketers need to use consumer research to understand their target audience before attempting to communicate with them.

■ Marketers can also use communications to generate learning in their target market.

■ Marketers can use communications to try to change attitudes towards their products and services, and to generate consumer 'intention to act' – intention to buy.

## Improving and developing own learning

The following projects are designed to help you develop your knowledge and skills further by carrying out some research yourself. Feedback is not provided for this type of learning because there are no 'answers' to be found, but you may wish to discuss your findings with colleagues and fellow students.

### Project A

Identify at least four different marketing communications using a variety of media. For example: posters, direct mail, on-pack promotional offers, magazine advertisements. For each, consider the following questions:

■ What device(s) did the marketer use to get your attention?

■ How is the message organised? Was it immediately clear what the message was, or what the marketer wanted you to do?

■ What types of personal influences and personalities might people have who find the message a. appealing b. unappealing c. irrelevant.

Set your answer out in table form, as follows:

| | Example 1 | Example 2 | Example 3 | Example 4 |
|---|---|---|---|---|
| Device used: | | | | |
| Message organisation: <br><br> Clarity: | | | | |
| Influences/ personalities: <br><br> ■ appealing <br><br> ■ unappealing <br><br> ■ irrelevant | | | | |

**Project B**

Look at the examples you identified in Project A. What attitude do you think the advertiser wanted you to form in each case?

Is this attitude cognitive, affective or connotative (or more than one)?

Accumulate further examples, illustrating the three different elements of attitude. These will help develop your understanding and you may be able to use them as illustrations in an exam answer.

**Project C**

Talk to colleagues in your marketing department. Identify examples of advertisements used and explore the attitudes that you were wanting the audience to form.

Make notes on your findings. How successful were these ads?

# Feedback to activities

## Activity 3.1

Wrong medium used. Check which magazines your targets do use. Also check whether there was any exceptional noise relating to that issue. Encoding could also be an issue, with poor execution of the message meaning people overlooked the ad.

Poor encoding. The MD may understand what he is saying, but his language and inability to put things in easy-to-relate-to terms has confused his staff. Suggest an alternative approach, e.g. interview with MD, written by staff member.

Lack of feedback: set up mechanism to gather data, e.g. ask people where they heard about you.

Source problem: this may occur in any organisation but is more important in some countries where the context of the message, i.e. who says it and how, is very important.

Receiver problem: have you correctly identified suitable recipients within your target market? Check your mailing data specifications and sources.

## Activity 3.2

- Associate product with well-known personality with appropriate characteristics (e.g. sophisticated or fun-loving).
- Set up in-store sampling opportunities.
- Use images and fonts on labelling to suggest the type of wine, e.g. rich in heritage or easy-drinking.
  Use text on labelling to explain about the contents.
- Use familiar music in TV and radio commercials and at promotional events to build a conditioned response in consumers.
- Create an association between the wine and a well-known characteristic or feature of the country of origin through images, music, usage etc.

## Activity 3.3

Many of us feel the desire for a new car and may not need any convincing about it. But many of us also dislike the prospect of actually making the purchase: we feel inadequate in our knowledge and fear demonstrating this to the vendor. We're also worried about being misled into buying a car that is mechanically unsound or stolen. We might be worried, too, about what our friends would say if we ended up with an unsafe or illegal vehicle.

# Session 4

# Internal and external audiences

## Introduction

In this Session we look deeper at the buying behaviour of external customers and consider aspects of perceived risk and involvement theory as they affect purchase decisions. We also look at buying decisions in organisations, and finally we look at internal audiences, and how communications can be used in internal marketing.

---

**LEARNING OUTCOMES**

At the end of this Session you will be able to:

■ Explain the consumer buying process.

■ Understand the importance of the components of perceived risk.

■ Explain organisational buying behaviour.

■ Understand the impact of corporate culture on marketing communications.

■ Explain the role that internal marketing can play.

---

## The consumer buying process

There are customers who browse and those who research a product and make comparisons before going shopping, and some who see something they like and make an impulse purchase. Marketing communications aim to attract customers' attention throughout the stages of the buying process.

There are consumers who identify a product they want to purchase, those who respond when the product is communicated to them through the media and those who take an active part in researching the best buy, comparing prices, after-sales service and value for money. Customers who undertake research may use magazines such as 'Which?', search the Internet and make detailed shopping expeditions.

You could present this as a spectrum from:

Browsers                          to       Detailed researchers
No specific product in mind                Specific product, price and value added

The buying process often follows a number of stages:

1. Recognising a need or want.
2. Researching alternatives.
3. Choosing the product.
4. Making a trial of the product.
5. Making a final decision.

Different levels of information and encouragement to buy are required at each stage of the buying process. For example, in purchasing of a computer, the initial process may be to single out a number of reputable brands, make a detailed information search regarding specifications and capacities and then visiting a store such as PC World to 'handle' the goods. The decision may be made on a mixture of price and after-sales support. Hidden persuaders such as design, added value and the influence of the salesperson may clinch the final decision.

Marketers are also interested in assessing not only the process of buying behaviour but also the likely repetition of purchase. Organisations need to assess sales forecasts and be able to predict, with some accuracy, the pattern of sales. Brand-conscious consumers are wooed to particular brands by their peers and through marketing communications. Brand loyalty allows the manufacturer some security in predicting future sales, which is why so many schemes such as loyalty cards, clubs and long-term promotions have become popular.

Marketing communications attempts to appeal to buyers throughout the buying cycle, by appealing to functional, symbolic and experiential needs.

---

**Activity 4.1**

Identify three products, one in the white goods market, one in the FMCG market and a major purchase such as a car or house.

Plot the various stages of likely purchasing behaviour.

---

## The components of perceived risk

Consumers attach a lot of self-importance to their brand choices and evaluate the risk of looking stupid through making the wrong choice. Take a teenager buying a new pair of trainers: peer group pressure plays a major role in the brand choice, as does the credibility of the brand itself.

There are a number of factors affecting brand choice:

- **Subjectivity** – the unique perception of the individual based on past experiences.
- **Categorisation** – the individual compartmentalises information related to their own organisation.

55

- **Selectivity** – the degree to which the individual filters information from the environment.
- **Expectations** – based on values and beliefs, what we expect from brand performance.
- **Past experiences** – triggered responses from memories of similar events, sights, smells and sounds.

Perceived risk is said to fall into the following categories:

- Performance risk
- Financial risk
- Physical risk
- Social risk
- Ego risk

It is a recognised fact that buyers are concerned about the risks associated with the outcome of any decision they make to purchase a product.

Let's take a pharmaceutical company trying to introduce a new drug to treat diabetes as an example. Potential users or customers of the drug may consider the following issues:

- Performance risk – will this drug treat diabetes in the way in which it is said to?
- Financial risk – can we afford these drugs? In the case of a country with a National Health Service, this will apply to the doctors involved in recommending or prescribing the drug, rather than the individual being treated.
- Physical risk – will this drug have adverse effects?
- Social risk – will this impress friends or colleagues? This type of risk is less likely to be involved with the adoption of new drugs.
- Ego risk – will the drug make me feel good about myself? Again, this is less likely to be involved with the adoption of new drugs.

Understanding that these risks exist enables marketers in the pharmaceutical companies to design communications that will help the buyer overcome the questions they face.

In the case of the introduction of new drugs, the results of tests undertaken can be used in just such a way, and the communications message will also be given source credibility by the use of the name/qualification of the eminent physicians carrying out the research and supervising the tests.

To minimise the risks associated with purchasing new products and brands, organisations employ methods that will encourage trust and satisfy needs for reassurance. For example, less well known brands will offer lengthy warranties and improved customer service options. PR can be used to gain credibility and third party endorsement. In the fashion industry, new designers give away free samples to celebrities in pop music and film to raise the profile and use the connection with a high profile individual to gain brand credibility.

Häagen-Dazs used a whispering campaign to help launch its ice cream in the UK. The company sent samples to high profile celebrities and gave away trial cartons at all the major events, such as horse racing etc. This proved an effective way of gaining credibility and encouraging market share. These tactics, coupled with a major advertising campaign and the use of PR, created a whole new market, positioning Häagen-Dazs as a fashion accessory.

With the emergence of the Internet, organisations can market a complete range of media through one central source. This adds weight to the offer and gives customers confidence to engage with the brand. The more involved the consumer gets with the product and brand, the more likely the risk is minimised and repeat purchase is likely.

In high-risk situations purchasers will seek out more information, and the use of point of sale and print media can be useful in detailing technical specifications and detailed technical data. Some consumers wish to make this search for information private until the time comes to speak to a retailer, while others spend long periods of time talking to sales personnel to gain extensive knowledge of the products. When consumers are buying a low risk product, they often use internal search mechanisms comparing established brands on price, packaging and point of sales displays.

---

**Activity 4.2**

Research the Internet for web sites that provide a complete buying experience, offering a range of 'added value' services alongside the products.

---

## Organisational buying behaviour

The organisation as a buyer goes through a very similar process to that which the consumer goes through. However, there are some differences. The stages of the process for an organisation are as follows:

- Need/problem recognition
- Product specification
- Supplier and product search
- Evaluation of proposals
- Supplier selection
- Evaluation

In the context of supplier and product search, the supplier selection may be influenced by formal systems and processes; organisations may operate 'preferred supplier lists' or have formal criteria which suppliers must meet.

The other key difference is the structure of the **Decision Making Unit (DMU)**. Consumers are influenced by many individuals in their decision to purchase, including their family group. However, in an organisation the buying centre is made of a number of individuals who are involved in the purchase decision, often in a more formal situation.

The members of this DMU are said to be:

**The user** – the end user of the product or service being considered.

**The influencer** – often a technical specialist, who advises on the suitability of the product or service.

**The decider** – the person making the decision. This may be the department head or the financial accountant.

**The buyer** – these may be individuals in a purchasing department, who may set the criteria for selection of suppliers.

**The gatekeeper** – this individual may control the information flow within the organisation. They may be technical specialists, secretaries or Personal Assistants.

These roles may be taken by any number of individuals, or may all be taken by one person. Companies communicating with organisations should not expect the DMU to stay the same for every transaction that is made. Some will be more complex than others, and as relationships and trust develops, these decisions will often be simplified.

## The role of internal marketing

The concept of internal marketing became popular in the 1980s in conjunction with the drive for improved customer service. Employees are instrumental in the creation of a customer-centred organisation and their attitudes and behaviour is key to changing organisational culture.

Organisational identity is concerned with the way individuals think and feel about the organisation to which they belong. Creating a sense of shared ownership of the organisational objectives is essential to fulfil a customer-focused strategy. Marketing communications can play a large part in getting this message across to the internal audience – using newsletters, conferences, seminars and Intranets.

Individuals identify with the organisational identity and gain self-worth from the association of working in a positive organisation. Corporate culture is based on the collective values and beliefs of the organisational leaders and staff, and describes 'the way we do things'.

Culture affects many customer-focused areas such as:

- The way the telephone is answered.
- The look and style of the reception and offices.
- Care afforded to visitors.
- Communications such as letters, faxes and emails.
- Orders and subsequent complaints handling.

Changing the culture is a challenge; many people are anxious about change and this inevitably creates major obstacles. There are a number of methods to support culture change which communicate a new way of working, such as:

- Training
- Team briefings
- Social events
- Internal communications
- Culture surveys

Internal marketing may focus on explaining the philosophy of marketing and how the customer plays the central role in enabling profits, and therefore increases job security. Attitudes need to be changed so that staff view customer service as a way of improving their own job satisfaction – what's in it for them?

---

**Activity 4.3**

Prepare a PowerPoint presentation for your own organisation/department, detailing the benefits of a customer-focused organisation and how the culture needs to change to meet the changing customer demands.

---

## The impact of corporate culture on planned communications

Consistent messages build trust and credibility with any audience, internal or external. Organisations that promote themselves as customer-focused and there to listen to customer complaints create **cognitive dissonance** when customer expectations are not fulfilled.

One of the current topics is the customer help-lines for technical support to IT solutions. There is nothing more exasperating than when the technical helper seems to speak an entirely different language, using terminology which is indigestible to the user. Not only that, but three hours later you have been round in circles and the support person takes you through pre-prepared actions which are entirely unrelated to your specific problem. This leaves you feeling disappointed with your purchase and no less knowledgeable as to how to get the product to work.

These inconsistencies between the marketing communications and the corporate culture give the brand and company a poor reputation. This situation arises when there is a conflict between the marketing strategy and the policies and training within the organisation. Are the staff really working to fulfil their role or do they have a real commitment to support the customer?

Other scenarios are likely if communication and planning are poor. What happens when the Marketing department launch a new product that is not ready for delivery and the Production department is unable to fulfil expectations? Worse still, the product could be faulty because insufficient inspection procedures were built into the planning time to market. Perhaps distributors have been chosen without thought to their capabilities to fulfil customer expectations, and little or no support is achieved.

Corporate culture affects the way that the customer perceives the product. The organisation is the brand.

The style of management and the organisational structure feed into corporate culture as enablers. If there is a hierarchical structure that discourages open communication then this may hinder integrated marketing communications. Structures are best built around processes, so that staff can experience 'whole work tasks' that include all the stages of transformation, giving better job satisfaction. Management style needs to be one of empowerment and encouragement, recognising good work and giving rewards to motivate improvement. Changing culture can take years.

When organisations partner or merge with other organisations, the customer is often faced with two cultures within the same organisation, which can send out confusing messages. Often a culture change programme is implemented alongside a new structure to embed the values and philosophies of the organisation.

Communication messages need to not only reflect the benefits and features of the product or process, but also need to encapsulate the organisational brand values and philosophies so that customers buy into the whole experience.

---

**Activity 4.4**

Working with a colleague, take two organisations from contrasting cultures and identify their organisational values and beliefs, then contrast the affect this might have on their customers.

---

# Case Study – Apollo Data Loggers

Apollo Data Loggers manufactures and distributes a range of equipment (both hardware and software) designed to monitor and capture data concerning temperature, humidity, damp, and shock. For example, growers of fresh produce need an accurate record of temperatures experienced during the growth, preparation and transportation of their produce. For freight carriers and transporters, data logging provides a means of verifying the conditions in which their customers' products are carried.

Apollo has established itself in the market partly through superior technology which, unlike its competitors, is capable of downloading data whilst it continues to record. Sales revenues have grown to approximately £3m but profitability, whilst respectable, remains unexciting at around 6%. The market is becoming more competitive, which in turn impacts on price. To avoid price competition and discounting, which eventually leads to an erosion of profitability, Apollo's marketing strategy requires a move to niche markets where premium pricing can be sustained.

To reach its markets, Apollo has developed a global network of over 40 distributors. These channel intermediaries provide their customers with solutions, but the decision making is often complex, involving all three parties: Apollo, the distributor and the client. This network can require vast amounts of information and the development of customised products to meet client requirements. For example, Apollo's distributors need information about the range of 42 mainstream products and the product revisions which occur with increased frequency. These revisions can be caused by customers buying equipment to support their own businesses, which is not compatible with their data logging equipment. Apollo is required, therefore, to update its own equipment constantly and communicate information about the revisions more frequently.

In order to communicate with and support its distributors, Apollo produces sales literature, manuals, product specifications, brochures and data sheets. In addition, data capture software needs to be made available and updated as necessary. Contact with the distributors is maintained by telephone, fax and email, and through visits by members of the sales force. Apollo is also well represented at leading exhibitions, either directly or indirectly through agents and distributors. There is little advertising, apart from some in the trade press, and public relations has been largely ignored.

In order to retain clients, build longer-term relationships and reduce costs, many manufacturers are looking to develop positive life-long relationships with their distributors. One way in the past has been to increase the switching costs for distributors. However, this is difficult unless there is some distinct and sustainable competitive advantage or reason to be aligned with a particular manufacturer. Correspondingly, distributors are looking for improved reliability, manufacturer commitment and integrity, as well as product expertise. To meet these requirements a shift in the form of the relationship between Apollo and its distributors is necessary, and to do this a more effective and efficient communication system needs to be introduced.

To date, Apollo's marketing communications strategy has been to use its distributors to present Apollo's products to their markets. This has often resulted in a fragmented and varied set of messages which are largely product-oriented and based on the provision of information, product attributes and benefits. The strategy is now being questioned, as some people claim that the current approach is slow and inefficient due to duplication and repetition which drives up communication costs. With increasing competition, a requirement for faster information flows and a need to present a more unified and focused identity to clients and distributors means that the marketing communications strategy is in need of review.

The information provided in this case is based on a case in Bickerton, Bickerton and Simpson-Holley 1998, *Cyberstrategy*, Butterworth-Heinemann. Information has also been provided by the company, whose name has been disguised. Some of the material has been adapted in order to provide a suitable context for the mini-case study and in no way is intended to imply good or bad management or even actual situations or current practice.

**Source:** *Integrated Marketing Communications Examination Paper*, December 2000.

**Questions**

1.  Apollo operates in a business-to-business environment. Explain how the organisational buying process might impact on communications from them and their distributors.

2.  How is Apollo's internal culture likely to impact on their marketing communications?

**SUMMARY OF KEY POINTS**

In this Session, we have looked at consumer and organisational buying behaviour, and covered the following key points:

■ Consumer and organisational buyer behaviour follows a process which is similar. However, it is important for those marketing to organisations to understand the differences that exist.

■ Marketers need to understand the levels of perceived risk buyers may experience and try to overcome these through their communications.

■ Communications can play a large part in internal marketing and in achieving a customer-focused culture.

## Improving and developing own learning

The following projects are designed to help you develop your knowledge and skills further by carrying out some research yourself. Feedback is not provided for this type of learning because there are no 'answers' to be found, but you may wish to discuss your findings with colleagues and fellow students.

**Project A**

Whether your organisation deals directly with consumers or is in business-to-business marketing, consider how the marketing communications uses links to the buyer decision-making process, and influences each stage.

Talk to colleagues in your marketing department about how effective it is at each stage.

---

**Project B**

Talk to colleagues in your marketing department about the impact your organisation's culture has on your marketing communications activity.

---

**Project C**

How much internal marketing is undertaken within your organisation? What impact does this have on achieving a customer-focused culture?

What tools are used to communicate with this internal audience? Make notes of your findings, as well as any improvements you feel are appropriate.

---

## Feedback to activities

### Activity 4.1

One of the major differences between consumer purchasing of low value goods and that of major purchases is time and repeat purchase. Consumers will take an average of 6 months to purchase a house, researching suitable properties, finding a lawyer and negotiating a mortgage. Buying white goods, such as a fridge, can take a few weeks to research the favoured make, model and retailer, and then it may take a week from purchase to receive the goods. FMCG goods could be an impulse purchase, such as some delicacy from the delicatessen counter, or a repetitive weekly buy such as eggs or milk.

### Activity 4.2

Many established brands such as Häagen-Dazs and Pizza Express now offer a whole experience, such as members clubs, promotions, special buys, information events etc. These brands have taken marketing communications to another level, using the Internet to create a whole integrated package of interactive inducements to buy their products.

www.pizzaexpress.com

www.haagen-dazs.com

www.starbucks.com

www.lancome.com

www.dove.com

## Activity 4.3

Benefits of a customer-focused culture:

- Improved relationships with customers.
- Customer loyalty.
- Customer retention.
- Improved supplier relationships.
- Informed product development.
- Less waste and rejections.
- Improved systems and processes.
- Better staff morale.
- Rewards and recognition.

A customer-focused culture takes more care in communicating internally and externally and customers are made to feel valued and important, leading to more transparent and less adversarial relationships. In turn this improves the credibility of the brand and creates better profit margins.

## Activity 4.4

Organisational values are often those of senior management who may then employ people with like-minded attitudes.

Some possible motivating values might be:

- Hard work reaps rewards.
- Customers are always right.
- Quality and improvements.
- Value added services.
- Excellent customer service.
- Empathy and listening.
- Training and self-development.
- Empowering individual initiatives.

Some less encouraging values might be:

- Discipline and hard work are mandatory.
- No investment in improvements.
- Little reward and recognition.
- Planning is a waste of time.
- Staff are instructed, not consulted.
- Staff must do as they are told.
- Innovations are not valued.

# Session 5

# Using a context analysis

## Introduction

This Session looks at the complexity of marketing communications, and how a context analysis can help make sense of the situation. It goes on to consider the way in which an effective marketing communications plan should be structured and presented.

---

### LEARNING OUTCOMES

At the end of this Session you will be able to:

■ Consider the different elements of marketing communications and identify linkages between these.

■ Explain how the findings of context analysis can inform the communications plan.

■ Present a structured communications plan.

---

## The elements of marketing communications and how they inter-relate

Marketing communications is concerned with transmitting a number of messages to a given target audience through a chosen communications medium. The meanings, implicit or explicit, need to reach the target audience, transmitted in such a way that the messages are acted upon so as to meet specific objectives.

To assist you in thinking about the process, a number of questions need to be answered:

1. What messages am I communicating?
2. Which medium is most suitable for these messages?
3. How can I best transmit the messages?
4. What do I want my audience to do as a result of having received these messages?

Teams will approach this process through studying the audiences' needs and wants through research and building a profile. The messages are then derived from the objectives of the marketing communications.

| Message | → | Media | → | Transmission | → | Action |

## Message

The message is often a combination of product and brand. The message could be concerning the success of the company and its rise in share prices, or even the appointment of a new director. These communication messages must also take into consideration the overall brand messages, which may be concerned with quality, customer service and perhaps innovation.

Product messages change over time throughout the product life-cycle. Launching a new brand may be concerned with creating awareness and trial; therefore companies have to educate the market quickly at the start of the life-cycle, whereas once the product is established, more complex benefit messages may be appropriate.

## Media

For the marketing communications to be successfully received by the target audience, appropriate media must be used. This is a combination of budget and resource restraints and researching the customer profiles, so that messages are tailored and delivered through a familiar medium and subsequently received and understood. It's a waste of resources and inappropriate to advertise business-to-business products and services through a mass-market media such as television; the budget will be wasted, messages diluted or often not received at all.

## Transmission

Timing is important and can be crucial for any campaign. There are two constraints: firstly, many products are seasonal and therefore communications need to be planned for transmission just before purchase, for example at Christmas and other special occasions such as Easter. Secondly, the media itself may need to be planned well in advance, such as buying exhibition space up to a year ahead of time. The customer buying cycle needs to be studied so that messages are received at the point of purchase.

## Action

What do you want your audience to do as a result of receiving the message? Do you want them to 'think' differently, as in a PR campaign to raise awareness about green issues and how your organisation is saving the planet, or do you want them to go out and buy your product? PR can be beneficial to gain credibility and transmit cultural messages about how a company works, whereas if you want immediate action you may choose to use an on-pack promotion to stimulate sales.

This simple process can help you plan campaigns more effectively, helping you think through the process of communication as well as the content.

**Activity 5.1**

Take a campaign from current media and develop a presentation illustrating the framework above.

There will be a number of different media and you need to highlight the likely 'interconnectivity' and how the various media reinforce one another.

## Context analysis and its impact on the marketing communications plan

A context analysis provides a picture of the world within which you and your customers are operating, which affects their buying decisions. It's also important to evaluate the organisational context and the resources and capacities that are valuable to carry out a marketing communications plan.

The key elements of any context analysis are the economic, social, cultural and environmental conditions that surround the organisation, products and brands. In any analysis of the context, qualitative and quantitative information provides a base on which to make judgements about your approach to marketing communications.

Factors to consider within the **economic** dimension include:

■ State of growth or depression within the country or countries of your customers.
■ Cost, quality and availability of alternative choices etc.

Factors to consider within the **social** dimension include:

■ Social profile of the country or countries of your customers.
■ Range of arts, culture, sports and leisure pursuits undertaken.
■ Level of skills and education in the workforce and among children etc.

Factors to consider concerning the **cultural** dimension include:

■ People's beliefs and attitudes to your products and services.
■ Cultural norms and values.
■ Customer buying behaviour.

Factors to consider in the **environmental** dimension include:

■ Green issues such as climate changes, air quality and the landscape.
■ Current approaches to land use, waste and water.
■ Range of biodiversity.
■ Levels of noise pollution.

Factors to consider about the **organisation**:

■ Vision and purpose of the organisation.

■ Resources, capabilities and capacities within the organisation.

■ Likely effects of any major communications campaign.

All the above factors affect what messages are transmitted and the way we choose to transmit them. External factors such as the economic wealth of a nation tell us how much disposable income is available, and this in turn tells us what is likely to be purchased and by which socio-economic groups. In a depression most people are concerned with basic necessities such as food, and luxuries are purchased less frequently. In recent years fast food outlets have often survived well when the economy has been depressed, as have supermarket chains.

Social and cultural influences tell us what type of products are most likely to be purchased by a given market and the type of communications that will be successful. To illustrate this point, young children in the developed world watch TV and see advertising about special offers, on packets of cereals for example, which appeal to them; the children in turn will influence the food shopping decisions made by their parents.

The organisations' ability not only to implement a marketing communications campaign but also meet the demand from the results is an important part of communications planning. Many campaigns fail because the product is not ready on the shelves or the demand has been underestimated, so the customers cannot purchase the products and services advertised.

---

**Activity 5.2**

Pick a product. List the economic, social, cultural and environmental factors you would need to investigate, which would impact on the buying decisions of your customers.

Which factors would impact most and how would they affect the style and content of your communications with your customers?

---

## The communications plan

Developing a communications plan through a number of process stages requires major decisions to be made in advance concerning the marketing strategy and the marketing communications mix.

## Strategy

The organisational **vision and purpose** sets the long-term strategic direction. If an organisation has its main purpose of providing healthcare to insurance paying publics, then it would be a major diversification to provide NHS funded dentistry. Strategic decisions provide a framework for communicating corporate messages about values and approaches to business, such as environmental concerns as with the Body Shop. Anita Roddick promoted her travels and concerns with underprivileged countries as a PR opportunity to launch new brands based on environmentally and ethically sound principles.

## Communication objectives

For a plan to have a direction that can be measured, **SMART** objectives lead action planning. Communication objectives are often concerned with the various stages of the **buying cycle AIDA (Awareness, Interest, Desire and Action)**. This cycle highlights the stages of sale, from becoming aware of a product's existence through to purchase. Different media are used throughout the cycle to stimulate demand. Other objectives may be concerned with company image, brand loyalty and supporting distribution networks.

## Marketing communication tactics

The choice of media is based on the stage of the **product life-cycle**, objectives for the campaign, customer profile and positioning. A number of media may be chosen, all of which, if planned effectively, can reinforce the other, resulting in the creation of an integrated campaign which will be more cost effective and have better results.

## Action planning and implementation

Once the decisions have been made, the action planning makes the plan come to life. This is the 'who, how and what' part of the plan, where resources are confirmed and budgets and time frames are developed. It may be at this stage that the plan is re-visited, due to lack of funds or unrealistic expectations regarding time frames. If the strategy is the destination, your action plan becomes the road map. At this phase, a test market may be set up to evaluate the communications plan in micro-form before national launch, testing media response.

## Evaluation and control

How can you improve if you don't know what you have achieved? Putting in controls is essential for further planning. Whether you need to re-design your plan due to unforeseen events such as September the 11th 2001 or create a new plan for next year, you need to measure the success of each individual aspect of the planning process.

Each product and market segment may need a separate communications plan, which is amalgamated into a corporate communications plan. One of the reasons for creating clarity at the strategic stage is that to have too many products and markets causes confusion and budgets get stretched very thin, as opposed to having synergy and thereby maximising resources.

Concentrating on particular segments can also be a dangerous strategy. If the market changes, differentiating yourself from the competition through carefully managed campaigns can be your major competitive advantage.

---

**Activity 5.3**

Develop a presentation describing the different questions you would need to ask at each stage of the planning process.

---

# Case Study – Woodstock Furniture

Woodstock Furniture is a privately owned company located in a fashionable area in London. The company makes bespoke, high quality kitchen and bathroom furniture. Kitchens account for 80% of sales and the average order value is £25,000.

The general kitchen furniture market in the UK is worth over £800 million but, of this, the bespoke market is only worth a static 1%. Woodstock's sales have fluctuated over its 22 years of trading and currently stand at £1.7 million per annum, with net profit at 6.9%. However, the balance sheet is weak and there is little opportunity to attract finance for promotional investment. Staff are very supportive of the company, appear to identify strongly with the customised approach and many have been with the company since its start up. However, many of the internal systems and procedures are old, slow and in need of updating, perhaps a reflection of the slower, detailed craftsman-like culture that identifies the Woodstock Furniture Company.

In recognition of some of the problems facing the company, the management has developed a marketing plan which seeks growth of 15% per annum to be achieved by market penetration and, in particular, the attraction of new customers. It now needs a marketing communication programme to develop a strong corporate brand. The problem is that profit margins are small and there is little to invest in developing the brand and competing with well-known high street outlets.

The competition, as Woodstock see it, have huge resources which can be used to invest in promotional campaigns to drive awareness and action. For example, these companies have authentic web sites, unlike Woodstock's site which is little more than an online brochure. Many of the large national standardised companies can produce promotional literature in large production runs and are happy to ignore wastage. Using expert photography of fake kitchens makes the quality and impact of the literature high. Woodstock's smaller budgets dictate that photographs of real customers' kitchens are required, which seldom look perfect and can even appear amateurish. It costs £4 to produce each of the Woodstock brochures so vetting of each request for literature is important, to avoid those people who ask for brochures but buy nothing. A high conversion rate is necessary and although 50% of quotations are converted into sales, Woodstock cannot afford this figure to be lowered.

Woodstock's customers do not want the standardised kitchen units provided by the larger, more dominant players in the market. They want kitchens made to measure and which complement the character of their homes. They look for attention to detail, design, craftsmanship and support when commissioning bespoke companies such as Woodstock. The target market is affluent, often has more than one home and relies on word-of-mouth recommendation when drawing up a shortlist of possible providers. For many, price is not the key issue; rather it is the capability to craft suitable furniture to match the required décor and house style. This requires a high degree of trust, which successful companies in this market are able to reciprocate and in turn generate commitment. Many of Woodstock's customers are celebrities, but because discretion and privacy is important to them, they often refuse to allow their names (and kitchens) to be used for Woodstock publicity. However, customer loyalty is extremely important, with over 60% of new business being driven from existing customers.

In recognition of this, Woodstock now believes that it is in the business of craftsmanship and the design and construction of customised furniture, rather than the business of making and installing kitchen and bathroom furniture. It has improved levels of support and service (having, for example, introduced annual maintenance contracts) and has high levels of customer satisfaction. The marketing plan states that prices are to be raised to capitalise on premium pricing opportunities and the high levels of demand inelasticity. The marketing plan involves forming relationships with architects and developers and creating cross promotions and alliances with firms operating in similar markets, such as conservatories, studies and staircases.

**Source:** Adapted from an article in the *Sunday Times*, 15th August 1999, in Integrated Marketing Communications Examination Paper, June 2000.

**Questions**

1.  Undertake a context analysis for Woodstock Furniture, drawing out the key issues from this analysis.

2.  Identify the key stakeholder groups that Woodstock Furniture should communicate with, and recommend the messages that might be communicated to each.

3.  Outline the stages of the communications planning process as they relate to Woodstock Furniture.

## SUMMARY OF KEY POINTS

In this Session, we have introduced the use of context analysis in marketing communications planning, and covered the following key points:

■ Some of the important issues in designing marketing communications are the message, the media and the audience.

■ Marketing communications is complex, and a context analysis can help make sense of this.

■ The context analysis looks at economic, social, cultural and environmental conditions that impact on the organisation, its brands and its products. It also looks at the organisation itself, and its customers and stakeholder groups.

■ The marketing communications planning framework – MCPF – consists of the context analysis, promotional objectives, marketing communications strategy, the promotional mix, the resources needed (human, financial and time/ scheduling) and evaluation and control.

## Improving and developing own learning

The following projects are designed to help you develop your knowledge and skills further by carrying out some research yourself. Feedback is not provided for this type of learning because there are no 'answers' to be found, but you may wish to discuss your findings with colleagues and fellow students.

**Project A**

Talk to colleagues in your marketing department about one of your recent advertisements. What message was it trying to convey?

What media were used to carry the message? Who was the target audience? How effective was this advert?

**Project B**

Carry out a context analysis of your own organisation's marketing communications situation.

What can you learn from this?

**Project C**

Talk to colleagues in your marketing department and compare a recent marketing communications plan to the framework used in this Session.

How does it compare? Could improvements be made?

## Feedback to activities

### Activity 5.1

This exercise should encourage you to evaluate the different media in terms of message. For example, a campaign featuring a food product will probably use mass market advertising, in-store displays and point of sale, plus an on-pack promotion. There may be competitions on the web site and a PR campaign in the marketing press. All these media have the ability to carry different types of messages.

### Activity 5.2

Some examples of such an analysis might be:

|  | Economic | Social | Cultural | Environmental | Organisational |
|---|---|---|---|---|---|
| **Luxury Goods** | Limited disposable income. | Fashion and profile of target audience. | Norms in peer group, attitudes to product usage etc. | Packaging and re-cycling. | Financial resources and in-house capabilities. |

## Activity 5.3

Possible questions might be:

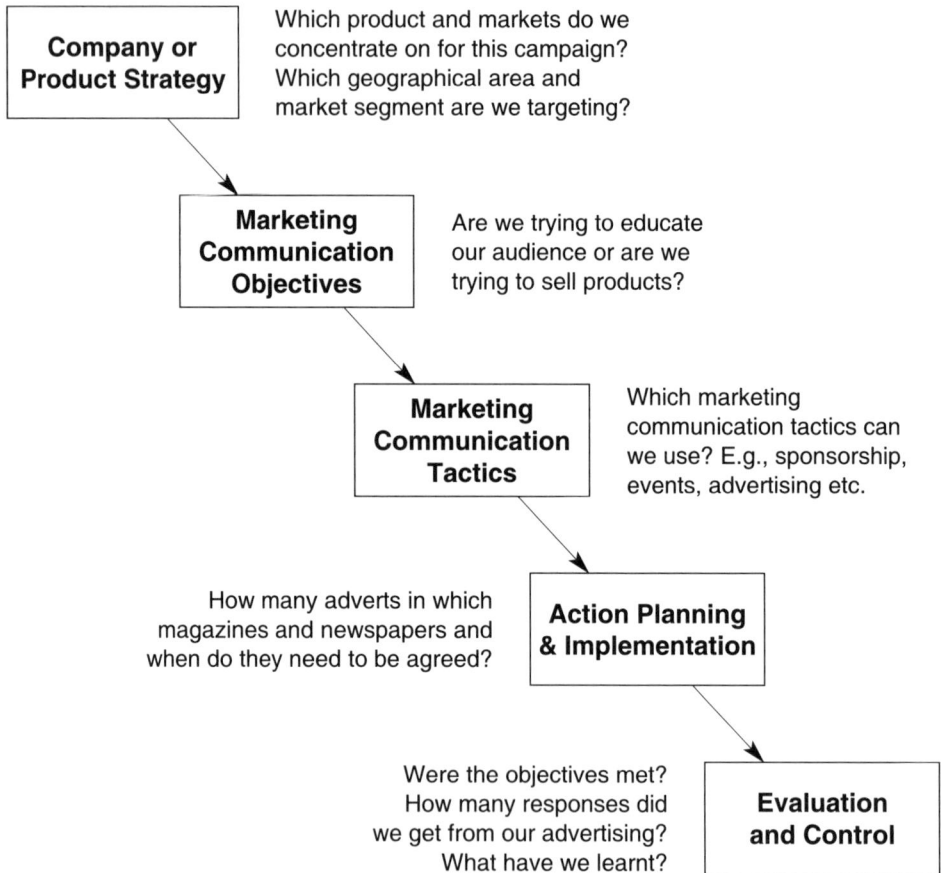

| Company or Product Strategy | Which product and markets do we concentrate on for this campaign? Which geographical area and market segment are we targeting? |

| Marketing Communication Objectives | Are we trying to educate our audience or are we trying to sell products? |

| Marketing Communication Tactics | Which marketing communication tactics can we use? E.g., sponsorship, events, advertising etc. |

| How many adverts in which magazines and newspapers and when do they need to be agreed? | Action Planning & Implementation |

| Were the objectives met? How many responses did we get from our advertising? What have we learnt? | Evaluation and Control |

# Session 6

# Segmentation, targeting and positioning

## Introduction

This Session looks at ways in which segmentation, targeting and positioning influence the marketing communications process, and how they can help make it more effective. Several segmentation methods are considered, with particular attention to psychographic segmentation. Perceptual mapping and positioning strategies are also explored.

---

### LEARNING OUTCOMES

At the end of this Session you will be able to:

■ Explain how segmentation and target marketing assists the development of marketing communications.

■ Explore various segmentation methods.

■ Understand and determine various positioning strategies.

■ Explain how perceptual mapping can be used.

---

## The role of segmentation, targeting and positioning

In the 1950s, most marketing communications were mass market, aimed at the whole population. As competition has grown, so organisations have found it necessary to target discrete groups so as to maximise opportunities for the communication messages to be heard and acted upon.

Organisations compete either by becoming the brand leader in a particular market or, as a follower, differentiating their brand in some way to gain competitive advantage. Creating brands aimed at specific target groups through segmenting the market can generate a significant advantage over the competition.

Segments need to be evaluated systematically so that comparisons can be made and the attractiveness of market segments assessed against the following criteria:

■ Size – will the sector be large enough to warrant developing a marketing mix for that segment alone? Marketing resources are always stretched so the segment needs to be significant enough to warrant separate attention.

■ Segment Growth – is the segment in a growth phase? Assessing the product life cycles of other products in the sector may highlight long term potential.

- Segment Profitability – other organisations operating in this sector will provide some evidence of the profitability.

- Customers' price sensitivity – if the segment is crowded with competitors and this group of purchasers are price-sensitive, there may not be significant margins to be achieved.

- Stage of Industry Life Cycle – opportunities exist as new market segments emerge. However, the cost of infrastructure and marketing may be too high.

- Pattern of demand – are there seasonal patterns or other cyclical patterns that will affect demand?

- Potential for substitution – there may be other products that do the same job or a potential for substitute products which might erode sales.

Marketing communications are designed to appeal to a significant audience. Customer profiling is the most common form of analysing customer motivations and the different variables that affect buying behaviour. It becomes complex when it is discovered that there are a number of decision makers for one purchase, such as buying a car or a house. Therefore, there may be a need for parallel communication activities which appeal to more than one sub-segment.

Customers can be reached through a number of different media. If we take the Internet as an example, there are a number of different types of user. For example, some surfers spend hours of their spare time jumping from one connection to another looking for interesting sites, while some more focused users know exactly which sites to look at because they have researched the URLs from other media. These groups also split into e-commerce buyers and those that don't yet trust or like the idea of buying on the Internet. In considering these complexities, we realise that one size does not fit all: we have to tailor communications that fit in with the group of customers we are trying to target.

---

**Activity 6.1**

Take a group of customers and analyse their buying behaviour in terms of sales channel. List the types of media which are likely to drive additional buyers through the channel.

What are the probable messages that will influence this customer group?

---

## Psychographic segmentation

Psychographic variables identify the values, beliefs and attitudes of a given group of people. Lifestyle and personality traits explain possible buying habits, which marketers use to target marketing communications more effectively.

As direct marketing increases, so does the need to differentiate consumers into sub-groups, clarifying segments by understanding customer characteristics and what motivates purchasing.

Look at the Harley-Davidson web site, harley-davidson.co.uk. Take a look at how they have classified their customers. The purpose of this exercise is to target the sub-groups of Harley-Davidson riders with specific products and services. Understanding consumer attitudes in relation to a brand enables more targeted brand strategies and communications.

Lifestyle refers to the way consumers try to achieve their life's goals. People join groups, both at work and during their leisure pursuits, which have different psychographic profiles. This information not only tells us about likely peer groups but also gives us a profile of their habits and consumption patterns.

These profiles can be achieved through customer surveys, information from promotional offers, web site contact details and general lifestyle information which is readily available, like magazines and government statistics.

---

**Activity 6.2**

Using the model above or any other that you have read about, take another brand known to you and design a presentation using as much information as you have to profile different customer sub-groups using psychographic variables.

---

## Positioning

Once an organisation has selected its target markets, it has to decide on what basis it will compete in the chosen segment or segments. Consumers have to be able to evaluate one product or brand against another and positioning helps customers distinguish competitive advantage.

Organisations can position products and brands by using a range of different associates, such as:

**Occasions** – when are the products used and in what context. For example, different wines may be chosen for celebrations from those drunk for normal social events.

**Personality** – Harley-Davidson products are positioned as a macho product with a free spirit.

**Usage** – convenience stores provide an ideal opportunity for late-night shoppers, and cereals are positioned as both a morning breakfast food and a late-night snack.

**Symbolism** – using a symbol with the corporate logo provides an association, for example Esso with the symbol of a tiger in a petrol tank which is intended to represent strength and power.

**Competitors** – some brands achieve cult status through advertising campaigns, such as the most recent Budweiser campaign where whole pubs could be heard to imitate the call, 'whassup!'

**Special interest** – environmental concerns and associated products, such as Ecover cleaning materials, appeal to specific interest groups.

**Price** – positions products for different market segments, as in own brands at supermarkets.

There could be a whole number of attributes that can be used by an organisation to differentiate their products and brands. Positioning is an idea or perception created in the mind of the customer and given an image. This may be a change in packaging, pricing, distribution or promotional messages and tactics. The customers need to be able to see a distinct advantage over competing products and brands.

Consumers often use leading brands as the main starting point for positioning, such as Heinz, or simply the most visible brand at the time. Customers respond to the profile and imagery, company reputation and publicity. Strategically, this makes it difficult for other competitors to enter the market, as they would have to invest heavily in positioning in order to be visible.

Re-positioning an existing product or brand may be necessary at the mature stage of the product life cycle to change the image; for example HP sauce which had an old-fashioned image.

Positioning establishes the product or brand in the consumer's mind as unique, providing a differential advantage over the competition.

---

**Activity 6.3**

Work with a colleague to gather information about four competing brands in the FMCG sector (Fast Moving Consumer Goods) and identify the differences in both product or service, brand and promotional communications.

What is the major differentiator in each case?

---

## Perceptual mapping

Perceptual mapping is a tool that can be used so that the organisation can visually identify its current marketing position versus the competition, and plot any future strategic changes.

The process has a number of steps:

1. Define the segments in a particular market.
2. Decide which segment or segments to target.
3. Define the most important consideration consumers use to distinguish products and brands.
4. Use attributes and other descriptors to create a map.
5. Plot competing products and brands.
6. Explore opportunities and threats to product/brand positioning.

The map uses two axes, representing key market attributes that reflect customer perceptions. These attributes could be price, quality, style or a range of other issues.

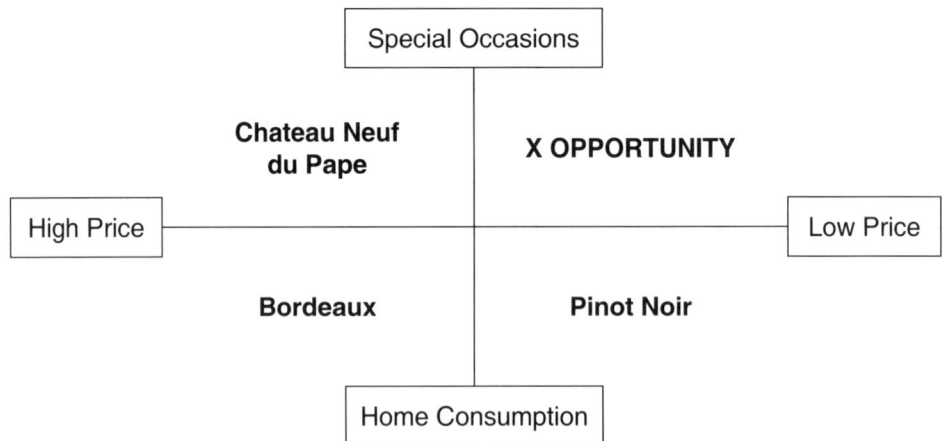

```
                    ┌─────────────────────┐
                    │  Special Occasions   │
                    └──────────┬──────────┘
                               │
   Chateau Neuf                │      X OPPORTUNITY
   du Pape                     │
                               │
┌────────────┐                 │                 ┌────────────┐
│ High Price ├─────────────────┼─────────────────┤ Low Price  │
└────────────┘                 │                 └────────────┘
                               │
    Bordeaux                   │         Pinot Noir
                               │
                    ┌──────────┴──────────┐
                    │  Home Consumption   │
                    └─────────────────────┘
```

A perceptual map of the wine market highlights the likely customer perceptions when choosing wine for different occasions. Other considerations would also affect the purchase such as packaging, shelf space and position, special offers etc.

A number of maps could be used showing different attributes, enabling the organisation to see clearly whether there are further gaps in the market to re-position the product or brand, or even launch a new one. For example, if we use the above map there may be an opportunity for a low-priced special occasions wine.

Positioning and re-positioning need to be handled with caution, as customers have built a relationship with a product and brand and you need to take care that sales do not diminish as a result of a poorly executed communications programme. Market research is essential to learn about people's attitudes towards both existing and potential new products and brands.

There are various approaches to distinguishing one product from another: it may be that using a particular functional feature to differentiate the positioning is enough, or an emotional selling proposition could be used, or of course a mixture of both.

---

**Activity 6.4**

Using a market sector of your choice, create a positioning map by brainstorming product and brand attributes and differentiators.

Make recommendations for a new competitor looking to enter the market.

---

# Case Study – Breakfast cereals

*This Case Study is taken from a past examination paper, and is used in Sessions 6, 7 and 9 of this Companion, with different questions adjusted to the content of these Sessions.*

The UK Ready-to-Eat (RTE) breakfast cereal market is worth £1,080 million and is dominated by three main manufacturers, Kellogg's, Weetabix and Cereal Partners. They hold 69% market share but are faced with a number of competitive pressures, one of which is the 21% share held by the own label distributors which is growing at 5% each year. The market is mature and is characterised by strong competition. Growth in the market has been slow with only product innovation and segmentation activities (e.g. chocolate flavours and children's products) showing above average performance. Branding in the RTE sector is extremely important.

| Manufacturer | Market Share by Volume % | UK Advertising Spend £m |
|---|---|---|
| Kellogg's UK | 42 | 55 |
| Weetabix Ltd | 15 | 15 |
| Cereal Partners Ltd | 12 | 18 |
| Own Label | 21 | 0 |
| Others | 10 | 14 |
| Total | 100% | £102m |

Table 1: Market Share and Advertising Spend for Three Leading UK Cereal Manufacturers

With high penetration levels (90% of households holding stock and 73% of consumers claiming to eat them for breakfast), opportunities for real growth appear to be limited. However, research has shown that regular eating of the right sort of breakfast can help us get the correct balance of foods we need.

The nutritional value of breakfast cereals and their impact on health, diet and weight, combined with their convenience, suggest that there are new opportunities for product development and marketing communications. This health orientation has helped broaden market opportunities through new products, for example the very successful launch of Nutrigrain cereal bars from Kellogg's for those who need to eat a mobile breakfast, maybe while travelling to work, and the promotion of breakfast cereals as an all-day snack food (which has been referred to as guilt-free snacking). The development of the Nutrigrain bars also demonstrates how Kellogg's has moved into new marketing channels (e.g. petrol forecourts) and is reaching new audiences.

The different strategies adopted by the leading brand manufacturers suggest that there is no single best way to use marketing communications in this market.

**Kellogg's** is the leading brand manufacturer but has been most affected by the growth of own label brands. Faced with declining market share it has just announced an aggressive marketing policy, slashing prices by 12% on its top six brands. It also intends to increase its advertising spend by 40%. In the past Kellogg's advertising has been based around a benefit-oriented message which aims to educate audiences about the nutritional values of its products. In doing so, Kellogg's acknowledges the role parents play in the decision-making process. Kellogg's also collaborates with the Government's Health Education Authority to raise awareness of the need for a balanced diet and the important role breakfast plays in our daily food intake.

The **Weetabix** company is privately owned and discloses very little about its activities. The Weetabix biscuit, the company's main brand, has a unique characteristic in that it turns very soft and mushy when milk is poured on it. Rather than work as a product disadvantage, this increases the product's utility as it makes it a suitable food for all ages; from babies as a weaning food, to young people as a quick and convenient snack food, through to those in their later years. In addition to specific brand advertising, which has been attribute-based, Weetabix aims to add value to its brands through the use of sales promotions, rather than focus on price reductions and discounts. For example, one promotion used
40 free drawstring tea bags banded on top of a Weetabix 48 pack, whilst another linked into an offer with Maxwell House coffee. Weetabix has been very profitable and the company does not want to be drawn into a price war.

**Cereal Partners** was formed through an alliance between General Mills and Nestlé and is the single largest producer of own label products. The core of its activities in the market has been brand extensions and relaunches of established brands. This is demonstrated through the extensions of its largest single brand, Shredded Wheat, into Fruitful, Honey Nut and Bitesize. It does not see price as a significant factor in the decision-making process, as it claims that research indicates that breakfast cereals are perceived to be a good value food. Its advertising messages are often directed at children and stress the taste and

| Manufacturer | Leading Brands | Brand Market Share by Value (%) | UK Advertising Spend £m |
|---|---|---|---|
| Kellogg's UK | Kellogg's Cornflakes | 9 | 8 |
| Weetabix Ltd | Weetabix | 7 | 9 |
| Cereal Partners Ltd | Shredded Wheat | 4.5 | 5 |

fun properties of its main line brands.

**Table 2: Market Share and Advertising Spend for Three Leading UK Cereal Brands**

**Note:** *Information for this case has been collected from a variety of public sources. The figures have been adjusted to enable clearer relationships to be observed. The material is not intended to imply good or bad management practice. This mini case is presented as illustrative material and is suitable for teaching purposes only.*

**Source:** *Integrated Marketing Communications Examination Paper,* June 2001

**Questions**

1. From the information in the Case Study, describe two potential segments for Weetabix.

2. Suggest attributes of the cereals mentioned in the Case Study that might be used to construct perceptual maps for the market.

3. From the information in the Case Study describe a potential target segment for the new Nutrigrain bar.

## SUMMARY OF KEY POINTS

In this Session, we have introduced segmentation, targeting and positioning, and covered the following key points:

- Breaking the total market down into segments – group of customers that share needs, wants and characteristics – helps target marketing communications more effectively.

- Customer profiling presents a means of analysing customer motivations and buying behaviour.

- Psychographic segmentation is particularly useful to the marketer, as it looks at values, beliefs and attitudes, and helps the design of effective communications.

- Products and brands can be positioned using a range of variables.

- Perceptual maps give a visual image representing consumer perceptions of products or services.

## Improving and developing own learning

The following projects are designed to help you develop your knowledge and skills further by carrying out some research yourself. Feedback is not provided for this type of learning because there are no 'answers' to be found, but you may wish to discuss your findings with colleagues and fellow students.

---

**Project A**

Talk to your colleagues in the marketing department about the segments that your organisation targets, and look at the various communications used to target each.

Can you make associations between the two?

---

**Project B**

Find out how your organisation profiles its customers. Is a database used?

How much do your sales force contribute to this process?

---

**Project C**

Talk to colleagues in your marketing department about the use of perceptual maps. Are there examples you can look at?

How have they been used?

Are there examples of communications that have been produced as a result of a mapping exercise?

## Feedback to activities

### Activity 6.1

If we take housewives as an example of a group of customers, they may use independent shops and supermarkets for food shopping. How will the media and messages differ according to the specific sales channel?

| Types of Buyer | Sales Channel | Message | Media |
|---|---|---|---|
| Housewife | Independent food shops | Ease of access<br>Fair prices<br>Friendly service | Posters<br>POS |
| Housewife | Multiple | Better prices<br>On pack offers<br>Loyalty cards | TV Advertising<br>Loyalty Magazine |

## Activity 6.2

There are a number of models that could be used, available in all the marketing textbooks. For example, the VALS System (SRI International).

Arnold Mitchell of the Stanford Research Institute developed this system in the USA, using 2,713 respondents to 800 questions to classify the American public into 9 value lifestyle groups. This framework suggests that individuals pass through various stages of development, each of which influences attitudes, behaviour and psychological needs. They move from being driven by needs (survivors and sustainers), to an outwardly directed hierarchy (belongers, emulators and achievers) to an inner directed hierarchy (I-am me, experientials, societally conscious).

The 9 groups are:

1. Survivors, who are generally disadvantaged and who tend to be depressed, withdrawn and despairing.
2. Sustainers, who are again disadvantaged but who are fighting hard to escape poverty.
3. Belongers, who tend to be conventional, nostalgic, conservative, and generally reluctant to experiment with new products or ideas.
4. Emulators, who are status conscious, ambitious and upwardly mobile.
5. Achievers, who make things happen and enjoy life.
6. 'I am me', who are self-engrossed, respond to whims and are generally young.
7. Experientials, who want to experience a wide variety of what life can offer.
8. Societally conscious people with a marked sense of social responsibility, who want to improve the condition of society.
9. Integrateds, who are psychologically fully mature and who combine the best elements of inner and outer directedness.

## Activity 6.3

This is a good exercise to link with a perceptual map.

| Product/Service | Qualities/Differentiator | Communication Tactics |
| --- | --- | --- |
| Heinz Baked Beans | Well-known quality brand with unique packaging | Heinz magazine In-store promotions |
| Sainsbury's own brand | Sainsbury's packaging Value for money | Shelf space Sainsbury's recipes |
| Happy Shopper | Low cost | Independent shops No marketing |

## Activity 6.4

Unless you are creating a new market, you are inevitably competing with a range of companies who are either positioned as market leader, market challenger, market follower or market nicher. The market leader may be dominant in terms of economies of scale, but may also have less flexibility to re-position itself in terms of new packaging, styling and promotional communications. Market nichers focus on specific market segments to improve market share, perhaps in one geographic location. Market challengers confront the major competitor head on, as in Burger King and McDonald's.

# Session 7

# Promotional objectives

## Introduction

This Session considers how marketing communications is shaped by corporate objectives and strategy. It looks at the need for the mission statement to communicate an appropriate message to all stakeholder groups, as well as how marketing objectives should help to achieve corporate objectives. It also investigates how promotional or marketing communications objectives can help to achieve marketing objectives.

---

### LEARNING OUTCOMES

At the end of this Session you will be able to:

■ Explain how the mission statement should impact on marketing communications activities.

■ Understand how marketing communications fits with corporate and business level strategies.

■ Explain how communications objectives contribute to the achievement of organisational objectives.

---

## The impact of corporate strategy and the mission on marketing communications

What is your organisation's mission? You don't know? Don't worry, you are in good company. Many businesses put little effort into communicating what the company's mission is to employees or other interested parties, assuming there is a mission at all. Yet the mission is meant to be there to encapsulate what the business is all about. A mission becomes a reference point: a navigation beacon to guide company strategy by and a benchmark against which to determine the appropriateness of activities.

Without doubt, much of the problems with mission statements lie with the people who made them. Too often they are bland, vague, uninspiring or could have been written by any business, including your competitors or people in a completely different industry. "We will be the best widget manufacturer in the world" says the company that fails to do anything about delivering the training, tools, work practices, recruitment policies, communications etc. to support its ambitious claim.

There is, though, no single way to write a 'good' mission. A mission may be short and pithy, and thus perhaps memorable and motivational. But often it is longer, providing much clearer direction for the business. It may talk about:

■ Purpose and priorities: what the company is in business for, e.g. creating shareholder value, and the relative importance of, for instance, growth and delivering customer satisfaction.

■ Strategies: an overview of how the business will achieve its aims, perhaps in relation to particular target markets, product types or technologies.

■ Culture: how the business operations will fit with the external environment, or what it will be like to work there.

■ Behaviours and values: uncompromising ethical or environmental stance, for instance.

The Body Shop's mission, for example, is a six-point statement sub-titled "Our Reason for Being". It talks about its role through campaigning for and creating social and environmental change. Balancing the needs of different stakeholder groups is specifically covered.

So the mission generally provides boundaries within which the business operates. Within these boundaries, objectives can be determined and strategy formulated to enable the objectives to be achieved. Strategy may relate directly to business operations, achieving growth organically or by acquisition, or focusing on particular market segments. It may also look at other issues which are indirectly vital to achieving market aims, e.g. total upgrade of IT infrastructure or revision of remuneration policy.

So where do communications come into all this?

Every aspect of the mission and the strategy will have an impact on one or more class of stakeholder. Sometimes the mission will specifically mention the interests of specific stakeholders, especially customers, shareholders and employees. Corporate communications are therefore vital as they provide the link between the company, with its mission and strategy, and its stakeholders. They need to understand the company's mission and strategy for many reasons. These include:

■ Identifying the kind of company they are, or want to become involved with. The mission may, for example, indicate values and objectives that are incompatible with a prospective employee's or shareholder's objectives.

■ Guiding activity, by stimulating a cascade process from which departmental and other objectives are determined.

■ Having check-points against which to gauge whether behaviours and activities are consistent with the company's aims.

These stakeholders will want to see that their expectations of the organisation are met, so great care needs to be taken, not just in developing strategy, but in communicating it effectively. Bear in mind that good communication is usually about dialogue, not monologue. The reactions of stakeholders need to be gauged in order to adapt communications (or even strategy) accordingly.

The business's stakeholders are **audiences** or **publics**, around which Public Relations (PR) activity revolves. Communications to these publics are discussed more fully in Session 10.

---

**Activity 7.1**

Find out what your company mission is. If it doesn't have one, write one that would be appropriate.

Who are the stakeholders the mission relates to?

What evidence is there within the business for each of the key statements in the mission. Suggest what else the business could do to support these statements.

---

## Marketing communications role in achieving organisational and business objectives

There is no single definition of marketing communications, and any consideration of the subject need to be taken in context. At one level marketing communications concerns the process of the exchange of information between an organisation and any of its publics. Public relations, for example, is viewed as one tool in the promotional mix, but its audiences and purposes are very diverse (see Session 10). On a more tactical level, some people view marketing communications as solely encompassing promotion of the organisation's products, services or other commercial offerings to its target customers. The difficulty with this view comes in trying to separate out the 'product' (or whatever) and other intangible factors which might influence buying behaviour, such as corporate reputation.

However, central to marketing is the concept of **exchange**. It is evident that, for marketing to work, two parties are needed, each of whom offers something that is of value to the other. For these transactions to occur, communication is essential between them. These communications can do any of the following:

Inform…people of what is on offer.
Persuade…people of the benefits of entering into the transaction.
Remind…people of a need or of previous benefits of a transaction.
Differentiate…your offering from someone else's.

These communication purposes can easily be remembered by the mnemonic **DRIP**.

It is easy to think of this exchange in the context of actual or potential customers. But it can be extended to cover any other stakeholders too. Information may become of value in its own right, offered in return for, say, endorsement (by a journalist), loan facilities (by a banker) or commitment (by an employee). Marketers may be directly or indirectly involved in contributing to any of these communications.

Many organisational goals directly relate to exchange. Strategies and objectives frequently relate to customers, e.g. building market share or enhancing the value of customer relationships. Marketing, and its promotional activity, clearly has a role to play here. But objectives may also relate to other stakeholders, for example though reviewing distribution networks or developing the supply chain. The whole image of the company – what its name or brands stand for – may be very influential in determining the course of negotiations, even if marketing people are not directly involved.

A corollary of this is that integration of messages, whether deemed 'marketing' or 'corporate'; is essential. Different audiences may be interested in different things, but the messages emanating from the organisation need to be consistent and synchronised to avoid confusion and uncertainty in the audience's mind.

### Corporate objective

Whatever corporate strategies or marketing activities there are, ultimately they should be there to satisfy the corporate objective(s). Usually this will be a financial measure, related to adding value for shareholders. Marketing can add real value to shareholders by:

■ Developing the business's assets, e.g. brands, or a loyal customer base.
■ Maximising profitable growth by creating superior offerings for customers.

In turn, marketing communications can play a pivotal role in creating these sources of value.

---

**Activity 7.2**

Based on the last sentence above, suggests two ways that marketing communications can play a role for each of the following added-value activities:

■ Brand building
■ Developing a loyal customer base
■ Creating superior customer offerings

---

# Corporate strategy and promotional objectives

Earlier this Session we touched on the company mission and its relationship to corporate strategy. These are two steps in the process of defining objectives for the business as a whole. The endpoint, from a marketing communications view, is the agreement of promotional objectives. Let us look at the whole process in more detail, splitting it into levels which constitute a hierarchy of objectives, illustrated below.

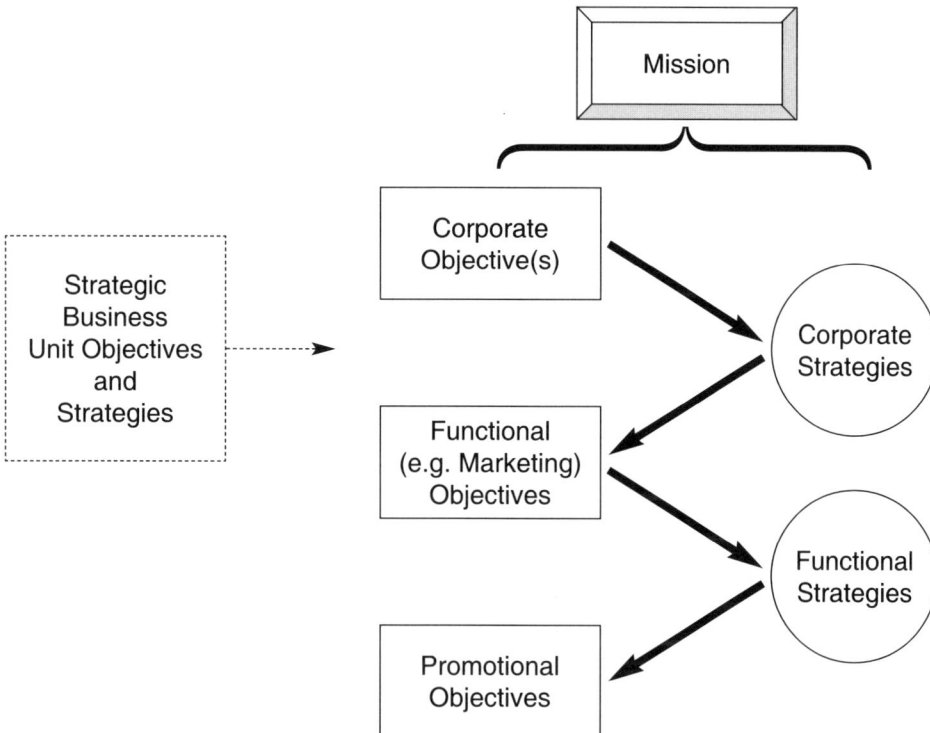

## Corporate objectives and strategy

Whereas the mission gives an overview of the company's aims, the corporate objectives set out its specific, measurable goal(s). For commercial businesses this will usually be a financial measure of particular interest to shareholders, such as profit growth or return on investment. Other types of business may use other measures: a not-for-profit organisation, for instance, may set targets based on making most efficient use of available resources.

Businesses often operate as a series of separate entities, perhaps split into operating companies or operating as autonomous geographical regions.

Separate financial or other objectives may be set for each of these Strategic Business Units (SBUs).

To achieve the corporate objective(s), the organisation will need to formulate strategies. These strategies will feed into the next level of objectives, set at functional level (or at SBU level, feeding into the SBU's functions).

### Functional objectives

At this next level, the different functions within the business (e.g. Marketing, HR, IT, Finance, Production) need to set objectives that will deliver the corporate strategy. A function will need to set goals both in relation to those strategies for which it has primary responsibility for delivery, and also those where its contribution is secondary. This requires willingness and ability to discuss plans across the business and to identify which departments will need to contribute to them. Examples of Marketing's primary objectives for a particular period might be:

- To increase total market share for a specified range of products to 7.0%.
- To generate 1,000 leads for Sales.
- To improve customer retention by 20%.

Again, as with corporate objectives, these objectives need to be translated into strategies to enable them to be met. There may be more than one strategy per objective.

### Operational objectives

From these strategies, supporting activities will be identified which might relate, in Marketing's case, to any elements of the marketing mix. It is at this level that promotional objectives will be set. Overall promotional goals may be established, but these may need to be broken down into even more detailed objectives as individual tactical activities are identified. The promotional objectives, then, fall at the end of the end of a line from the corporate objectives, but it should be a possible to trace a direct chain of related links between those two points.

Two further points are worth noting. First, what is a strategic decision at one level may be seen as a tactical one at another. Thus Marketing may make a decision to withdraw a particular product as part of a review of product strategy. At a corporate level this may be viewed as a tactical decision derived from a cost reduction strategy.

Second, the time scales involved tend to get shorter as the hierarchy descends. While no business can afford to be inflexible, the mission and corporate financial objectives are unlikely to change very frequently and may do so only as part of radical change. Corporate strategy may take a medium-term view, perhaps using a rolling three year plan, which will be adjusted occasionally in response to changing market and other conditions. The functional view will tend to be shorter term, probably based on an annual planning cycle. Operational activities may also be planned annually but are subject to short-term change as operating conditions fluctuate.

---

**Activity 7.3**

The following information is extracted (slightly adapted) from the Summary Listing Particulars issued by mmO$_2$, the mobile communications company, when it demerged from BT in 2001.

**Goal (corporate objective)**

Our goal is to create shareholder value through above-average sector growth in revenue and earnings.

*Corporate Strategy*

The key elements of our strategy to achieve this goal are to:

- Emphasise operational performance and execution:
    - Focus on higher value customers in all of our business.
    - Achieve competitive scale in Germany and the Netherlands.
    - Focus on customer retention and conversion.
    - Focus on cost efficiencies.

- Achieve greater integration by managing our business cohesively:
    - Implement and exploit new branding.
    - Integrate product and network development and management.
    - Leverage technology.
    - Enhance procurement efficiencies.

- Lead in new data services through GPRS (General Packet Radio Service) and UMTS (Universal Mobile Telecommunications System) technologies:
    - Implement leading edge technology for data services.
    - Build services and applications pipeline.
    - Enhance mobile data services for business customers.
    - Leverage Genie [mobile internet] offering.

Extract used with kind permission of mmO$_2$

Select three of the above 12 sub-strategies for which Marketing might have primary responsibility for delivery. Suggest a Marketing objective for each (there is no need for specialist knowledge of mobile communications or mmO$_2$ – just use a creative, common sense approach).

Suggest one strategy and two supporting promotional objectives for each Marketing objective.

---

# Case Study – Breakfast Cereals

*This Case Study is taken from a past examination paper, and is used in Sessions 6, 7 and 9 of this Companion, with different questions adjusted to the content of these Sessions.*

The UK Ready-to-Eat (RTE) breakfast cereal market is worth £1,080 million and is dominated by three main manufacturers, Kellogg's, Weetabix and Cereal Partners. They hold 69% market share but are faced with a number of competitive pressures, one of which is the 21 % share held by the own label distributors which is growing at 5% each year. The market is mature and is characterised by strong competition. Growth in the market has been slow with only product innovation and segmentation activities (e.g. chocolate flavours and children's products) showing above average performance. Branding in the RTE sector is extremely important.

| Manufacturer | Market Share by Volume % | UK Advertising Spend £m |
|---|---|---|
| Kellogg's UK | 42 | 55 |
| Weetabix Ltd | 15 | 15 |
| Cereal Partners Ltd | 12 | 18 |
| Own Label | 21 | 0 |
| Others | 10 | 14 |
| Total | 100% | £102m |

Table 1: Market Share and Advertising Spend for Three Leading UK Cereal Manufacturers

With high penetration levels (90% of households holding stock and 73% of consumers claiming to eat them for breakfast), opportunities for real growth appear to be limited. However, research has shown that regular eating of the right sort of breakfast can help us get the correct balance of foods we need. The nutritional value of breakfast cereals and their impact on health, diet and weight, combined with their convenience, suggest that there are new opportunities for product development and marketing communications. This health orientation has helped broaden market opportunities through new products, for example the very successful launch of Nutrigrain cereal bars from Kellogg's for those who need to eat a mobile breakfast, maybe while travelling to work, and the promotion of breakfast cereals as an all-day snack food (which has been referred to as guilt-free snacking). The development of the Nutrigrain bars also demonstrates how Kellogg's has moved into new marketing channels (e.g. petrol forecourts) and is reaching new audiences. The different strategies adopted by the leading brand manufacturers suggest that there is no single best way to use marketing communications in this market.

**Kellogg's** is the leading brand manufacturer but has been most affected by the growth of own label brands. Faced with declining market share it has just announced an aggressive marketing policy, slashing prices by 12% on its top 6 brands. Kellogg's also intends to increase its advertising spend by 40%. In the past its advertising has been based around a benefit-oriented message which aims to educate audiences about the nutritional values of its products. In doing so, Kellogg's acknowledges the role parents play in the decision-making process. Kellogg's also collaborates with the Government's Health Education Authority to raise awareness of the need for a balanced diet and the important role breakfast plays in our daily food intake.

The **Weetabix** company is privately owned and discloses very little about its activities. The Weetabix biscuit, the company's main brand, has a unique characteristic in that it turns very soft and mushy when milk is poured on it. Rather than work as a product disadvantage, this increases the product's utility as it makes it a suitable food for all ages; from babies as a weaning food, to young people as a quick and convenient snack food, through to those in their later years. In addition to specific brand advertising, which has been attribute-based, Weetabix aims to add value to its brands through the use of sales promotions rather than focus on price reductions and discounts. For example, one promotion used
40 free drawstring tea bags banded on top of a Weetabix 48 pack, whilst another linked into an offer with Maxwell House coffee. Weetabix has been very profitable and the company does not want to be drawn into a price war.

**Cereal Partners** was formed through an alliance between General Mills and Nestlé and is the single largest producer of own label products. The core of its activities in the market has been brand extensions and relaunches of established brands. This is demonstrated through the extensions of its largest single brand, Shredded Wheat, into Fruitful, Honey Nut and Bitesize. It does not see price as a significant factor in the decision making process as it claims that research indicates that breakfast cereals are perceived to be a good value food. Its advertising messages are often directed at children and stress the taste and fun properties of its main line brands.

| Manufacturer | Leading Brands | Brand Market Share by Value (%) | UK Advertising Spend £m |
|---|---|---|---|
| Kellogg's UK | Kellogg's Cornflakes | 9 | 8 |
| Weetabix Ltd | Weetabix | 7 | 9 |
| Cereal Partners Ltd | Shredded Wheat | 4.5 | 5 |

**Table 2: Market Share and Advertising Spend for Three Leading UK Cereal Brands**

**Note:** *Information for this case has been collected from a variety of public sources. The figures have been adjusted to enable clearer relationships to be observed. The material is not intended to imply good or bad management practice. This mini case is presented as illustrative material and is suitable for teaching purposes only.*

**Source:** *Integrated Marketing Communications Examination Paper,* June 2001

## Questions

1. Explain why objectives are needed as part of the planning process, differentiating between corporate, marketing and promotional objectives.

2. Suggest marketing objectives for each of Kellogg's, Weetabix, and Cereal Partners Ltd, based on information in the Case Study.

3. Based on the marketing objectives you have developed in (1), suggest one promotional objective for one product from each company.

## SUMMARY OF KEY POINTS

In this Session, we have introduced communications objectives, and covered the following key points:

■ Organisations set objectives at all levels of the planning process to give shape to clear goals for achievement.

■ Promotional objectives help achieve corporate and marketing objectives by achieving the promotional requirements of the marketing mix.

■ Promotional objectives are set to differentiate products from those of competitors, remind the target audience of the products benefits, inform them of its existence, and persuade them to buy.

## Improving and developing own learning

The following projects are designed to help you develop your knowledge and skills further by carrying out some research yourself. Feedback is not provided for this type of learning because there are no 'answers' to be found, but you may wish to discuss your findings with colleagues and fellow students.

---

**Project A**

Talk to colleagues within the organisation to identify how well the mission statement of your organisation is known. Is internal marketing used to communicate mission, vision and objectives and plans?

If so, how often and through which methods?

---

**Project B**

Talk to colleagues in your marketing department and consider the links between corporate, marketing and promotional objectives.

How well do they support each other?

---

**Project C**

Talk to your marketing manager about your organisation's promotional plan.

Look at the promotional objectives that are within it.

Link these back to marketing objectives.

Categorise the promotional objectives using the DRIP mnemonic.

---

## Feedback to activities

### Activity 7.1

Answers will, of course, vary, but you will not be alone if you find it hard to directly link the mission to day-to-day activity. Ask friends if their organisation has a mission too and make comparisons. Can you identify a link between successful businesses, however you want to measure success, and mission statements?

## Activity 7.2

### Brand building:

- Creating a consistent set of brand values to be evidenced in all external communications.
- Developing links with partners, e.g. through commercial or charitable sponsorship, to support brand image.

### Developing a loyal customer base:

- Use regular communications as a strategic tool to build relationships with customers.
- Developing reward schemes to incentivise 'loyalty' and to understand customers better.

### Creating superior customer offerings:

- Using communications to persuade customers of the superior features, benefits or value of your product.
- Careful use and evaluation of communication activity, minimising wastage to reduce costs and/or maximise profits or investment capital.

## Activity 7.3

1. Focus on higher value customers in all our businesses.

   **Marketing objective:** To increase market share of high value customers to XX% within 12 months.

   **Strategy:** Target business buyers/users in large corporations, to increase sales of our new technology, and raise usage rates of existing users.

   **Promotional objectives:**

   - Increase awareness of our latest technologies among corporate telecommunications buyers by XX% .
   - Obtain X,000 members to new loyalty scheme for high-use corporate mobile technology users.

2. Focus on customer retention and conversion:

   **Marketing objective:** Increase retention rate by x%

   **Strategy:** Increase attractiveness of annual renewal offerings.

   **Promotional objectives:**

   - Increase response rate to annual renewal invitation mailing by XX%.
   - Raise awareness of enhanced renewal benefits amongst target audience by XX%.

3. Implement and exploit new branding:

**Marketing objective:** To make the mmO$_2$ brand the first choice amongst the majority of buyers in our target audiences by December 200X.

**Strategy:** Increase brand visibility and cement brand values in target audience's minds.

**Promotional objectives:**
- Re-brand all customer-facing material (signage, stationery, equipment etc.) by [date].
- Agree and implement new corporate promotional campaign by [date].

(N.B. Specific campaign objectives will need to be set. Care will need to be taken to integrate this and any other promotional activity).

# Session 8

# Push, pull and profile strategies and e-promotion

## Introduction

In the last Session we considered promotional objectives and their role in the overall achievement of the corporate plan. In this Session we go on to look at strategies for targeting consumer markets, the trade, and other stakeholder groups.

Finally, we look at the way in which electronic promotional techniques can help with the achievement of push, pull and profile strategies.

---

**LEARNING OUTCOMES**

At the end of this Session you will be able to:

■ Identify appropriate pull, push and profile strategies for various situations.

■ Explore appropriate marketing communications for business-to-business markets.

■ Explore 'corporate image' – personality, identity and reputation.

■ Explain how Internet and e-commerce activities relate to both consumer and business-to-business markets.

---

## Pull and push strategies for particular situations

When deciding communication strategy, the marketer can identify three main types of audience: the end-user of the product, who may be an individual consumer or a business; intermediaries, who operate between the producer and the end-user; and **stakeholders** who may have no direct interest in the product but who have an interest in the organisation itself. Different communication strategies are required for each audience.

A **pull strategy** is aimed at the end-user. It seeks to create demand from the target audience, so that products are **pulled** by them through the **marketing chain**. This demand may be for products directly, but an individual may also pull for information, for example. An individual approaching a retailer for a product he or she has seen advertised on television, and an Internet user searching for product details on a firm's web site are both examples of pull by consumers.

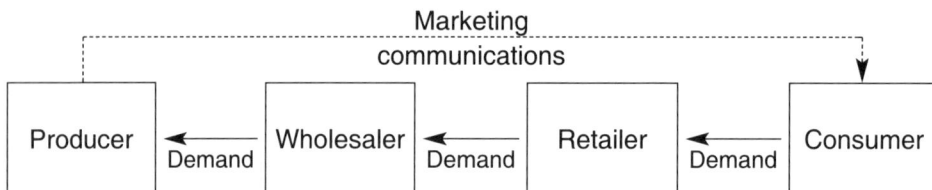

**Figure 8.1 Pull strategy.**

A **push strategy** is targeted at intermediaries, such as wholesalers, retailers, dealers and agents. Push activities aim to persuade the intermediary to **push** the product along the marketing chain by stocking it, displaying it or advocating it. The push may be to the next intermediary in the chain, if there is one, or to the end-user. Rotary Watches has developed a trade-only web site, which gives product information and allows on-line ordering. This is a cornerstone of their growth strategy; they say they have "[retailer] relationships to die for".

**Figure 8.2 Push strategy.**

A **profile strategy** is aimed at stakeholders (who may include intermediaries and end-users), and seeks to influence their perceptions of the organisation. Examples might concern communications about the business's financial performance, ethical stance or community involvement.

## Promotional tools

### Pull strategy

A wide variety of tools are available to support pull strategies. Many factors will determine the appropriate mix, including promotional objectives, the type of end-user, the nature of the market and the nature of the product. In particular, for high-involvement products, the early emphasis will be on tools that convey information and motivate the receiver to find out more or perhaps seek a demonstration. For low-involvement situations, methods may be chosen to suit less information-demanding messages, with a higher emphasis on brand and product recognition. In business-to-business markets the emphasis will generally be on supporting a rational buying process by what may be a more complex decision-making unit. The Internet is playing a rapidly growing role in this market.

Thus, while there is no universal rule, the most important pull strategy tools are likely to be:

| Business-to-business: | Personal selling<br>Exhibitions<br>Trade advertising<br>Web sites<br>Marketing PR (trade focus)<br>Direct mail |
| --- | --- |
| Business-to-consumer: | Advertising<br>Personal selling<br>Sales promotions<br>Direct marketing (post, telephone, e-mail etc.)<br>Web sites<br>Marketing PR  (consumer focus) |

**Push strategy**

Push strategies revolve around the nature of the relationships between businesses in the **marketing chain**. Communications must not only persuade, but must underpin the relationship of mutual support. Personal selling will often be vital, supported by trade advertising and sales promotions. The latter may be targeted directly at the intermediary, or at helping him or her move the product along the marketing chain. Extranets, with or without support from personal relationships, are playing an increasing role in communications between businesses; this will be covered further at the end of this Session.

**Strategy mix**

An organisation may use a mixture of push and pull strategies to achieve its goals, aiming to stimulate interest in both consumers and intermediaries. Timing is important. A **push** campaign will need to precede a **pull** one if, for example, a financial advisor is to respond effectively to demand for a new investment product which a customer has seen advertised in a newspaper. Marketers will also need to consider the balance of power in push/pull decisions. For example, food manufactures may have to use promotional budgets to respond to demands by retailers for bigger discounts and more point of sale material, rather than spending on consumer advertising, if their products are to get shelf space.

Whilst push and pull communications will have different objectives, it is essential to take an integrated approach so that consistent messages are communicated, and attitudes generated, amongst the different audiences.

---

**Activity 8.1  Time to Push or Pull?**

Think about a product or service you are familiar with. Write a memo suggesting how the balance of push and pull strategies might change over its lifetime.

---

## Communications for business-to-business markets

The business-to-business market (B2B) has many differences from the consumer ones.

- There are generally a smaller number of actual or potential buyers.
- The size of orders is usually larger.
- The decision making unit is often complex, involving buyers, users, technicians and others. A specialist purchasing department may be involved.
- The decision-making process tends to be more complex, formal and lengthy.
- The product is often complex or requires technical understanding.
- The product and other features of the deal, such as delivery or payment terms, are more likely to need to be modified or adapted to individual buying organisations' needs.
- Company money is used for the purchase, which means buyers are open to greater scrutiny and accountability.
- The overall buying process tends to be more rational, whereas emotions may play a larger part in consumer behaviour. In both cases, however, decisions are made by people, who inevitably have their own opinions and motives.

These differences mean that a different mix of communications methods is needed for B2B situations compared to B2C.

The most important element of the mix is personal selling. A salesperson, probably as part of a larger sales force, is able to target the relatively few, and possibly geographically dispersed, buyers. Given the general requirement for adaptation, he or she is able to understand the very specific situation and needs of the buyer, explain the product's technical aspects, and negotiate whatever special terms are appropriate. Business order may be very valuable, and the selling organisation will want to invest in maintaining the relationship with buyers. Salespeople can do this and also keep customers abreast of new developments. A salesperson is thus able to facilitate moving existing and potential customers through the stages of the AIDA model (Awareness – Interest – Desire – Action). Particular attention can be paid to Key Accounts who may be important because of size or frequency of orders, or because of their market position or the technologies they use.

Running a salesforce is costly and this may absorb much of a business's promotional budget. Investment in developing a brand or in running large scale above-the-line campaigns is therefore likely to be less important. That is not to say that other elements of the mix will not be used, but they will tend to be in a supporting role.

Direct marketing is playing an increasing role in B2B activities. Identifying the relatively small number of buyers makes targeting reasonably straightforward, though care needs to be taken to reach those who really are influential in the buying process. Direct marketing also helps the salesperson by maintaining the B2B relationship between calls (particularly for non-Key Accounts), and generating leads or 'warming up' a prospect prior to a request for an appointment.

Written communications, for example direct marketing, advertising or promotional literature, will tend to have a bias towards rational, information-based messages. The aim is to appeal to buyers' logic, at least giving them reasons to consider putting the selling organisation onto their list of possible suppliers.

Exhibitions and events such as conferences and seminars also play an important part in B2B marketing. They give opportunities for businesses to reach target audiences easily, in situations that allow a mix of presentation of written material, demonstrations and personal selling. Exotic or interesting locations can attract prospects – cruise ships are a popular choice for conferences, literally supplying a captive audience.

Attracting media attention may also play an important role in marketing plans. Independent endorsement of your products can be very influential and could be achieved at very low cost.

The use of new media in B2B situations was discussed in Session 3.

---

**Activity 8.2**

You are the owner of a newly established business supplying machinery to the fabric industry. You have marketing experience, but will have to allocate your time to a range of other activities within the business as well as marketing. There are no other marketing staff, but you have allowed a first year marketing budget of £60,000.

Suggest how you would allocate this sum.

---

## Trust and commitment as components of channel based communications

No organisation operates in a vacuum. It needs to be constantly alert to the changing demands of all its stakeholders, not just its customers. One key set of relationships is with other organisations in the marketing channel.

Some organisations produce and distribute direct to the public, but most are part of a chain forming a marketing channel, comprising intermediaries such as agents, wholesalers, dealers, distributors and retailers. Each organisation brings different strengths to the relationship, so that each can share in the benefits that others contribute These chains usually comprise discrete organisations (there are exceptions to this such as vertical marketing systems), and, as such, each organisation has its own objectives and has an over-riding motivation towards self-interest.

But at the same time most organisations recognise that they have a degree of interdependence with other organisations in the chain. Collaboration, by working towards mutually agreed goals, is likely to bring many advantages. Effort is not wasted working towards conflicting ends: activities can be co-ordinated to maximise their impact, and greater understanding brings strengthening relationships and the potential for more business.

To make these relationships work requires a focus on effective communication. Organisations need to spend time understanding each other's goals, systems, procedures, resources and relationships. Understanding will be particularly important in relation to operational communications, such as ordering and invoicing systems and marketing communications – the **push** communications discussed earlier this Session. Indeed, the push communication strategy requires particular emphasis on effective channel based communications. Intermediaries are the focus of attention in these strategies. If they are to be motivated to push the product to the next channel member, then there needs to be a thorough understanding of their requirements and expectations.

Effort needs to be put into establishing and **maintaining** this understanding, which means developing mechanisms for regular communications. Very importantly, underpinning any relationship there needs to be a feeling of trust. This means each party acting in the belief that the other is also committed to the relationship, and that each party is acting with integrity and honesty. In addition, each channel member needs to demonstrate that it is committed to an ongoing relationship. Organisations are not going to make any significant investment of time, money, I.T. resources, etc., in building relationships if they are going to be fleeting. Common values and recognition of the benefits of working together are vital ingredients if trust and commitment are to be built. But the ability and willingness to communicate are particularly important: failure to do so is likely to lead to failure of the relationship. Conversely, effective communication is likely both to be evidence of trust and commitment and to contribute to it.

## The components of corporate image – personality, identity and reputation

An organisation, like a person, can be said to have an 'image'. The **corporate image** is the way a stakeholder perceives an organisation in response to cues about it. Whilst the organisation may create these cues in an attempt to mould the image, ultimately the image depends upon the perceptions of others. Thus, in response to what we have learnt about a business, we may say it is 'bureaucratic', or 'caring', or appealing to a different target market from ourselves. This may or may not reflect reality, or how the organisation sees itself, but this is the picture we have built up. Following the atrocities in the USA on 11 September 2001, the budget airline easyJet slashed fares to attract customers and placed full-page advertisements asking governments to ignore the major airlines' pleas for financial dispensations. easyJet not only won much business but also enhanced its image, appearing responsive, customer-centric and willing to play David against Goliaths.

Image is composed of two components. First, **personality**. Corporate culture plays a big part in developing personality and, in turn, culture may reflect the personalities of real people such as Richard Branson (Virgin), Simon Woodroffe (Yo! Sushi) or other past or present role models within the business. The organisational planning process, e.g. formal and structured, or informal and more spontaneous, also influences the business's personality.

Second, image is created through **corporate identity** – the external face of the organisation. By paying attention to this identity, the business can exercise considerable influence over the cues that create its image. Use of the elements of the promotional mix inevitably helps to create this identity, but so do other cues:

- Symbols of the organisation, such as its name, Head Office and stationery, all give clues about it, and may be changed when a company wishes to alter its image.
- Staff behaviour, especially in customer-facing departments and service organisations.
- Communication style, for example open and friendly, or media-shy and secretive, also projects the business's identity to the outside world.

Organisations are increasingly aware that their image matters, and are proactive in managing their identity. But they cannot wholly control it. Barclays Bank came in for much criticism following its national campaign focusing on the bank being "Big". The intention was to create an image of global presence and strength, which might have particular appeal to larger investors and institutions. But the campaign coincided with many branch closures and many people took the "Big" claim to be arrogant and insensitive.

## Reputation

Reputation is an attribute that takes much longer to build than image. Images can change in the relatively short term, but reputations take time to forge; they are based on trustworthiness, reliability and responsibility. Organisations fight hard to maintain a good reputation, once gained, and it can engender real loyalty in the organisation's following. Marks & Spencer and the BBC have both taken many knocks in recent years. However, one can sense a will for them to succeed amongst many people who respect them and believe their good reputation deserves to continue, regardless of any short-term problems.

## Profile strategy

The management of an organisation's corporate communication objectives is known as a profile strategy. The strategy involves communicating about the organisation as a corporate entity to its stakeholders. This contrasts with push and pull strategies where just distributors and end-users respectively are the objects of attention, though these groups may also be the target of profile strategies. The organisation will need to monitor its stakeholders' views. Where a gap exists between the desired and actual perceptions of the organisation, communication programmes to correct the situation will need to be put into place. This requires the business to listen to its audiences, adapting its position if necessary.

---

**Activity 8.3**

With the help of colleagues or fellow students, build a library of examples of profile communications. You will usually find these in print media, especially broadsheet newspapers and trade press, although you will see other examples , for example outdoor and broadcast media.

Think about the following:

Who do you think your examples are targeted at?

What prompted the company to pay for this type of communication?

Does it link with any other activity (e.g. web site content) or is there a lack of concurrent activity (e.g. no advertising for the organisation's products or brands)?

---

## Internet and e-commerce activities appropriate to B2C and B2B markets

Whether one is talking about B2B or B2C markets, the Internet has many applications.

At a basic level it is a shop window. Businesses can display their wares, using graphics and text. Site visitors can drill down into whatever level of detail the site allows. Non-product information, such as a profile of the company, may also be available.

Solely using the Internet in this way, however, ignores its transactional capability. This is one of the Internet's advantages over most other communication media. Indeed, the Internet is a **pull medium** where the customer usually initiates the site visit, or at least consents to it. So it is reasonable to expect that a customer's interest may go beyond just pulling general information, to finding out how it might relate to their specific circumstances. At this level, transactional capability can go from relatively simple requests, such as finding a quotation for a new home insurance policy, through to being able to complete a purchase transaction – an exchange of goods and services in return for money. Online ordering is commonplace, although reticence still exists amongst some buyers who are concerned about security.

Transactional capability goes further than this though. Organisations' sites can allow individuals and businesses to undertake far more complex enquiries and transactions, effectively bringing other channel members' own IT facilities into their home or office. Individuals can conduct all their banking business, short of withdrawing cash, from home, while businesses can have access to a complete range of data and facilities concerning their relationships with suppliers and distributors. Ordering, billing, stock monitoring, order tracking, even enquiries about end-users can all be undertaken online.

Think of all the bits of paper that *aren't* flying around, and the speed with which information can be exchanged. For businesses, in particular, the potential costs-savings are enormous and this is one reason why, in terms of transaction volumes and value, the B2B market already outstrips B2C and will continue to do so. For example, Ford, General Motors, Siemens Automotive and many others have set up an e-workplace (www.covisint.net) to conduct supply-chain management for the motor industry. DaimlerChrysler says that their investment in e-business has already been recouped through cost savings, and have placed orders for an extraordinary 43% of future component requirements following online bidding by aspiring suppliers.

The ramifications for marketers are enormous – think about your role if you were trying to market components to DaimlerChrysler or other car-makers. Space doesn't permit fuller discussion here but there is no element of the marketing mix, including promotions, that is not going to have to be rethought in the light of growing B2B e-commerce, particularly where there is little opportunity for product differentiation.

The B2C market is also developing rapidly. Whilst there are many web-only sites trading, there is evidence that many consumers find the combination of Internet and conventional trading outlets attractive – the "bricks and clicks" approach – meaning that you can visit your supermarket *and* buy on-line. This means taking an integrated approach to the Internet, seeing how it can complement, rather than replace, other activities. But whatever you do with your site, you want to:

- Encourage people to visit it, using different methods of traffic generation.
- Encourage people to re-visit it, by making it worthwhile and interesting to explore.
- Encourage dialogue, to help build relationships with customers and also to...
- ...learn about your customers by inviting them to supply information, or by other means.

E-commerce is still young, with opportunities continually opening up. E-mail, interactive TV, kiosks, and intranets are just some of the other tools revolutionising marketing. Even text-messaging is a proven commercial medium, increasing traffic in shops by informing consumers of special offers or, in the case of Channel 4, prompting viewers when their favourite shows are on, which helps viewing figures and advertisers.

Marketers need to be wholly attuned to the opportunities of e-commerce and how they can be integrated with other activities. If you aren't, your competitors are.

## Case Study – Canine Treats

The UK's dog treating market is currently worth £74 million, with the biscuit category accounting for £23 million. Biscuits are the oldest manufactured pet food and represent the 'traditional' way of treating a dog.

However, over the past decade the treating category has grown dramatically with the introduction of meaty sticks and pieces (£24 million) and, in the last five years, added value chews (£27 million). With consumers having many more products to use for their 'treating' occasions, Bonio, despite maintaining its leading position in terms of value and volume share, was under extreme competitive pressure.

According to James Knott, brand manager for Friskies Petcare, Bonio has always symbolised and owned bone functionality and enjoyment for dogs. The essence of the brand is the bone icon and its key attribute is that it offers vital crunching exercise that soft meals cannot provide. Gnawing helps maintain healthy teeth and gums, preventing plaque and tartar build-up, while the calcium supplement helps build strong teeth and gums.

## New brand positioning

Growing concern that Bonio would become a generic within the biscuits treating category, offering little more than the cheaper competitors' alternatives in terms of differentiation, led Friskies to consider ways of combating further threats.

The brand objectives for 2000 were to drive growth of Bonio Biscuits by increasing frequency of use; to protect and build on the products core credentials of oral hygiene with a proven USP; and to differentiate the Bonio offering from Pedigree and private labels.

The decision was made to relaunch and reposition the brand. To achieve this, the company's R&D facility was asked to come up with a biscuit formula which could be proven to fight plaque and tartar. The result was a product that could be shown to reduce the build-up of plaque by 20% and tartar by 25%.

## On-pack promotions

A large proportion of the marketing budget in 2000 was spent on investing in promotions that added value to the brand. "Without any above-the-line support, we were forced to find new and exciting ways to communicate our brand message to users and lapsed users," says Knott.

"The key to success lay in selecting a mechanic that actively encouraged both dog and owner to interact with the brand and the promotion". The resulting 'Bonio Lick and Win' promotion used humour to encourage the owner to come into contact with the issue at the heart of the promotion – the dog's mouth.

The owner was required to get their dog to lick a bone-shaped game card to reveal a win/lose message. The prizes were simple cash prizes, including one for £10,000. This was followed in 2001 by a promotion in a similar vein – 'Bonio Clean Up and Win', a card game within the biscuit box. Friskies also modernised its packaging. An impactful design was created to stand out more on retailers' shelves.

## The future

Friskies Petcare recently launched BIG Bonio and Bonio Breathfresh into the market, both designed to drive loyalty, penetration, frequency of brand purchase and feeding occasions. The company is currently looking into a number of brand extensions in the UK. In terms of international brand exposure, the product formulation and Bonio 'bone icon' have been launched across Europe. However, this is featured under a separate brand name – Bonzo. Whilst Bonio has a strong brand awareness in the UK, this recognition does not exist pan-Europe. In the UK, Bonio continues to hold brand leadership in the dog biscuit market in terms of value and volume share and rate of sale. "Our challenge over the last two years has been to drive a level of excitement into a product area that is perceived as boring," says Knot.

## Measuring effectiveness

The campaign's results increased both volume and value market share.

| Grocery | Total 2000 Value (£ in actuals) | Total 2000 Volume (Kg actuals) | Total 1999 Value (£ in actuals) | Total 1999 Volume (Kg actuals) |
|---|---|---|---|---|
| Friskies Bonio | 6,970,435 | 4,017,416 | 6,051,259 | 3,650,261 |
| Friskies Winalot Shapes | 5,098,709 | 3,693.683 | 5,222,766 | 3,760,533 |
| Pedigree Markies | 3,518,349 | 1,672,332 | 3,546,575 | 1,659,369 |
| Own label | 2,965,110 | 2,434,767 | 3,428,169 | 2,562,915 |
| Pegigree Biscrok | 1,159,002 | 636,006 | 1,332,571 | 732,747 |

Source: AC Nielsen

**Source:** Canine Treats, *Marketing Business*, February 2002.

**Questions**

1.  Basing your answer on the information in the Case Study, suggest a pull strategy and associated promotional mix for the launch of the repositioned 'Bonio'.

2.  Basing your answer on the information in the Case Study, suggest a push strategy and associated promotional mix for the launch of the repositioned 'Bonio'.

2.  Basing your answer on the information in the Case Study, suggest a profile strategy and associated promotional mix for the launch of the repositioned 'Bonio'.

## SUMMARY OF KEY POINTS

In this Session, we have introduced pull, push and profile strategies, and covered the following key points:

■ An organisation's communications strategy is a combination of pull, push and profile strategies.

■ Pull strategy is targeted at end customers, whether consumer or business-to-business, and is designed to 'pull' them to the product or service.

■ Push strategy is targeted at the trade/channel members, and is designed to 'push' products through the channel.

■ Profile strategy is targeted at wider stakeholders, and is designed to communicate the identity of the organisation.

■ Electronic media can assist to communicate with all three audiences.

## Improving and developing own learning

The following projects are designed to help you develop your knowledge and skills further by carrying out some research yourself. Feedback is not provided for this type of learning because there are no 'answers' to be found, but you may wish to discuss your findings with colleagues and fellow students.

## Project A

Talk to colleagues in your marketing department about the pull, push and profile strategies that are currently used.

How well are these strategies integrated?

Are messages consistent, and do the tools used support each other?

## Project B

If your organisation currently uses a channel of wholesalers and retailers to distribute your products, think about the impact a decision to offer your products through the Internet would have on them.

Talk to colleagues in your sales or marketing departments and get their views on this issue.

List the main considerations your organisation would have to make.

## Project C

One of the best ways to learn about ways to use the Internet is to visit sites. Here are the addresses of some of the top UK brands. Visit some of them and make notes on:

■ what they use the sites for.

■ how they build dialogue and relationships.

Do the sites enhance your understanding of the brand?

www.interflora.co.uk
www.yourbaby.com
www.dhl.co.uk
www.audi.co.uk
www.thesun.co.uk
www.tampax.com
www.persil.co.uk
www.americanexpress.co.uk
www.wedgwood.co.uk
www.thomascook.co.uk

# Feedback to activities

## Activity 8.1

Your approach will vary for different product/service types and how they are distributed. Some of the general points you might make are included in the following non-specific memo.

## M E M O

**To: Marketing Manager**

From: B. Rains

Date: September 2002

Re: Push and pull strategies for X product

Here are my thoughts on the mix of push and pull strategies required for the promotion of our new product.

**Introductory phase**
In the early stages there may be an equal emphasis on push and pull strategies.

The first activity, however, would be pre-launch. This would be aimed at the trade, to ensure intermediaries are familiar with the product's features and benefits and are in a position to deal with enquiries and demand for supplies. Personal selling is likely to play an important part here, supported by exhibitions at key trade fairs, a pre-launch trade advertising campaign, promotional incentive schemes and trade press PR. Following launch, push activity would continue alongside pull communications such as advertising and sales promotion, to ensure both consumer interest and supply and endorsement by distributors.

**Growth phase**
As demand grows, less emphasis is likely to be put on push activity. Repeat purchases and word-of-mouth recommendation would support pull activity, creating increasing demand. Intermediaries would be familiar with the product and able to respond to consumer pull. Push activity may be needed, though, to counter competitor responses and reinforce differentiation. Extranet-based information, ordering etc., could support push relationships.

### Established phase

Faced with increasing choice as the product and its competitors become established, tactical pull activity, such as advertising or direct marketing, would be needed to maintain consumer interest and extend the product's life. Equally, intermittent push activity may be appropriate to remind intermediaries of the product and maintain exposure.

### Decline phase

Once the product moves into decline, considerable effort may be needed to persuade intermediaries to stock or promote it and the marketer will need to decide at what point the costs of doing so outweigh the benefits.

### Activity 8.2

Emphasis in first year will be in finding prospects and turning them into customers. This means the marketing priorities will be lead-generation activity, and following these leads up.

Appointing an experienced salesperson makes sense. He or she will probably have existing contacts and can spend time finding prospects and converting them into buyers. Suggested remuneration basis in the first year: basic salary + sales related bonus. A lease car and other costs, National Insurance and expenses, will need to be budgeted.

Other marketing activity should be focused on:

- Lead-generation activity such as exhibitions and carefully targeted direct marketing. Comparisons between buying or hiring exhibition equipment would be considered to maximise spend on actual attendance at events.

- Development of promotional literature that can be presented to prospects.

- Low-cost activity to raise awareness amongst your target market, e.g. generating trade press coverage through letters, press releases, articles etc., and networking.

- A web presence would be valuable – initially as brochure site, built using in-house skills – and may become increasingly important over time. Customer requirements would need to be gauged and resource allocation may have to be diverted into building a more sophisticated site. However, this is unlikely to generate many leads early on, which is our first priority.

Suggested budget breakdown

|  | £'000 |
| --- | --- |
| Salary | 22.5 |
| On-costs and expenses | 4.0 |
| Car + costs | 5.0 |
| Bonus | 10.0 |
| Exhibitions (equipment and attendance) | 14.5 |
| Direct marketing activity | 1.0 |
| Literature | 2.0 |
| Other costs | 1.0 |
|  | 60.0 |

**Activity 8.3**

The motives for profile communications vary.

They may be linked to corporate activity, e.g. preparing for, or fighting off, a take-over.

Sometimes they will ask stakeholders, perhaps MPs, to lobby on behalf of the organisation's interest.

Increased scrutiny in recent years relating to corporate social responsibility has led to this being a regular theme of profile communications too.

Profile communications sometimes link with news events or activities: the success of a sponsored event or team, for example, may lead to advertising soon afterwards, reminding audiences of the relationship between the success and the business.

# Session 9

# Promotional mixes and messages

## Introduction

This is the first of two Sessions that looks at promotional tools and how they are used to communicate promotional messages. This Session looks at the role of advertising within the mix, and ways in which it is thought to influence buyers. It goes on to consider the use of emotions and feelings within advertisements.

The next Session looks at the other promotional tools and how they combine to form the communications mix.

---

**LEARNING OUTCOMES**

At the end of this Session you will be able to:

■ Explore the role of advertising in various markets.

■ Explain how advertising is thought to influence consumers.

■ Understand strong and weak theories of advertising.

■ Explore the use of emotions in advertising messages.

---

## The role of advertising

Advertising's traditional role, as a vehicle for reaching mass-market audiences, is changing. Reasons include:

■ increasing fragmentation of broadcast and print media, in particular the multiplicity of new TV channels.

■ the rapid growth of the Internet and other new media.

■ the growth of capabilities, in other areas such as direct marketing and promotions.

■ the increasing importance of hard-to-reach audiences such as the under 25s.

■ the growing need for accountability in marketing spend (it is not always easy to identify a direct, measurable link between advertising costs and benefits).

■ increasing demand for interactivity and personalisation in communications.

This is not to say advertising is on the ropes; the industry has delivered year-on-year real growth (over £17bn was spent on advertising in 2000, though data for 2001, awaited at the time of writing, may show it was a more difficult year for various reasons).[3] But where advertising was once the first and most obvious tool that marketers drew on, particularly in consumer markets, now it has to fight harder to justify its place alongside other elements of the promotional mix. Heinz famously switched much of its TV advertising budget to direct marketing in the 1990s, seeing it as a better way to reach its target audience, while other big names such as Unilever[4] and Procter & Gamble[5] have since announced changes to the way they allocate promotional budgets. So there has never been a more important time for marketers to understand the diversity of tools available and to be aware of the opportunities to use different promotional mixes in different business circumstances. Now, more than ever, marketers must be able to deliver integrated messages across a range of platforms.

## Business to business (B2B)

The business market is different from the consumer market in many ways, which students will have studied elsewhere. These differences lead to other forms of communication offering advantages over advertising. Personal selling is the dominant element of the mix. Though expensive, it suits the complexity of typical B2B decision-making processes. It enables each customer's differing needs to be addressed separately and favours the development of long-term relationships. The relatively few number of buyers and ease of finding out about them makes direct marketing another effective mechanism. Advertising is not unimportant but often it will play a supporting role rather than the main one. In particular, coverage in trade publications can be used to build awareness, provide information and create leads, opening the door for the salesperson.

## Services marketing

This is a diverse sector, ranging from the one man business to the international finance house. Any of the range of promotional tools available may be suitable, as if one were marketing a product. But of course, unlike a product, services are not tangible and are based upon a promise to deliver. Advertisements, then, will often aim to reassure, or will stress security, from "Established 20 years" in the local jeweller's classified advert in a free newspaper, to HSBC's 2002 "The World's Local Bank" campaign, ensuring you know that that their international expertise (which symbolises size and strength) is being applied for your personal benefit in the home and on the High Street.

Continuity of strong brand images, e.g. McDonald's golden arches and the AA's (Automobile Association's) black and yellow symbol, and personal endorsements both also help to overcome consumer uncertainties. People are a key part of services delivery, so internal advertising and attention to ensuring that staff live up to external advertising's claim is vital.

[3]Advertising Association, 2/4/02.
[4]Press release, www.unilever.com, 12/2/02.
[5]Marketing Week, 2/12/99.

### Not-for-profit marketing

The not-for-profit sector makes much use of advertising, e.g. Red Nose Day posters, and the powerful 2002 NSPCC campaign showing a cartoon child being battered. The Family Planning Association's 1969 Pregnant Man image is familiar to many who never even saw it originally.

Budgets are often an issue in this sector, both in terms of raising funds and in justifying spend on advertising (or other communication options), as opposed to spending directly on the cause in question – public scrutiny may be strong. Achieving sponsorship for media costs is one approach to the former problem, as are specific fund-raising activities: the NSPCC has an appeal running to fund its £250m Full Stop campaign spend. Sometimes media owners may be persuaded to supply free or reduced-price space or time.

Being very clear about objectives, and undertaking a thorough cost-benefit analysis, is critical to justifying campaign expenditure. But as advertising can be costly, other forms of communication are often the preferred medium. PR, often using human interest stories, direct marketing with clearly defined target audiences and ease of measurement of results, and promotions linked to consumer products, may all take precedence over advertising. Web sites, viral marketing, word of mouth and personal selling by staff as ambassadors for the organisation are all low-cost options too.

---

**Activity 9.1**

Allocate some time, ideally with the campaign manager and/or the advertising agency, to research an advertising campaign that your organisation has run. What stages were there? What documents and other material were produced in the development process? How were results measured?

Would the campaign strategy have been appropriate if you had worked in a different sector – consumer, B2B, not-for-profit, services, or public? Why?

---

## Strong and weak theories of advertising

Do you ever see an advertisement, or a series of them, and as direct result, feel persuaded to purchase the product or service it relates to? Alternatively, do you find advertisements to be just one of a range of stimuli that contribute to a longer, more considered decision-making process that ultimately leads you to purchase? Perhaps you can recognise both circumstances.

In essence, these questions capture two key theories about the impact of advertising – the strong theory and the weak theory.

## The strong theory

The assumption that advertising alone can lead people all the way from lack of awareness of a product through to purchasing it has underpinned much promotional activity in the past. It implies that, by getting the formula for advertising right, consumers' understanding, attitudes, and behaviours can be altered and they will go on to buy.

This theory assumes that advertising can **persuade**. Consumers effectively have a passive role in the buying process and, provided they are led though the right steps along the way, what they learn from adverts will be sufficient to make them think and act in new ways. Even better, their long-run behaviour will change and they will continue to buy brand X after the first purchase.

## The weak theory

This theory suggests that the whole process is rather subtler. Advertising may play a role in the buying process but it will not, alone, persuade people to change their buying behaviour. Instead, it becomes one of range of influential factors, including stimuli from other elements of the promotional mix. Adverts won't capture our attention long enough, if at all, to change our view of a particular brand or product. But they will help us feel more comfortable with it once it is in our mind, and after we have made a purchase.

Weak theory says that initially adverts help reinforce attitudes we have developed through processing information from various other sources – perhaps past experience of the brand, a friend's recommendation, or a mention in a press article. Adverts will remind us of what we know about the product and, if we are interested in finding out more, may help to increase our understanding of it. Advertising also helps with product identification. Cumulatively, the effect of this information from advertising and other sources is that, when faced with a buying opportunity, our familiarity with the product and its characteristics will make us more inclined to buy it. Following purchase, advertising again reinforces our views and helps to keep the product at the front of our mind for when we are considering a repeat purchase. Adverts thus help make our buying decisions habitual, until stimuli in relation to a competing product weave their way into our mind.

Thus, assuming weak theory, the consumer's role is initially one of active processing of information from several sources, weighing up arguments and discriminating, before choosing one option or another. Advertising's role is to tilt the process in the advertiser's favour. Subsequently the consumer becomes more passive and adverts help to reassure and remind him/her about his/her decision.

**Strong versus weak**

Is either theory the right one? Well, neither can be wholly right. The strong theory implies that increased sales are the inevitable result of properly conducted advertising, but this means that there can be perpetual growth of individual brands and of markets as a whole, which is clearly not possible. On the other hand, we can think of instances where advertising alone may prompt new buying behaviour, such as reacting to a direct response TV or off-the-page advertisements, or being persuaded to consider an exciting new product advertised in the press. Daewoo cars made a highly successful entry into the UK car market in 1994. Though Daewoo did deploy other elements of the promotional mix, it was the widespread advertising campaign (which first addressed consumers' ignorance of the Daewoo brand, and then explained the company's innovative way of operating, compared to traditional car retailers) that convinced many UK consumers to buy a car from this hitherto unknown brand.

The strong theory, then, probably applies well in situations where new brands and other innovations are involved. But if, as is usually the case, advertising is about known products and brands then, to be effective, the advertising needs to be integrated with messages communicated in other ways.

---

**Activity 9.2**

Some well-known consumer brands are switching part of their advertising budget to other elements of the promotional mix.

Make notes on what you think this implies about their attitude towards the strong and weak theories of advertising?

---

# Cognitive processing and advertising

Cognitive processing is the term for how we process information in our minds to form judgements, attitudes and opinions. Cognitive processes are the thoughts we have along the way. If we can understand the theory behind these processes, then we can apply this knowledge to the practice of creating effective advertising.

When we are confronted with a communication we may form judgements on three different levels.

**Product/message processing:** these are the thoughts about the product itself and what we are being told about it. Do we accept what is being said about the product, does it reinforce existing attitudes we have somehow formed, or contradict them? Intuitively you will realise that advertisers want to create messages that are consistent with, and support, the consumer's existing understanding.

**Source processing:** do we find the source of the information credible, likeable, trustworthy etc. If so, this will increase the likelihood of our accepting the message.

**Execution processing:** what do we think about the style of the advert itself, regardless of content? Does it come across as funny, moving, awesome or triggering some other kind of emotion or feeling? Triggering an emotion within us helps to engage with the advert beyond the most superficial level. It also creates a response to the advert (positive or negative) which we may consciously or unconsciously transfer to the product itself.

Though we may consider communications on three different levels, these do not have equal weight all the time. Think about the difference between deciding to buy a laptop computer and a canned drink. Which elements of cognitive processing would dominate your thoughts?

With the laptop you will be motivated to find out about its features and benefits; you may read material about it, seek opinions and undertake research on the Internet. Messages and information about the product in advertisements will take on significance for you as you use them to support, develop or challenge the opinions you are forming. This is an example of **high-involvement decision-making**, where people have the interest and motivation to consciously seek and interpret information about the product. The fact that, for example, an advert is cleverly constructed will make little, if any, difference to your opinion (though this cleverness may help you to notice the advert in the first place).

Buying a can of drink is, usually, a **low-involvement process**. Though some people may be interested in finding out about the sugar content or where the drink was made, most people will use very limited thought processes to form an opinion about it. These shallow thought processes rely on **peripheral cues** – incidental pieces of information that have lodged in your mind which are not about the product itself. So the impression left by that witty execution of a drink advert you liked may trigger a positive response to the product when you see it. The fact that, through product placement, your movie idol used the brand in a film you saw last week also left its mark on you.

The advertiser needs to get into the head of the people who are buying the product. What cognitive process will our target audience be going through? Is this likely to be a low-involvement purchase, a high involvement one, or something in-between? Perhaps you will need research to find out, and you may find the answer varies for different buyers of the same product. If your audience is motivated towards high involvement then messages about the product and its features and benefits will dominate your advertising. If involvement is going to be low then methods of stirring emotions and feelings are likely to be more important.

Source-related thought processes may be relevant in both circumstances: independent research may help validate your claims in a high involvement process; a voiceover from a fashionable TV presenter may add peripheral credibility to a low-involvement situation.

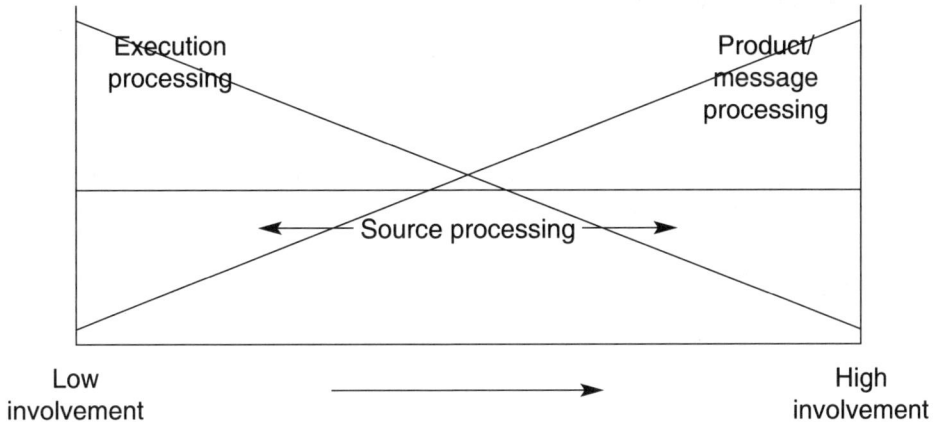

**Figure 9.1: The relative importance of cognitive processes in high-involvement and low involvement decision-making.**

---

**Activity 9.3**

Think about these products and services. Are these most likely to be low-involvement or high-involvement decision-making situations?

1. Frozen vegetables for a domestic consumer.
2. Paper towels for a domestic consumer.
3. Paper towels for the central buyer of an NHS Hospital Trust.
4. A marketing text-book for a CIM student.
5. A pension product for a 40 year old self-employed businessperson.
6. A car.
7. Wedding banqueting facilities.
8. Climbing boots.
9. Carpet slippers.
10. The different target audiences for your company's products.

## How is advertising thought to work?

With our understanding of weak and strong theories of advertising, and of cognitive processing, it is possible to put together an overview of how advertising is thought to influence individuals. But perhaps it is worth briefly considering traditional theories which nowadays are viewed as less appropriate.

One of the best known theories, developed for personal selling but subsequently applied to advertising, was AIDA:

Attention ➔ Interest ➔ Desire ➔ Action

This suggested that advertising could move individuals through sequence of phases, first grabbing their attention to the product, and leading through to purchase.

Another common sequential model suggested the following phases:

Awareness ➔ Knowledge ➔ Liking ➔ Preference ➔ Conviction ➔ Purchase

Both models assume that advertisements can persuade people to move through the sequence, but this is not now generally accepted. Indeed, people may not go through all the stages at all, particularly if we accept the concept of low-involvement decision-making. The models also present practical problems of how one ascertains and measures what particular point the audience is at.

### Current Thinking about Advertising

So how *is* advertising thought to work?

If you think about the number of advertising messages you are bombarded with daily – TV, outdoor, radio, Internet, press etc. – you will realise that only a tiny percentage make an impression on you. Though you may see many adverts, your mind filters out most of them. Those that register have some kind of significance for you. This may be because they relate to your current situation, for example, you might start noticing holiday adverts when you are thinking of booking a break. Maybe the advert's execution makes a particular impact on you, or perhaps the novelty of the subject matter stimulates your interest. It's unlikely you will remember all the adverts's content but, if it is of sufficient significance, your cognitive processing will identify relevant part(s) of the message and these will make their way into your long-term memory. This information enables you to make associations, with past learning about this product/brand, or in the future. A repertoire of meaningful moments from advertising, and other sources, is built up so that you effectively compile a mental database of information, experiences and emotions relating to the product. You then consciously or subconsciously draw on this when, for example, you compile a shortlist of products from which to choose before making a purchase, or make a spontaneous purchase at the point of sale. Advertising's role is to create new meaningful moments for you to store and recall later. Re-seeing ads or messages reminds you of moment you have stored before, reinforcing their significance for when you draw on them for a first or subsequent purchase.

An important point for marketers to remember is that we need to make it easy for consumers to make associations between the different cues they have collected in relation to a single product or brand. Just as it is hard to form a clear and simple view of a customer's relationship with our organisation if we have entered several variants of their name onto different parts of our computer database, so we cannot easily make sense of our mental database if we have received conflicting messages about the brand. Integration of messages between advertising and other parts of the promotional (and marketing) mix is vital is we are not to confuse, and lose, the consumer.

---

**Activity 9.4**

You have been asked to make a brief presentation to the Managing Director on the way that FMCG advertising is thought to work.

Prepare five slides covering this topic. Each slide should include a heading and bullet points (not extended text).

---

## Emotions in advertising

Stop for a few seconds to think of a personal moment that has had significance in your life.

Inevitably your recollections will include the emotions and feelings you had at that time – happiness, pain, worry, excitement, belonging or whatever. Emotions bring our experiences to life, giving them three dimensionality which helps imprint them in our mind.

Advertisers will often aim to create the stirring of emotions in their work. This has many benefits.

First, the device that is used to stir the emotion may be the very thing to capture your attention in the first place. The 2001 press and poster advert for the perfume Opium, featuring a picture of the naked, supine model Sophie Dahl, certainly turned heads and stirred a few emotions! (It also generated a great deal of word-of-mouth interest and unpaid media coverage, but that's another matter).

Second, it may be the element in our cognitive processing that makes the advert's execution significant to us. Not only does it strike a chord in some way, but that very feeling then helps to embed the advert into our memory.

Finally the emotion may be replayed in our mind, bringing to the surface its associations with the product or brand. Next time we experience that emotion, for whatever reason, there may be a subtle recollection of the product. Conversely, further experience of the product may invoke the emotion.

What type of emotions and feelings are effective in creating good advertising? The important point is that we must **like** the advert, as research has shown clear linkage between people's liking and their intention to buy. But liking doesn't necessarily mean that the ad must stir feelings of enjoyment within you. Some of the most powerful ads create emotions that we may consider negative. Remember the 1986 advert by Lynx, who campaigned against the fur trade? "It takes up to 40 dumb animals to make a fur coat. But only one to wear it," they said. Emotions of anger and contempt were whipped up, but people 'bought' the message. Since 1984, Benetton has run international campaigns, many of which have stirred up shock, surprise, horror, and even political indignation by forcing taboo subjects into the open. But they are memorable and talked about and have created great awareness, helping to build what has become a major international brand.

So liking an advert does not necessarily means that it is 'nice'. Enjoyment can be a criterion for success, but so can other feelings which make the advert stimulating, relevant, meaningful or valuable to the individual. Creating empathy, not apathy, is the advertiser's goal.

## Case Study – Breakfast cereals

*This Case Study is taken from a past examination paper, and is used in Sessions 6, 7 and 9 of this Companion, with different questions adjusted to the content of these Sessions.*

The UK Ready-to-Eat (RTE) breakfast cereal market is worth £1,080 million and is dominated by three main manufacturers, Kellogg's, Weetabix and Cereal Partners. They hold 69% market share but are faced with a number of competitive pressures, one of which is the 21 % share held by the own label distributors which is growing at 5% each year. The market is mature and is characterised by strong competition. Growth in the market has been slow with only product innovation and segmentation activities (e.g. chocolate flavours and children's products) showing above average performance. Branding in the RTE sector is extremely important.

| Manufacturer | Market Share by Volume % | UK Advertising Spend £m |
|---|---|---|
| Kellogg's UK | 42 | 55 |
| Weetabix Ltd | 15 | 15 |
| Cereal Partners Ltd | 12 | 18 |
| Own Label | 21 | 0 |
| Others | 10 | 14 |
| Total | 100% | £102m |

Table 1: Market Share and Advertising Spend for Three Leading UK Cereal Manufacturers

With high penetration levels (90% of households holding stock and 73% of consumers claiming to eat them for breakfast) opportunities for real growth appear to be limited. However, research has shown that regular eating of the right sort of breakfast can help us get the correct balance of foods we need. The nutritional value of breakfast cereals and their impact on health, diet and weight, combined with their convenience, suggest that there are new opportunities for product development and marketing communications. This health orientation has helped broaden market opportunities through new products, for example the very successful launch of Nutrigrain cereal bars from Kellogg's for those who need to eat a mobile breakfast, maybe while travelling to work, and the promotion of breakfast cereals as an all-day snack food (which has been referred to as guilt-free snacking). The development of the Nutrigrain bars also demonstrates how Kellogg's has moved into new marketing channels (e.g. petrol forecourts) and is reaching new audiences. The different strategies adopted by the leading brand manufacturers suggest that there is no single best way to use marketing communications in this market.

**Kellogg's** is the leading brand manufacturer but has been most affected by the growth of own label brands. Faced with declining market share it has just announced an aggressive marketing policy, slashing prices by 12% on its top 6 brands. Kellogg's also intends to increase its advertising spend by 40%. In the past its advertising has been based around a benefit oriented message which aims to educate audiences about the nutritional values of its products. In doing so, Kellogg's acknowledges the role parents play in the decision making process. Kellogg's also collaborates with the Government's Health Education Authority to raise awareness of the need for a balanced diet and the important role breakfast plays in our daily food intake.

The **Weetabix** company is privately owned and discloses very little about its activities. The Weetabix biscuit, the company's main brand, has a unique characteristic in that it turns very soft and mushy when milk is poured on it. Rather than work as a product disadvantage it increases the product's utility as it makes it a suitable food for all ages; from babies as a weaning food, to young people as a quick and convenient snack food, through to those in their later years. In addition to specific brand advertising which has been attribute based, Weetabix aims to add value to its brands through the use of sales promotions rather than focus on price reductions and discounts. For example, one promotion used 40 free drawstring tea bags banded on top of a Weetabix 48 pack, whilst another linked into an offer with Maxwell House coffee. Weetabix has been very profitable and the company does not want to be drawn into a price war.

**Cereal Partners** was formed through an alliance between General Mills and Nestlé and is the single largest producer of own label products. The core of its activities in the market has been brand extensions and relaunches of established brands. This is demonstrated through the extensions of its largest single brand, Shredded Wheat, into Fruitful, Honey Nut and Bitesize. It does not see price as a significant factor in the decision making process as it claims that research indicates that breakfast cereals are perceived to be a good value food. Its advertising messages are often directed at children and stress the taste and fun properties of its main line brands.

| Manufacturer | Leading Brands | Brand Market Share by Value (%) | UK Advertising Spend £m |
|---|---|---|---|
| Kellogg's UK | Kellogg's Cornflakes | 9 | 8 |
| Weetabix Ltd | Weetabix | 7 | 9 |
| Cereal Partners Ltd | Shredded Wheat | 4.5 | 5 |

Table 2: Market Share and Advertising Spend for Three Leading UK Cereal Brands

*Note:* Information for this case has been collected from a variety of public sources. The figures have been adjusted to enable clearer relationships to be observed. The material is not intended to imply good or bad management practice. This mini case is presented as illustrative material and is suitable for teaching purposes only.

**Source:** *Integrated Marketing Communications Examination Paper*, June 2001

**Questions**

1. Evaluate the marketing communications strategy of each of the main brand manufacturers, commenting on the role of advertising.

2. Suggest how Weetabix Ltd might use marketing communications to counter the new promotional strategy announced by Kellogg's.

## SUMMARY OF KEY POINTS

In this Session, we have introduced the role of advertising in the promotional mix, and covered the following key points:

■ Advertising's role as a mass communications tool is changing, but remains an important one.

■ Advertising has a role to play in business-to-business, services and not-for-profit markets as well as consumer markets.

■ Strong and weak theories of advertising put forward contrasting views – that advertising is a powerful persuader, and advertising is just one influence on the buyer. In fact, a combination of the two is probably right.

■ Cognitive processing plays a large part in the way customers perceive adverts.

■ Using emotions in advertising can arouse strong feelings and capture the audience's attention.

## Improving and developing own learning

The following projects are designed to help you develop your knowledge and skills further by carrying out some research yourself. Feedback is not provided for this type of learning because there are no 'answers' to be found, but you may wish to discuss your findings with colleagues and fellow students.

**Project A**

With colleagues in your marketing department, look at your organisation's latest advertisements. In which media were they placed?

What messages were they designed to convey? Make notes of your findings.

---

**Project B**

Following on from Project A, identify what evaluation methods were used following the ad campaign.

How effective were the ads in achieving promotional objectives?

---

**Project C**

Over the coming weeks, work with your colleagues or fellow students to build up a library of advertisements. Take cuttings from magazine and newspapers, make notes about broadcast ads and make notes on, or photograph, outdoor material. Try to collect examples from several different types of source – upmarket, downmarket, FMCG, B2B etc.

Separate the ads. into those that aim to create feelings and emotions in the reader/viewer/listener and those that don't.

Which of the ads were effective for you? Why?

Can you see any patterns emerging between which ads stimulate emotion (or aim to) and those that do not?

---

## Feedback to activities

### Activity 9.1

Items produced will depend upon the organisation's processes and the media being used, but may include:

Creative brief.
Media brief.
Concept development material.
Pre-Testing material, and resultant research information.
Proofs.
Media schedule.
Control and evaluation information.

It is unlikely that the strategy would have been appropriate for another sector, or even for another product within the same sector. Start point (e.g. brand awareness, new or existing product/service), objectives, promotional mix, budget, and target audience are amongst the many variables that would affect a campaign's transferability between sectors.

## Activity 9.2

The strong theory implies that increased spending on advertising will lead to increased sales. Though there may be an effect of increased sales for new brands, the reality is that ever increased spending on advertising will bring diminishing returns. So companies that are switching budgets to other promotional elements are implicitly recognising that advertising, based upon strong theory, can yield no additional profits.

Even under the weak theory there is a limit to how much reassurance and reinforcing of attitudes is needed via advertising. Successful strategies come from balancing the effect of advertising with the benefits of other elements of the promotional mix.

If the weak theory is assumed, the organisation must believe that the limit of the benefits of their advertising has been reached (or exceeded) and resources can be utilised more effectively by developing other elements of the promotional mix, supported by the remaining weak-theory advertising.

## Activity 9.3

1. Low involvement, but consumers seeking organic products may be more involved.
2. Low involvement, but consumers seeking eco-friendly materials and production methods may be more involved.
3. High involvement: ascertaining size, performance, cost, availability etc. may be very important.
4. Towards high involvement: most students will want to make some checks that the book meets certain criteria they have set. Source processing may be important.
5. High involvement.
6. Generally high involvement: but past experience, and the way that cars are often extensions of our positions and personalities may mean a short-cut process.
7. High involvement.
8. High involvement: performance is important, source processing may play an important role.
9. Carpet slippers: low involvement (and easy to create warm, comfortable feelings in the execution).

Answers will vary. Do you use different styles of advertising for different products/audiences?

**Activity 9.4**

Here are some suggested slides.

---

# What is Advertising?

■ Method of:
Informing
Influencing
Reminding
Persuading (sometimes)

■ Can help, amongst others, to:
Create awareness
Position
Differentiate
Generate dialogue

---

# What Advertising Is Not

■ Guaranteed to move consumers
from unawareness to purchase

■ The only promotional tool we
should consider

---

# Strong Theory vs. Weak

- **Strong Theory:**
  Says advertising is *persuasive*
  Most applicable for new brands/products

- **Weak Theory:**
  Advertising cannot *change* views/behaviour
  Ads help reinforce, remind, familiarise
  Requires integration with other methods

# Cognitive Processing

- Product/message processing
- Source processing
- Execution processing
- Balance depends on audience and product
  ☐
  High involvement or Low involvement?
- Possible research requirement

# Likely Effect of Advertising

- Most ads filtered out
- Remainder may create meaningful moments
- Stored in "mental database"
- Works with other stimuli to develop
  and reinforce attitudes
- Influences:
  Purchase
  Repurchase

# Session 10

# Promotional mixes and messages – 2

## Introduction

This is the second of two Sessions looking at the tools of the promotional mix. This one looks at all elements of the mix except for advertising, and explores the role that each tool plays to support others. It also considers how each tool might be evaluated.

---

**LEARNING OUTCOMES**

At the end of this Session you will be able to:

■ Explain the role of various tools within the promotional mix.

■ Understand loyalty programmes and customer retention issues.

■ Identify the main audiences to which public relations activities are directed, and PR's role in managing crises.

---

## How sales promotion is used within the promotional mix and how it might be evaluated

Sales promotion is a below the line element of the promotional mix, which may be aimed at a variety of audiences. Some examples of sales promotion methods are given below:

| Audience | Examples |
|---|---|
| Consumers | Coupons<br>Samples<br>Point-of-Purchase (PoP) material<br>Premiums (free or reduced cost merchandise, in-pack, on-pack or via application)<br>Price reductions<br>Competitions |
| Intermediaries (distributors, retailers etc.) | Buying allowance (temporary price reduction)<br>Free merchandise<br>Merchandise allowance<br>(paying for special promotional efforts)<br>Push money (incentivising personal selling) |
| In-house salesforce | Motivation programmes<br>Achievement awards |

**Table 10.1 Sales Promotion Methods**

Unlike advertising, which generally aims to build positive longer-term brand associations to influence buying behaviour, sales promotions are primarily about persuading people to alter short-term behaviour. Thus, they are often oriented towards prompting people to take action, and *now*. Action-oriented uses for sales promotion for different audiences might include:

## Consumers
Encouraging trial, or re-trial.
Persuading people to change brand.
Increasing existing usage or finding new uses.
Short and long-term behaviour change by encouraging and rewarding 'loyalty'.
Detracting from competitor activity.

## Trade
Shifting surplus stocks.
Giving shelf space.
Providing a more prominent display.
Generating endorsement and recommendation.

## Sales force
Incentivising sales activity.

Sales promotion can be used in other ways that do not necessarily prompt immediate action.

■ **To collect customer data:** increased personalisation of communications, for example, via the Internet and through direct mail, which requires data-gathering. On-pack offers and competitions in the press may be used for this purpose. Information may also be turned into leads for a sales force or agents. An award-winning promotion by the national radio station Talksport involved sending a single sports shoe to targeted individuals in charge of advertising in businesses, after gathering their personal details including shoe size. The individual got the other shoe when they had a meeting with a Talksport sales executive, and the campaign proved very effective.

■ **Generating publicity:** creative execution can often attract media interest, and promotes word-of-mouth communication. The effect on sales is less immediate but helps develop brand awareness and interest.

## Integration
Although any promotional tool can, theoretically, be used on its own, sales promotions' focus on short-term behaviour has often led to it being used in a stand-alone capacity. Promotions can be used as an isolated, quick response to rapidly changing market conditions, and in-store display material is likely to have a

more immediate effect on short-run buyer behaviour than PR or advertising. But effective promotions are often supported by other mechanisms. For example, the budget airlines' response to the US atrocities of September 2001 was an immediate discounting of fares, supported by advertising and extensive publicity. Sales soared over the following months. Indeed, the sales promotions industry is now recognising that integration is becoming increasingly important as the opportunities to reach customers become more diverse. Promotions planners now work alongside colleagues specialising in CRM (Customer Relationship Management), advertising, event management, new media and other disciplines.

An important aspect of integration is that sales promotions must not detract from the brand positioning, and should ideally enhance it. For example, short-term price reductions or "tacky" premiums can negatively impact a consumer's perception of a brand's value and standing. At the very least, promotions should be consistent with customer expectations. A 2002 Royal Mail promotion for its Special Delivery Service offered a Mini Cooper as a competition prize. The target audience was SMEs and SOHOs (single office/home office). Not only did Royal Mail see similarities between the car's image and their own (e.g. value for money, quintessentially 'British', and traditional but not old-fashioned), but they also felt that offering a higher value prize, such as a Porsche, would be too 'far-fetched'; people would think they had no chance of winning, and the promotion wouldn't fit with the price point of the £3.50 service.

## Evaluation

As always, the results of sales promotion activities need to be assessed against objectives. Examples might concern shifting stocks to create space for new supplies, building awareness of a new service or shifting demand patterns to smooth seasonal variations.

Sometimes, though, particular care needs to be taken in judging the effect of promotions. Increased sales in a period do not necessarily mean extra sales viewed over a longer term, nor extra revenue or profit. Individuals may have brought forward purchases which they were going to make later. Discounts might benefit those who were going to buy the product anyway. Or they might be taken up by promiscuous switchers from other brands, who simply chase the cheapest options. Only a handful of people might choose to buy who would not otherwise have done so – and even fewer will necessarily turn this into long-run behaviour.

---

**Activity 10.1**

A colleague is excited about the sales promotion he has just organised for your company, which sells cameras off the page direct to the public. The effect of the promotion was to more than double sales over three months from an expected 5,600 to 14,000 by discounting the normal £100 price by 25%. The normal sale price reflects a 100% mark-up on the buying-in price from the manufacturer. (Post, packaging, insurance etc. are paid directly by the consumer and can be ignored here).

Research data indicates the profile of buyers was as follows:

- those intending to purchase the cameras anyway during the period: 40%.

- those who were intending to buy in the next period, and brought forward their purchase: 20%.

- those who bought solely because of the discount: 20%.

- those who were going to buy a competitor's product but chose your company's instead: 20%.

Is your colleague right to be excited?

---

## The role of Public Relations in the promotional mix and how it might be evaluated

The boundaries of Public Relations (PR) are not easy to define. The Institute of Public Relations says, "PR practice is the planned and sustained effort to establish and maintain goodwill and mutual understanding between an organisation and it publics". We will look in more detail at those 'publics' in the next section, but they include investors, customers, pressure groups, the community, suppliers, distributors, regulators, opinion formers, local and national government, competitors, employees and others. The media are an essential addition to this list, but note that PR isn't just about media liaison, which is how it is often portrayed.

Given this breadth of responsibilities, companies create a variety of structures to meet their PR needs: Corporate Communications, Public Affairs, Investor Relations and Publicity are amongst the many departmental titles you may come across. But, regardless of definition, ultimately what PR comes down to is building effective relationships with specific audiences. Good PR helps to develop a positive company image, build reputation and strengthen credibility. Although PR is not specifically product-focused, it does help create an environment in which it is easier to sell products and services. Footwear producers such as Nike and Reebok go to great lengths to counter accusations of exploitation of less developed countries in manufacturing. A negative **corporate** image threatens their **product** sales.

PR does include **marketing** communications responsibilities, and often these will have a media focus. Creating publicity for a new consumer product launch, generating editorial coverage for a new B2B service, or implementing a diverse range of longer-term activities aimed at differing publics in order to build a brand are all examples of PR. In general, organisations will separate out these product and brand marketing responsibilities from corporate communications, giving marketing managers responsibility for them alongside other elements of the promotional mix. As always, when looking at this mix, it is essential to integrate messages. PR must complement and support other activity, whatever form it takes, not operate independently from it.

### PR advantages

Used effectively, PR can offer several advantages over other promotional tools. For example, there is the real advantage of the effect of unpaid media exposure. Independent editorial coverage is generally perceived as carrying more weight than, say, advertising, as positive coverage suggests implicit endorsement by a third party. The non-financial price for this is that the organisation loses control of the message once it reaches the media. A journalist may not put the message over in the way that you want it; their copy may contain errors, or editorial reaction to something you have said may be critical. Potentially it's out of your hands – though if your PR activity extends to building relationships with journalists, rather than just sending out press releases, you are far more likely to be able to influence how stories, good or bad, are handled.

Another advantage of PR is that it can be a very low cost promotional tool. For this reason smaller businesses may find it particularly useful. Gaining media exposure through well-executed press releases or becoming known as an expert in your field can cost very little. Ultimately, though, PR is as expensive as you want it to be: staffing and/or agency costs, literature production and event organisation can run up large bills.

So how do you know if your PR is good value for money? Well, it must be measured against the **SMART** objectives you have set in relation to your different audiences. These objectives could be as diverse as defusing the arguments and activities of a lobby group, or collecting a specified number of leads through applications for an information leaflet.

Audience research can play a part in evaluation: pre- and post-testing and tracking can all be used to monitor changes in audience awareness and attitudes etc. Where PR activity is taking place alongside other elements of the promotional mix, you will want, if possible, to identify the effect of the different elements and whether some have been more effective in reaching certain audiences. Nochex, an email money transmission service, uses an online question to identify where consumers heard about their service. Results showed that PR proved highly effective in their low-budget 2001 launch.[6]

Media monitoring and evaluation can also be used, maybe with the services of specialist agencies. These can go beyond merely measuring column inches or air-time; tracking techniques and software can weight the coverage for favourability, prominence and source, i.e. whether the coverage was media-inspired or originated by specific PR activity by the business. Analysis can be undertaken of the message's **reach**, while Advertising Value Equivalents (AVEs) can be calculated to see how much similar coverage would have cost to buy as advertising.

---

**Activity 10.2**

Develop your knowledge of PR. The Institute of Public Relation's web site (www.ipr.org.uk) includes useful information on the nature of PR and the breadth of activities that it encompasses. There are also daily news updates and a helpful reading list.

See if you can access publications which keep you up to date on industry developments such as the IPR Journal or PR Week. The latter has a particularly useful Campaigns column – real case studies which clearly set out the situation, objectives, strategy and plan, measurement and evaluation methods and campaign results. Their web site (www.prweek.com) also has valuable campaign examples.

---

## The main audiences targeted by Public Relations and how it might be used in crisis management

The previous section mentioned that there are many different publics in PR. Separate objectives and communications strategies will need to be established for each audience, though there will certainly be overlaps in the messages and media used. Remember that a member of one type of public may well see a message aimed at a different public too. Consistency is therefore vital and requires co-ordinated effort within the business.

Table 10.2 sets out who the main publics are and why they need to be considered.

| Main Public | Reasons for targeting |
|---|---|
| Those with a financial interest:<br><br>Shareholders: (institutional, e.g. pensions fund and unit trusts managers, and individual); bankers, brokers, analysts and advisers, indirect investors, e.g. pension fund members. | Shareholders have voting rights in the business. A single institution may hold several per cent of a public company, and collectively, institutions can wield considerable power. Their views can influence strategy and even Board membership (e.g. Stelios Haji-Ioannou stepping down as easyJet chairman in 2003 following City pressure). Lack of institutional confidence can undermine a business. Analysts etc. specialise in understanding companies and comparing them to others in the same or different sectors. They are a very influential community. Bankers' confidence will need to be maintained to retain (or obtain) loan facilities and secure favourable terms. Good credit ratings can make a big impact on the bottom line. Indirect investors will want to be reassured that their finances are safe. Lobbying by worried group members could deter institutional investment. |
| Those whose relationship concerns the product, service etc.<br><br>Customers, users etc. (existing and potential).<br><br>Opinion leaders.<br><br>Supporters, e.g. of charities. | They will want the reassurance that they are buying/have bought from a business that meets any of a range of criteria relevant to them, such as trustworthy, efficient, ethical, responsible, financially sound, credible etc.<br><br>Corporate PR helps eliminate negative views of the business and builds up positive images. This removes one uncertainty from the consumer's decision-making process and/or eliminates a source of post-purchase dissonance.<br>Marketing PR creates similar attitudes towards the brand, product, service etc.<br><br>Publicity gives opportunities to build awareness and develop attitudes. |

| Suppliers, business partners and distributors. | Increasingly important as businesses outsource and/or become more interdependent (e.g. through **JIT** operation) to gain competitive advantage. Building long-term mutually beneficial relationships requires growth of confidence in, and understanding of, each other's businesses. |
|---|---|
| Local community, including residents, MPs, local councillors, schools, clubs, businesses and professional organisations. | Good local image eases recruitment and facilitates business exchange.<br><br>May make it easier to make changes to premises or operational activities that require planning approval, and may head off pressure groups.<br><br>Remember that local people may fall into another category of public too, e.g. potential buyers.<br><br>Word of mouth very important. |
| Government, regulators including quangos and bureaucrats. | Retaining their confidence may smooth out problems before they arise.<br><br>Gives opportunities to influence debates, and understand and plan for changes.<br><br>Direct or indirect government endorsement, consultation etc. builds your credibility amongst other publics. |
| Industry bodies and competitors. | Again, gives opportunities to influence debates.<br><br>Builds corporate image which may put you at a competitive advantage: become recognised as the 'leader', influential, authoritative, creative, substantial, the 'best' provider etc. |
| Pressure groups and representative bodies, including trade unions and lobbyists. | Smoothes relationships which could otherwise impact sales, restrict progress, divert management attention etc.<br><br>Co-operative approach can facilitate more efficient operations. |

| Media:<br>broadcast, print, new media. | Highly influential in reaching other publics.<br><br>Can create awareness, inform, prompt dialogues (e.g. C2B, C2C), lobby and much more. Can strongly influence **attitudes**. |
|---|---|
| Employees, including existing and potential ones. | Perhaps the most important public. Think of your own position: how well do you understand the business you work for, and how well do your team do so? Spend time thinking about your and their needs, and the reasons for them.<br><br>If the organisation's employees don't understand and believe in what it is doing, no-one else will. |

**Table 10.2 PR audiences**

## Crisis management

On the face of it, crisis management is a reactive process. An unexpected event occurs and the organisation must react. For example, if there is an industrial accident and death or serious injury occurs, or glass fragments are found in your product on supermarket shelves, or the IT system crashes and all order details are lost. The time following such an incident is when your organisation's abilities will be most in the spotlight, and when you have the maximum opportunity to either enhance your credibility and reputation, or possibly damage it irreparably.

The time following the incident may be very short before your publics form their opinion. That is why the key to crisis management lies in preparation, long before you ever need to react. Planning for crisis management involves many steps, including:

- Getting the right team together to develop the plan and be ready to implement it.
- Envisaging a wide range of circumstances of varying degrees of gravity ('scenario planning').
- Identifying and prioritising the relevant audiences for each type of crisis and anticipating what their information needs will be.
- Preparing equipment, documentation, processes, etc.
- Testing and rehearsing scenarios.

PR training is invaluable and spokespeople must be clear from the outset about the right and wrong things to say. "No comment" breeds distrust and suspicions of incompetence. Being seen to be exercising control of the situation is important, as is recognising the legitimate interests of your different publics.

A well-handled crisis can enable a company's reputation to be recovered or even enhanced. Perrier was able to regain market dominance following withdrawal of 160 million bottles world-wide due to benzene contamination fears in 1990. It did, however, require a hugely costly PR and promotional campaign.

---

**Activity 10.3**

A definition of 'marketing' is "the management process which identifies, anticipates and supplies customer requirements efficiently and profitably."

Make notes on the extent to which you think this definition could apply to the practice of public relations generally.

---

## The role of sponsorship within the promotional mix and how it might be evaluated

In March 2002, Unilever, one of the UK's largest companies and owner of household names such as Birds Eye, Pot Noodle and Persil, announced that it was planning a "dramatic increase" in spending on sponsorship as a proportion of its $4bn (£2.6bn) annual spend on communications. It said its brand teams would be looking at sponsorship as a key strategic tool, rather than merely a secondary or tactical one.

Their move reflects an increasing recognition in business generally of the potential value of sponsorship and reinforces a view that sponsorship is a promotional tool in its own right, alongside the traditional elements of the promotional mix (advertising, personal selling, sales promotion and public relations).

But even if sponsorship is being viewed as a separate tool, it should integrate with other elements of the mix. Think of some different types of sponsorship deal:

■ Association between commercial partners for mutual benefit, for example Vodafone and Manchester United, Tiger Woods and Nike.

■ Funding or provision of other resources to not-for-profit organisations, events and activities e.g. the Flora London marathon and the 2002 Commonwealth Games, whose many sponsors include BUPA, Manchester Airport and Adecco.

Both present ample opportunities for PR, facilitating the building of relationships between an organisation and its publics. Corporate hospitality opportunities are likely to be offered as part of commercial art and sport sponsorship deals. Funding a local community initiative is likely to bring goodwill to a business, whether the motive is altruism or something more.

Personal selling may be incentivised by opportunities to attend events or meet stars tied into sponsorship deals. Also, sales promotions offer opportunities for commercial businesses to 'theme' their promotions, or demonstrate their caring side by linking point-of-sale material, packaging or direct mail to national charity initiatives.

But whereas the above opportunities are obviously complementary, advertising and sponsorship cover may have similar objectives. In Session 9 we discussed how advertising is thought unlikely to be a dominantly **persuasive** medium. Sponsorship too is not thought to have a significant persuasive effect. Instead it helps to build awareness, reinforce familiarity and strengthen the brand or corporate image that is aiming to be projected. To this end, like advertising, thorough understanding of your audience and their motivations and preferences is vital to effective implementation of a sponsorship strategy. Used correctly, sponsorship's image-building benefits can have a multiplied effect, as users/viewers etc. not only become exposed to the brand and its associations, but process them cognitively in a context to which they are already receptive (i.e. through their interest in the sport, event, personality etc.).

## Measurement

Measures must be put in place in order to assess the benefits from sponsorship activity. This can be used to identify benefits in absolute terms, and as a basis for comparisons with other promotional opportunities.

As with other promotional tools, research can identify changes in attitudes and awareness, though it may not always be easy to separate out the effects of sponsorship and other activity.

The value of media coverage can be compared against the equivalent cost of buying that exposure. Sometimes that exposure cannot be bought in other ways at all: an audience may be too fragmented, or legal restrictions may inhibit non-sponsorship activity. The latter is one reason for the attractiveness of tobacco sponsorship of Formula 1 motor racing, although EU regulations mean that F1 tobacco sponsorship is to end by 2006.

Other benefits can be measured too, e.g. the value of associated corporate hospitality opportunities, or number of visits to a promoted web site, and consequent business written.

Whatever measures are used, the business will want to see a projected and actual return on its investment, usually expressed as a multiple of the sponsorship costs. A minimum figure might be 'x 2', and it could be many more. The retail group Kingfisher's three year sponsorship of Ellen MacArthur, the round-the-world yachtswoman, cost £1.8m but gave benefits worth many times this figure following her success. They have now renewed the deal for five years.

---

**Activity 10.4**

You are giving a short talk to your marketing team on the reasons for the growth of sponsorship as a communications tool. What key reasons would you identify?

---

## The role of personal selling within the promotional mix, and how it might be evaluated

Personal selling is a very expensive element of the promotional mix. Expenditure items may include:

- Salespeople's salaries, commissions and **on-costs**.
- Non-commission incentives.
- Training – essential to maintain skills and knowledge.
- Transport.
- Premises and associated costs, though nowadays many salespeople have no office base.
- Communications technology – used by all, but particularly important where there is no office base.
- Demonstration goods and materials.
- Supporting administrative and management infrastructure.

It is essential, therefore, for personal selling activity to be concentrated where it is going to be most effective, allowing other elements of the promotional mix to meet communication needs when personal attention is not necessary.

Personal selling, then, lends itself to certain situations.

Firstly, it is proven to be more effective in the later stages of the buying process. Advertising, sponsorship or other tools may be effective at creating awareness and stimulating interest in a product. But as the individual progresses with the process of evaluating the options against his or her needs, the more useful personal selling becomes in explaining benefits and overcoming objections. This can make all the difference between someone choosing to progress to trialling a product or not.

Of course, not all purchases require the assistance of a salesperson in the later stage – most of us are probably capable of buying a chocolate bar on our own! So, secondly, personal selling is most valuable in more complex decision-making situations. In these high involvement situations, individuals have the motivation and ability to undertake searches for information about a prospective purchase. Compared to personal selling, the other communications tools may well be inadequate to explain what the product is capable of, or how it can be used in an individual's situation. Remember also that people are generally seeking benefits, not features. A salesperson is able to translate how a complex product feature can actually give real day-to-day advantages in a buyer's specific situation.

It is not surprising then that personal selling is a significant feature of B2B markets. Here the decision-making may be complex. Several different parties' requirements may need to be satisfied, complex evaluation criteria met, and non-standard adaptations delivered. Other communications mechanisms are simply not capable of covering all the permutations or coping with the dialogue required. Though the growth of new media for B2B transactions is growing, as are remote communication technologies such as video-conferencing, some would argue that these can never be a substitute for face-to-face relationships. A 2002 British Airways campaign warns businesses about the orders they are losing by relying on technology while their competitors conduct client meetings across a table.

### Evaluation

Salespeople and sales forces, you will not be surprised to hear, are likely to be assessed on measures related to sales. This might relate to sales by product, customer segment, order value, commission generated or a similar measure. Other evaluation criteria might relate to:

- Inputs to the processes for successful selling, e.g. total calls made or presentations delivered.

- Outputs from sales, e.g. profitability or persistency, for example in financial services, where salespeople may be measured on how long business stays on the books.

But these quantitative measures overlook qualitative aspects of seller-buyer relationships, which are particularly important if an organisation claims to be marketing oriented. Selling is not just about the short-term, but is about understanding customer needs, building relationships and delivering real satisfaction. Enlightened companies, such as IBM and Eveready, therefore include assessment criteria that relate to customer satisfaction and delivery of a quality service, based on feedback sought from customers, not just sales performance. These criteria can directly affect individuals' remuneration. Such an approach is particularly important where Key Account Management (KAM) operates. Most businesses are particularly dependent on a handful of main customers. Careful attention needs to be paid to retaining and developing these strategically important relationships.

---

**Activity 10.5**

Sales forces can be structured in various ways, notably covering different:

- geographical areas.
- products or ranges.
- customers or customer types.

Your boss has asked for your views on the relative merits of these methods. Based on an industry of your choice, draw up three slides that set out the main advantages and disadvantages, and a fourth making your recommendation.

---

## Loyalty programmes and customer retention

'Loyalty' is a much-used word in marketing. It is also a much-abused one. Do customers really feel loyal to brands, just like you feel loyal to your friends? If customers keep on coming back to the same supplier, does it mean they are loyal, or could there be another explanation? If customers do feel some sense of loyalty to a brand, does it mean they always use it? If we consider a sequence of degrees of loyalty, for how many companies that you regularly use are you an 'advocate'?

Prospect → Customer → Client → Supporter → Advocate

As the answers to these questions might imply, loyalty and customer retention are not necessarily the same thing.

Companies are keen to retain customers, partly because it is generally cheaper to persuade them to make a repurchase than it is to turn non-users into buyers. The extent of savings is arguable and varies between markets, though figures of five or ten times are often suggested. Small increases in retention levels have been shown to grow over time into very substantial increases in profits.

From a communications viewpoint, sheer logic suggests that fewer steps are involved in the buying process when customers already have experience of the product and of its brand associations. And 'fewer steps' translates into lower costs, particularly on promotions.

But a supplier may continue to enjoy repeated custom for many reasons. A business traveller may use the same airline on every trip because it is more convenient, rather than because he feels loyal to it. Pure inertia may prevent you shopping around for a different business stationery supplier – the one you use is convenient and "OK". Or you may be a hostage, trapped into continuing to use a particular brand of IT software or consumables because anything else is incompatible with your hardware. Supermarket loyalty cards, which generate discounts for customers, have not necessarily delivered the benefits that some companies were expecting. Asda decided not to issue a card and Safeway have ditched theirs. Their view is that the costs of running card schemes can be more effectively channelled into delivering other benefits for customers. Tesco, though, credits its card with delivering significant business benefits. Besides upping business volumes, these benefits include offering opportunities to gather data about customers. It is this data – together with other research, both quantitative and qualitative – that can make a major contribution to understanding customers. In turn this can lead to better relationship-building and business retention.

Whether we are talking about supermarkets or any other type of business, developing these relationships means organising to be truly focused on **customer needs**, not just offering short term promotions to attract short-term business. What are the priorities of different customer segments? What problems do they have – buying from you or elsewhere – that you could tackle creatively? How do you make the experience of dealing with your organisation pleasurable, memorable or whatever? Remember that relationships are built on emotions, not transactions, so how can you create those feelings in your target segments? And bear in mind that just satisfying your customers probably isn't enough. Customers expect to be satisfied, so it doesn't become a differentiator unless they either become dissatisfied or experience exceptionally high levels of satisfaction.

To create loyalty, then, requires two shifts in what has been the traditional view taken by some businesses. Firstly, the focus must move from customer acquisition to customer retention. Of course, this doesn't mean ignoring new prospects –
you have to replace customers that you will inevitably lose, even if your business is faultless – but it requires a change of emphasis. Secondly, it requires a focus on meeting carefully identified needs and desires. Dangling short-term carrots may deliver business benefits but it does not necessarily translate into loyalty.

**Activity 10.6**

Two growing businesses each have 1000 customers. Business A concentrates on acquisition of new customers. It loses 40% of its customers each year, but acquires new ones equal to 50% of its start-of-year customer base. The equivalent figures for business B, which focuses on customer retention through a variety of methods, are 20% and 30%. In addition, a referral scheme leads to 10% of B's customers generating one new customer each year.

a. How many customers do the respective businesses have at the end of year 5?

b. What benefits might business B see, as well as increased customer numbers?

# Case Study – AP Engineering

AP Engineering (AP) is a privately owned civil engineering company, employing approximately 4,200 people in the Asia Pacific region. The company designs and manages the building of major civil engineering projects in a variety of vertical market sectors.

The company wins contracts by bidding for client-specified projects and offering the best (perceived) value for money. The problem with this approach is that the appointed civil engineering company has limited input to the original requirement/specification and, as soon as the project is completed, its involvement is normally terminated. Perhaps even more importantly, the margins earned on such projects are notoriously slim, so that in order to grow the business, higher margins need to be generated.

Following a review of the business, AP's new strategy is based upon a total engineering service, one which centres on client needs and their total project requirements, rather than the previous engineering/product focus. In other words, the company now adopts a relationship marketing approach. The emphasis is upon providing added value by shifting the offering both upstream and downstream. Therefore, AP Engineering now provides three connected offerings.

a. The front-end work, which involves undertaking the planning and risk analysis work for its clients.

b. The core work, which is about the design and build aspect of the project.

c. The tail-end work, which is essentially Facilities Management.

Among the many advantages this strategic approach presents, there are two significant benefits. The first lies in the substantially higher margins that the front and tail-end work attracts. The second concerns reducing wastage of resources, by being able to help accurately define the client problem at the earliest possible stage in the project life cycle.

In order to develop and implement this strategy, AP has had to evolve a new skills mix, namely Asset Management and Facilities Management skills. AP chose to purchase a number of small consultancies and formed alliances with other targeted companies specialising in these particular skill areas.

Whilst this might sound reasonably straightforward, AP has had to address further issues concerning the development of a suitable commercial culture for the established employees and those new to the enlarged organisation. The company now views each project as a commercial activity and all employees must adopt increased levels of commercial awareness, e.g. project risk assessment, the importance of working within budget and invoicing on time. In addition, the employees of the newly acquired organisations have to be incorporated into the values and corporate philosophy of the new company culture. A further issue concerns the way the company presents itself to clients and other key stakeholders.

The organisation is deliberately seeking to develop closer client relationships based upon trust and empathy. It has done this by improving understanding of its clients' business, by getting involved right from the start of a new project, by completing projects on time and within budget, and by a willingness to share sensitive information. It also helps that the AP Engineering brand is highly visible and has developed a credible reputation based upon clients' perceived value.

The level of communication frequency between client and AP Engineering varies across the life of a project. There is a great deal of communication at the outset of a project, as the brief is determined by all parties. As the project moves to the design phase, the level of communication tends to fall. However, projects often run tight on their deadlines; hence inter-organisational, and even intra-organisational communication levels intensify in an attempt to resolve on-site problems as quickly as possible.

The company realises that personal contact is the most significant communication tool used in the development and maintenance of client relationships, but the company is undecided about its communication strategy, and has asked you, in your capacity as Marketing Communications Consultant, for your advice.

**Source:** *Integrated Marketing Communications Examination Paper*, December 2001.

**Questions**

1. Identify and justify a communication strategy for AP Engineering for the next year.

2. Which tools of the promotional mix might best be used to implement this strategy? Why?

3. List the issues that AP might consider before implementing an integrated marketing communications policy.

## SUMMARY OF KEY POINTS

In this Session, we have looked further at promotional mixes, and covered the following key points:

- The main tools in the promotional mix, in addition to advertising, are sales promotion, public relations, personal selling and sponsorship.

- Each has a different role to play, but all are important.

- Sales promotion is associated with short-term increases in sales.

- Public relations plays a key role in profile strategy, and in crisis management.

- Sponsorship can be targeted and is useful in supporting the other tools in the mix.

- Personal selling is very important in communicating with business-to-business markets and where very complex products and services are involved.

- Marketing overall has taken a shift from transactional marketing to relationship marketing, and it is now important for promotions to support customer retention (as opposed to just acquisition).

## Improving and developing own learning

The following projects are designed to help you develop your knowledge and skills further by carrying out some research yourself. Feedback is not provided for this type of learning because there are no 'answers' to be found, but you may wish to discuss your findings with colleagues and fellow students.

---

### Project A

Talk to your colleagues in the marketing department and look at ways in which public relations is used. Is it used in the profile strategy? Has it ever been used in crisis management?

---

### Project B

Look at the use of sales promotion within your organisation's promotional plan. To what extent is it used as a consumer incentive, as an incentive for the trade, or as an incentive for the sales force? What promotional objectives is it used to achieve?

---

### Project C

Does your organisation use personal selling in the promotional mix? How is the sales force organised? Talk to colleagues in the sales force about ways that other marketing promotions support them in meetings sales objectives. Make notes of your findings.

## Feedback to activities

### Activity 10.1

We need to establish first the contribution to fixed costs and profits per camera sold:

To calculate the buying in price:

Buying in price + 100% mark up = sales price.

Therefore 2 x buying-in price = £100

Buying-in price = $\dfrac{£100}{2}$ = £50

Contribution per camera:

| | |
|---|---|
| Without discount: | £100 – £50 = £50 |
| After discount: | £75 – £50 = £25 |

**Expected future contribution without discount:**

| | |
|---|---|
| During the period: | 5,600 (i.e. 40% of 14,000) x £50 = £28,000 |
| Brought-forward purchases: | 2,800 (i.e. 20% of 14,000) x £50 = £14,000 |
| Total: | £42,000 |

**Actual contribution during promotional period:**

| | |
|---|---|
| Sales x contribution: | 14,000 x £25 = £35,000 |

| | |
|---|---|
| Net effect of promotional strategy: | |
| Expected contribution: | £42,000 |
| Actual contribution: | £35,000 |

Your colleague's promotional strategy has cost the company £7,000 even though sales rose substantially.

### Activity 10.2

Building up a library of case studies will help develop your understanding of PR and give you ideas that you could legitimately adapt to answer exam questions. Remember CIM papers are all about **applying knowledge**, so the more real examples you have studied, the easier it will be to demonstrate your knowledge.

## Activity 10.3

There are some very close parallels between the definition of 'marketing' and PR practice, in particular its customer focus.

Marketing requires a focus on customer needs. Different customers have different requirements, so segmentation is essential. The needs of each segment need to be identified and the mix of tools available to the marketer must be adapted accordingly, including using different communication tools.

PR also requires careful segmentation of its publics. Again, each will have its own needs and perspectives and the organisation must adapt its approach accordingly. The product will vary for each audience (e.g., a long-term growth strategy for institutional investors, proof of the safety of processes and equipment used, for a pressure group), therefore meaning that the mix of communication methods used must also be varied.

## Activity 10.4

Points to cover in your talk would include:

- Growing media advertising costs.
- Opportunities to avoid advertising clutter. (Interestingly Unilever say that they intend to be very strict about their sponsorship criteria: "We won't escape advertising clutter just to find ourselves in sponsorship clutter").
- Offers opportunities to target specific audience segments that may be hard to reach in other ways.
- Increased global reach of events and media.
- Increased emphasis on using sponsorship to deliver results, such as real brand-building benefits.
- Increased emphasis on accountability and measurability of promotions, allowing sponsorship benefits to be demonstrated.
- Recognition of growing opportunities to integrate with other communication methods, e.g. DM and sales promotions.
- Recognition of growing opportunities to use sponsorship to develop relationships with various publics.
- Can underpin response to demands for increased corporate citizenship.

## Activity 10.5

Your answer will vary for different situations, particularly in relation to your final choice. Here are some suggested non-specific points.

**Advantages**

## Geographical Structure

**Pro**
- Simple to operate.
- Can exploit synergies between businesses in the area.
- One salesperson per customer.
- Low travel costs.

**Con**
- Requires broad product knowledge.
- No account taken of salesperson's suitability for different types of account.

## Product-Based Structure

**Pro**
- Detailed product knowledge developed.
- Facilitates greater understanding of applications for customers.
- Management can allocate right people to right user type.
- Facilitate internal relationships with product managers, production etc.

**Con**
- Customer may be visited by several salespeople from same company.
- Any duplication of company effort means wasted time, costs etc.
- Potentially inflexible, e.g. if a customer/ salesperson experience a personality clash.

# Customer-Based structure

**Pro**

■ Thorough understanding of customer needs.
■ Better opportunities for relationship-building.
■ Can match salesperson to different types of account, e.g. for small business experience; national accounts.

**Con**

■ Again, risk of duplication of effort if different buying organisations have several relationships.
■ May miss/ignore opportunities outside target group.

# Recommendation

Customer-based structure + Geographical structure

**Customer-Based**

■ Focus on key accounts (giving 60% of total business).
■ Relationship building is key.
■ Only one, experienced, salesperson for any account (i.e. dedicated KAMs).

**Geographical**

■ Remaining accounts (40% of total business).
■ Prospecting for new accounts.

Main advantage: balances customer focused approach with need to keep costs acceptable.

## Activity 10.6

| | Business A | Business B |
|---|---|---|
| **Customers (start of year 1)** | **1000** | **1000** |
| Gain | 500 | 300 |
| Lose | 400 | 200 |
| Referrals | – | 100 |
| **Customers (start of yr 2)** | **1100** | **1200** |
| Gain | 550 | 360 |
| Lose | 440 | 240 |
| Referrals | – | 120 |
| **Customers (start of yr 3)** | **1210** | **1440** |
| Gain | 605 | 432 |
| Lose | 484 | 288 |
| Referrals | – | 144 |
| **Customers (start of yr 4)** | **1331** | **1728** |
| Gain | 666 | 518 |
| Lose | 532 | 346 |
| Referrals | – | 173 |
| **Customers (start of yr 5)** | **1465** | **2073** |
| Gain | 732 | 622 |
| Lose | 586 | 415 |
| Referrals | – | 207 |
| **Customers (end of yr 5)** | **1611** | **2487** |

The different strategies make a significant difference to customer numbers after five years.

Making projections is an important part of business strategy, and can directly influence the viability of plans. Bear in mind that all projections are dependent upon making assumptions and you must be able to justify these.

b. Some other possible advantages for B, because of its better customer relationships, include:

■ larger order sizes.
■ more opportunities to up-sell.
■ more opportunities to cross-sell.
■ opportunity for premium pricing.
■ ability to capitalise on economies of scale.

# Session 11

# Budget and resource issues

## Introduction

This Session explores issues around budget setting for promotional activity and plans. It looks at various options for setting budgets, and, in particular, at the role share of voice (SOV) plays in achieving competitive advantage in communications terms.

---

### LEARNING OUTCOMES

At the end of this Session you will be able to:

■ Understand the role of the promotional budget.

■ Examine various communication budgeting techniques.

■ Explain how share of voice (SOV) can be used as a strategically competitive tool.

---

## The role of the communications budget

Communications budgets matter to all organisations whatever their size. Microsoft is said to be spending $500m (around £350m) to launch its Xbox games console world-wide.[7] Cadbury's spent £6m on UK advertising for its new *Dream* white chocolate bar in 2002.[8] Meanwhile, a small owner-run high street restaurant may have only a few hundred pounds or so to get its name across to the public. Whoever controls the budgets for these organisations will want to make sure that they use the financial resources they are controlling to the best effect.

Unfortunately, setting a budget is not a science. There is no general rule that says if you spend £x on communications you will get benefits worth £y (though in some areas, such as direct marketing, statistical modelling and simulation using IT software can generate quite accurate predictions of  response levels and consequent business volumes). However, by exercising judgement, learning from experience and adopting a mix of budgeting techniques it is possible to arrive at an appropriate budget figure.

Budgeting for communications for a department or a campaign involves two key decisions:

■ How much will we spend on communications overall?

■ How will we allocate that budget between different elements of the promotional mix?

[7] BBC news online 15/11/01.
[8] Marketing Week 29/11/01.

Depending on the budgeting techniques used, either of these decisions may come first. A top-down management approach will allocate an overall budget, from which decisions will then be made about how it should be allocated to different products, brands, channels, promotional tools etc. A bottom-up approach considers the individual communications needs for campaigns, and the total of these comprises the overall promotional budget. Often there will be a mix between the two approaches, as a compromise is negotiated between what the marketing managers wish to do and what they will be allowed to spend.

Whichever approach is used, the budget planner must consider several factors:

■ What are the communications objectives to be achieved? As we considered in Session 7, these must derive from the marketing objectives and, ultimately, the corporate objectives. If the outcome of budget allocation decisions does not enable you to demonstrate clear linkages between objectives and spending, then the outlay cannot be justified. Key factors that will impinge on how much you will need to spend include the type of communications needed, extent of competition, nature and distribution of your audience and the type of product.

■ What resources are available? Not only must the budget be realistic in terms of the financial resources that are actually available, but it must also be consistent with the human and other resources required to make it deliver maximum value.

■ What experience can we draw on? Which spending has proved effective in the past and which has not, both for us and for our competitors? (This requires evaluation to be carried out for all activities: constant scanning of competitor activity and accessible records to be kept of this information).

■ Competitive position? What is our position relative to our competitors in terms of promotional budgets, market share (or other relevant measures) and spending patterns (see Session 11)?

■ Environmental factors: economic growth, consumer confidence etc.

The communications budgeting process, like budgeting processes elsewhere, brings several benefits:

■ It forces attention on objectives and plans, not least by requiring these to be made in the first place. The budgets must be subject to a "reality check," requiring realistic benefits to be estimated for realistic outlays. **Opportunity costs** will need to be weighed up, and decisions made about alternative strategies.

■ It provides benchmarks against which campaign activity can be monitored and control action taken.

■ Evaluation of final campaign results against objectives provides an input into the planning process for future communications activity.

■ It gives a basis for communication to managers and other stakeholders to enable them to understand relative priorities and to help co-ordinate their activities.

---

**Activity 11.1**

Study the Student Briefing pages of The Advertising Association's web site (www.adassoc.org.uk), in particular Briefing no. 6. This gives valuable information on the UK media, advertising costs and how much is spent on advertising by different market sectors.

Try to find information, from the Internet, print or broadcast media, agencies, publications or within your own organisation, to indicate costs of other forms of promotional activity.

---

## Budgeting techniques

Many different techniques may be used to set marketing budgets. Table 11.1 describes these and sets out their advantages and disadvantages.

| Method | Description | Pro | Con |
|---|---|---|---|
| Arbitrary | Budget decisions made by senior person, but with no real consideration of context or strategy. Figure may be plucked out of the air. | Quick, flexible. | No relationship to task in hand, or market realities, so budget may be wholly inappropriate. |
| Affordable or "All-we-can-afford". | The organisation's non-communications fixed and variable costs, plus an allowance for profit, are deducted from revenues. What is left is what the business can afford to spend on communications. | Relatively easy to calculate. Largely risk-free as non-comms. costs are accounted for before spending on promotional activity. | Again, no relationship to objectives or markets.<br><br>Comms. are likely to be the first area squeezed if actual financial results differ from budgeted ones. |

| Intertia | Rather than re-calculate, this year's figure is simply the same as last year's. | Easy to calculate.<br><br>May have a grounding in reality, if previous figure was appropriate. | May have little relationship to objectives or market, especially if these change significantly.<br><br>Encourages a "use it or lose it" approach, rather than rational decision-making. |
|---|---|---|---|
| Media multiplier | As for inertia, but an allowance is made for increases in media costs. | As for inertia, with the added advantage of having some relationship to real costs. | As for inertia. |
| Percentage of sales. | Comms. budget is calculated as a percentage of value of sales – either historical or forecast.<br>% may be based on company or industry norm, or be arbitrary. | Easy to calculate. | Suggests comms. expenditure should fall if sales do and vice versa, but the reverse may be appropriate.<br><br>Approach based on historical sales doesn't recognise that marketing drives sales, not vice versa.<br><br>Still fails to relate to market opportunities. |

| | | | |
|---|---|---|---|
| Competitor comparison (and Competitor Parity) | Comparison is made against individual competitors/the industry as a whole, often in terms of the ratio of communications (usually advertising) spending to sales.<br><br>Your organisation can identify how it compares with industry/category averages and specific competitor information to benchmark how much you should be spending to achieve particular market share targets.<br><br>Using Competitor Parity your budget equals that of competitor(s). | May ensure the company is not at a competitive disadvantage.<br><br>Easy to calculate if competitor data available. | Comparisons assume competitors' strategy is similar to yours.<br><br>Takes no account of how efficiently and effectively money is used.<br><br>Competitor data may be hard to come by, especially for non-advertising expenditure. |
| Profit maximisation. | Keep on spending on comms. until the point where extra spending equals extra revenue, i.e. there in no more profit generated by comms spend. | Attractive in theory as it seeks to maximise profit. | Assumes a direct and immediate link between comms. activity and results, but in reality there are time-lags between the two, and other factors will influence the communications/ sales relationship. |

| | | | |
|---|---|---|---|
| Objective and task | A bottom-up approach which reviews each promotional objective, and identifies the tasks, and associated budget, to achieve each one. | Directly links the budget with the promotional objectives to be achieved.<br><br>Gives benchmarks against which to monitor achievement of goals. | Hard to determine exact expenditure to achieve required goals.<br><br>Required budget may be unrealistically high. |

The reality of budget setting is that no single method will necessarily be used exclusively. All methods have their disadvantages and the application of more than one technique gives scope for negotiation and judgement in determining a final budget figure.

As stated before, learning and experience must play an important part in budget development. This understanding can come from past budget setting and allocation, but another valuable source of information is through experimentation. Budgets can be allocated to test marketing, for example launching a product in a representative test area before national roll-out, or trialling variations of a direct marketing pack on a small sample of the target audience. Lessons learned can be applied to adjust budgets before scaling them up for the full campaign.

---

**Activity 11.2**

As newly appointed Communications Manager reporting directly to the Marketing Director, you have been invited to a meeting with her to discuss how you propose to set your communications budget for the forthcoming year.

Make preparatory notes on key issues relating to your preferred method, including a suggested process.

---

## Share of voice

In the previous section we briefly looked at competitor comparison as a method of budget setting. We will look at this in a little more detail, as it leads us to an important concept, **share of voice**, which can be used strategically within the business.

Study of different industries, business sectors or individual businesses will show that each spends a different amount on advertising as a proportion of its sales.

The relevant figure is known as the advertising to sales ratio or A/S ratio, calculated as:

$$\frac{\text{Advertising spend (£)}}{\text{Sales (£)}} \times 100$$

Knowing A/S ratios enables us to compare our advertising spend against that of competitors. We can assess, for example, whether we are spending more or less than the industry average. If our ratio is more than is typical for our type of business then it suggests that our money is not working as hard as other businesses'. This could be because our creative approach is less effective, or maybe we are less able to take advantage of economies of scale, for example in media buying, than others.

### Share of voice

From data about our business sector as a whole, we can identify what proportion our organisation spends on advertising in relation to the sector total. This is our share of voice (or SOV). For example, if we spend £10m on advertising compared to a total for our sector of £80m, then we have a 12.5% SOV. It follows that whichever organisation has the largest share of voice is likely to be most noticed in the marketplace. This, however, assumes that the effectiveness of advertising is based upon its quantity but, of course, marketers constantly strive to make their advertising 'punch above its weight' by, for example, maximising **perception** (Session 3), and by effective integration of advertising messages with other elements of the communications mix.

**Share of voice** can be considered alongside **share of market** (SOM). As a general rule one would expect the organisation with the largest SOV to have the largest market share, both because it probably has the revenue to fund large-scale advertising, and because it has an interest in maintaining its position. Other players in the market might also have an ad-spend roughly commensurate with their market position. When SOV is the same as SOM there is said to be equilibrium, but there may be many situations where the relationship between SOV and SOM is not a direct linear one, as in the following examples:

### Higher SOV than SOM

- A challenger is launching an attack on the market leader's position in a big-spending ad campaign to capture market share.

- A new entrant is mounting a launch campaign to gain a foothold in the market.

- The brand's advertising is less effective than its competitors, or is addressing obstacles such as trying to recover from a PR disaster.

## Lower SOV than SOM

■ A large player is capitalising on its position by leveraging economies of scale.

■ The brand is in decline; sales may still be reasonable but ad-spend is being diverted elsewhere.

■ Advertising is low-key: a well-established brand is temporarily coasting, allowing the amount saved to increase profits or be used elsewhere.

The higher a brand's SOV, the more likely it is to be noticed, all other things being equal. If a brand wants to be noticed then its best chance to secure a high SOV is when its competitors are underspending on advertising, i.e. have a relatively low SOV, for whatever reason. Equally, efforts to boost SOV by large-scale spending when your competitors are doing the same will end in your efforts being diluted – you may spend a fortune to finish up with exactly the same SOV because your proportion of total market spend remains constant. Further, you may want to take steps to ensure your SOV position is consistent with your SOM, or SOM ambitions. Unnecessary overspending on SOV when you have a small SOM is wasteful. Conversely, you may well want to increase spending to defend your position if your SOV does not adequately reflect SOM.

SOV, then, becomes a strategic tool for the marketer, enabling you to make judgements based both on your own organisation's needs and on responding to the strategies of your competitors. Monitoring their activities is important so that you can gauge when it could be effective to boost your SOV, e.g. in the period before competitors plan to launch a new product, or while management attention and budgets are diverted on defending a take-over bid.

---

### Activity 11.3

You work in a consumer durables sector worth £75m p.a. of which your brand has £15m. The sector A/S ratio is 10%, and you spend £1m on advertising p.a.

1) How does your A/S ratio compare to the sector?

2) What is your SOV and SOM?

3) How much would you need to spend to bring your ad-spend into equilibrium with your market share (assuming the total market ad-spend is unchanged)?

4) Suggest some reasons for the difference between the figures in (2).

What danger might you face if you maintain your position?

---

# Case Study – Car Communications

You are Marketing Communications Manager for a car manufacturer that is about to launch a new car. The code name for the car is **Zen** and it is set to replace a car that has been one of the top brands in your country for the past 30 years. The Zen is a mid-market family hatchback and you are considering which overall communications strategy you will recommend to the Marketing Director.

One of the problems facing all car manufacturers is market congestion and the increased level of choice available to car buyers. Part of this congestion is caused by an increase in the level of car imports. These cars might have a higher specification or perceived image, but the net result is downward pressure on prices. Indeed, price wars are a common occurrence and better avoided if possible.

The launch of a new car is traditionally a very risky and expensive operation. The usual approach is to use a pull strategy with massive consumer-orientated advertising, beginning with a launch at a significant motor show, with bright lights, a rotating platform and plenty of journalists to give a strong public relations boost. Direct marketing and sales promotions commence after this to provide for a co-ordinated campaign. Decisions about the level of mass advertising are often influenced by share of voice and share of market statistics.

Ownership trends indicate that many families now own two or sometimes three cars, and in an ideal world every car manufacturer would like each driver to always replace a car with another from the same manufacturer. To assist the development of this level and type of loyalty, it is crucial to understand buyer motivations and the location of exactly where car-buying decisions are made. Despite huge efforts, research has failed to determine all the answers to these questions. However, suspicion is growing that the critical buying decision is made at the car dealership. If this is the case, then perhaps more emphasis should be given to a promotional push campaign, focusing on the dealer network. For example, Volkswagen developed the Retail Concept and formulated a totally new look for its dealers. Vauxhall flew 16,000 dealers from around the world to Morocco for a three day conference to launch the Vauxhall Astra.

It is also becoming clear that corporate branding is a much under-used concept in this market. With the lack of market differentiation, the increasing influence of corporate ethics can provide competitive advantage. Might there be an opportunity to use corporate branding throughout the organisation's network of employees and dealers? It could provide a competitive advantage by establishing exactly what the company's brand stands for, and for everyone involved to communicate the same message. Marks & Spencer and Virgin have established strong corporate brands and have avoided the expense and complexity of supporting individual product brands. Up until now your company has sold cars, not a brand.

**Source:** *Integrated Marketing Communications Examination Paper*, June 1999.

---

**Questions**

1. Explain the main ways of setting promotional budgets, making a recommendation for the company in the Case Study.

2. Examine the key strategic factors that need to be considered when determining the level of financial resources to be allocated to the launch campaign.

---

## SUMMARY OF KEY POINTS

In this Session, we have introduced the importance of setting marketing communications budgets, and covered the following key points:

- Promotional budgets are important as they help to manage the financial resources invested in a campaign.

- Several factors need to be considered when setting budgets – these include the objectives to be met, the financial resources available, previous experience, external factors, and what competitors are doing.

- There are many options available for setting budgets, but the most commonly used are not always the most effective.

- Share of voice is an important strategic method of using promotional budget to achieve competitive advantage.

## Improving and developing own learning

The following projects are designed to help you develop your knowledge and skills further by carrying out some research yourself. Feedback is not provided for this type of learning because there are no 'answers' to be found, but you may wish to discuss your findings with colleagues and fellow students.

---

**Project A**

Talk to colleagues in the marketing department about how your organisation sets its promotional budget.

Is a top-down approach used, or is the objective and task method employed?

---

**Project B**

Who is consulted when setting the budget for promotional plans and campaigns?

Should others be involved?

What advantages would this offer?

---

**Project C**

Look at the list of factors for consideration in setting budgets in the Session above.

Identify specific issues that have impacted on the amount of resource allocated to the promotional plan in your organisation.

List these, and discuss them with colleagues to check their accuracy.

---

## Feedback to activities

### Activity 11.1

It is valuable to build a database of realistic costs of promotional activity as part of your exam preparation. Any of the exams in the Diploma syllabus could ask you to determine budgets for a campaign at one level or another, particularly as part of the Integrated Marketing Communications and Analysis & Decision modules. While you cannot always be expected to deliver precise costings, you are expected to suggest budgets that are realistic, given the objectives to be achieved and the likely resources of the organisation specified in the question. Failure to do so will cost credibility and marks.

**Activity 11.2**

Preferred method: objective and task.

Reasons:

- Directly relates objectives to the task we wish to achieve.
- Clear relevant benchmarks to monitor achievement against and learn from.
- Doesn't require trade-offs requiring dropping or diluting of some objectives to meet others.

Requires:

- Careful calculation of resources required for the job.
- Drawing on company, staff and personal experience, and research.
- Willingness to negotiate if total projected budget higher than acceptable.

Suggested process:

1. Determine promotional objectives, derived from corporate and marketing objectives.
2. Determine tasks to meet them.
3. Cost tasks and determine overall budget.
4. Test for reasonableness
   - against industry data.
   - against projected sales revenues and profits.
   - against any corporate financial constraints, and other resource implications.
5. Reconcile budget in light of step 4, e g. adjust upwards/downwards, review objectives, obtain agreement to non-standard position, consider alternative approaches.
6. Detailed planning – task allocation, timing, milestones etc.
7. Monitor budgets and take control action as necessary.

**Activity 11.3**

1. Your A/S ratio is £1m/£15m = 6.7%, one third less than the sector average.

2. The sector spends £7.5m on advertising i.e. 10% of £75m. Your SOV is therefore £1m/7.5m = 13.3%.
   Your SOM is £15m/£75m = 20%, so your SOV is significantly less than your SOM.

3. To bring your ad-spend into equilibrium you would need to spend 20% of the total market spend of £7.5m i.e. £1.5m.

4. You are one of the market leaders and have economies of scale that others cannot match.
   The period in question is one of underspending between high-spending campaigns.
   The sector is in decline and you are diverting resources elsewhere.

5. Underspending may enable competitors to capitalise on the position by boosting their own SOV, in a bid to capture market share from you.

# Session 12

# Managing and developing brands

## Introduction

Branding is an important strategic issue in many organisations today, and marketing communications plays an important role in the development of positive brand associations for buyers. Strong brands can create a clear competitive advantage for organisations, and in this Session we explore branding in some depth, including marketing communications' contribution to building and supporting brands.

---

**LEARNING OUTCOMES**

At the end of this Session you will be able to:

■ Understand the role of branding.

■ Explain the characteristics of brands.

■ Explain how branding can be used to achieve competitive advantage.

■ Explain brand extension and brand stretching.

---

## The importance of branding

A successful brand is one that creates and sustains a positive image in the mind of the buyer over time. The elements of a brand are both direct, as in the logo or trademark, and indirect, relating to the culture of the organisation and their values towards the customers.

Customers differentiate competing products through their brand associations, used to communicate their competitive advantage. Buyers learn to trust a brand for quality, delivery, reliability and satisfaction. Perceived risk is reduced, as customers stay with their tried and tested brands, eliminating the possibility of disappointment.

The benefits of a strong brand are:

■ Faster time to market with new products.

■ Barrier to competitor entry.

■ Forecasting repeat purchase.

■ Increased price possibilities.

■ Reduction in launch and marketing costs.

- Commitment from all stakeholders.
- Enables organisation to glue disparate outposts together.
- Signifies a particular type of culture, providing clear signs about beliefs, attitudes and behaviour.
- Acts as a guarantee to customers regarding quality promises.

Organisations with a strong brand will include its value on their bottom line, so that when they come to sell the company it acts as a guarantee to the purchaser that sales will continue and customers will remain loyal to the brand. The brand signifies the following to a potential purchaser:

- Earning potential.
- Customer base.
- Projected sales.
- Past history.
- Stock market health.
- Reduction in marketing costs.
- Brand extension opportunities.
- Licensing opportunities.

When Orange launched their mobile phone brand, through extensive advertising and press coverage, they won 22% of a busy market within 18 months. In the telecommunications market consumer choice was predominantly made on coverage, but now branding has moved to another level with the introduction of new applications and services. Companies like Virgin, who have a strong brand presence in other markets, have successfully won a major shareholding in the mobile market (up to 80% of new users to the network).

The value of a well-known brand cannot be underestimated, not least of all because it acts as security to the peaks and troughs experienced in the economy and the guarantee that, although sales may fall, a well-known brand still has the lion's share.

---

**Activity 12.1**

Pick three major brands and research their brand development strategies. Reflect on what lessons have you learnt from this exercise.

---

## Types of brand

A brand is a promise to its customers; a relationship that cannot be betrayed. Companies spend huge amounts of money on brands, in developing them, launching them and supporting them.

There are a number of types of branding:

### Manufacturers' brands

Brands such as Cadbury's and Nestlé use their brand status to achieve distribution and shelf space. Pull communication strategies build demand and stimulate channel members to stock the brand.

### Own label

Most supermarkets and now some department stores stock own label goods. This means that economies of scale can be achieved, with manufacturers using excess capacity. Own label goods do not require the same level of marketing communication investment and, as a result, retailers can offer own label goods as a reasonable price. Consumers associate the brand values of the store with the products and know that they will have been manufactured at a known label source.

### Product brands

Branded products such as the Ford Mondeo or the Vauxhall Astra benefit from the umbrella company brand and all that becomes associated with the product brand. This type of branding is essential for market segmentation and appealing to different target audiences.

### Characteristics

The following characteristics help to establish the brand in the mind of the customer:

The brand should:

- Be eye-catching and gain attention.
- Connect with the positioning and perceptual map.
- Link to a visual image which helps memorability.
- Communicate something about the product.

A brand is a symbolic device; espousing whatever brand values the organisation believes in and grounded in the business philosophy.

Creating a new brand name and identity requires considerable care and is endowed with many emotional values. With today's globalisation opportunities, Internet brands in particular need to be cross-cultural and convey one meaning in many different languages.

---

**Activity 12.2**

Take some well-known brands and identify the major brand values that are being communicated through all their campaigns. Position these brands against their competition to establish competitive advantage.

---

## Differentiating the brand

A product from one manufacturer may be so similar to that of another's that consumers are indifferent as to which one they buy from.

Take for example Esso, BP, Shell and Elf – why would you choose one brand over another? This is a commodity product and therefore it's often the service and associated added value that you gain from the brand experience which helps you decide one brand over another.

### Brand semiotics

- **Utilitarian** – the practical aspects of the product and brand, its reliability, effectiveness, fitness for purpose etc.
- **Commercial** – conveying meanings about value for money and cost effectiveness.
- **Socio-cultural** – the social benefits of buying the brand, such as status, membership of aspirational groups etc.
- **Mythical values** – for instance Harley-Davidson and its strong relationship to the film *Easy Rider*.

Mythical values are the stories and values associated with a brand, such as the freedom from modern industrial life as in *Easy Rider*. Hovis is associated with the corner bakery and the communities we once lived in.

The association with values can differentiate one brand from another, and research can be carried out to segment customers according to their values and beliefs.

Research carried out by Gordon and Valentine (1996) into retail buying showed that consumers segmented retail buying in the following way:

- Convenience stores conveyed an image of disorder and feelings of guilt and confusion, as shoppers purchased goods they had forgotten to buy in the supermarket.
- Supermarkets represented planned shopping and conveyed an image of domestic management and functionality.
- Petrol stations carried a dual meaning of planned petrol purchase and impulse buying in the shop.
- Airports encouraged impulse purchases for travellers seeking to treat themselves.
- Off-licences provide an environment for experimentation and to buy drinks without feeling guilty.

This research gives the buyers in retail organisations the key customer purchasing strategy, and therefore highlights which brands would be usefully stocked.

Adding value to the brand is a culmination of a range of activities and experiences. The whole marketing mix adds to the brand image and must be regarded as the focus for the whole marketing effort.

---

**Activity 12.3**

Taking a brand such as Levi's, draw up a storyboard highlighting some of the myths in visual form that are associated with the brand.

---

## Brand development

A brand has much the same lifecycle challenges as a product and needs to adopt different strategies over time. The innovators and risk-taking segments adopt brands and then, once in a growth phase, additional distribution is sought. When a brand becomes mature, it may be time to look for new markets and maybe even consider a re-launch to create more interest.

The diagram below is an adapted Ansoff's matrix for brand development, highlighting the strategic choices.

Brands such as Virgin have launched new products to new markets, building on the goodwill achieved from the main brands such as Virgin Megastores and Virgin Atlantic. These were diversification strategies and extremely high risk, as Richard Branson discovered when buying into the railway market. However, a less risky venture was promoting the Virgin first class options to gain the business passenger market.

**Adapted Ansoff's Matrix**

|  | **Existing** | **Modified/New** |
|---|---|---|
| **Existing** | Penetration | Brand Development |
| **New** | Market Development | Diversification |

*Markets* (vertical axis label) — **Brand** (horizontal axis label)

Organisations spend vast amounts of money to re-launch their brand, sometimes with very little visible difference. The organisation will have undertaken a complete audit as part of the process and it may be that internal culture changes are the most significant results of a re-launched brand. A re-structure or merger may require an organisation to demonstrate, both externally and internally, the brand values, and reinforce the philosophy of the organisation. A brand is a symbol and can be used to good effect to flag changes that are wide reaching and not just concerned with selling more products.

---

**Activity 12.4**

Dotcom brands have come under scrutiny over the last couple of years as share prices tumbled and sales plummeted. What caused this drop in confidence? How could this have been avoided?

---

## Brand strategies

When organisations develop new products, the branding decision will be taken according to the general branding strategy. Multi-brand companies will always create new brands for new products, while for other companies the decision will rest on the profile of the target market. It's expensive to launch a new brand, so companies may choose brand extensions or brand stretching.

**Brand extensions** are used to launch new improved products into the same broad market, such as Pretty Polly extending its range from tights and stockings into lingerie, and Nescafé introducing the Cappuccino coffee product. The value of this approach is that a well-known brand will have the funds to launch an advertising campaign which will win shelf space. The values of the brand extend to the new and modified products and customers feel safe in choosing the brand over the competition because of their long-standing relationship and customer satisfaction.

**Brand stretching** takes place when a brand is stretched into a completely new market, such as Virgin moving from records to travel, financial services, telecommunications and soft drinks. This is a high-risk strategy and only works if a similar target audience will buy across all product areas; therefore, their loyalty is traded on for new product areas. Regarding the example of Virgin trains, this was not the case and any amount of brand loyalty couldn't make up for the poor infrastructure, which resulted in an inability to meet customers' satisfaction and expectations.

There is a danger that brands can overextend and lose focus. Care must be taken to examine gaps in the market that can be filled by an existing brand whilst maintaining its core values and messages. There have been many failures in new product development where insufficient research was undertaken before launching, for example Nestlé and the Kit-Kat ice cream, which has been withdrawn from the market. Consumers did not have the same 'experience' eating the crisp snack in an ice cream format.

---

**Activity 12.5**

Identify some successful and unsuccessful brand extensions, making note of the learning points for success and failure.

---

# Case Study – Car Communications

*This Case Study was used in the last Session to explore budget and resource issues. It is used again here because of the branding issues that are raised.*

You are Marketing Communications Manager for a car manufacturer that is about to launch a new car. The code name for the car is **Zen** and it is set to replace a car that has been one of the top brands in your country for the past 30 years. The Zen is a mid-market family hatchback and you are considering which overall communications strategy you will recommend to the Marketing Director.

One of the problems facing all car manufacturers is market congestion and the increased level of choice available to car buyers. Part of this congestion is caused by an increase in the level of car imports. These cars might have a higher specification or perceived image, but the net result is downward pressure on prices. Indeed, price wars are a common occurrence and better avoided if possible.

The launch of a new car is traditionally a very risky and expensive operation. The usual approach is to use a pull strategy with massive consumer-orientated advertising, beginning with a launch at a significant motor show, with bright lights, a rotating platform and plenty of journalists to give a strong public relations boost. Direct marketing and sales promotions commence after this to provide for a co-ordinated campaign. Decisions about the level of mass advertising are often influenced by share of voice and share of market statistics.

Ownership trends indicate that many families now own two or sometimes three cars, and in an ideal world every car manufacturer would like each driver to always replace a car with another from the same manufacturer. To assist the development of this level and type of loyalty it is crucial to understand buyer motivations and the location of exactly where car buying decisions are made. Despite huge efforts, research has failed to determine all the answers to these questions. However, suspicion is growing that the critical buying decision is made at the car dealership. If this is the case then perhaps more emphasis should be given to a promotional push campaign, focusing on the dealer network. For example, Volkswagen developed the Retail Concept and formulated a totally new look for its dealers. Vauxhall flew 16,000 dealers from around the world to Morocco for a three day conference to launch the Vauxhall Astra.

It is also becoming clear that corporate branding is a much under-used concept in this market. With the lack of market differentiation, the increasing influence of corporate ethics can provide competitive advantage. Might there be an opportunity to use corporate branding throughout the organisation's network of employees and dealers? It could provide a competitive advantage by establishing exactly what the company's brand stands for, and for everyone involved to communicate the same message. Marks & Spencer and Virgin have established strong corporate brands and have avoided the expense and complexity of supporting individual product brands. Up until now your company has sold cars, not a brand.

**Source**: *Integrated Marketing Communications Examination Paper*, June 1999.

**Questions**

1.  The Case Study mentions that previously your organisation has sold cars and not a brand. What would be the difference in promotional strategy if this was to change?

2.  Decide upon a promotional strategy for your company in support of the launch of the Zen. You should argue the benefits for your strategic approach.

3.  Which promotional tools are said to be most appropriate at the beginning of the product life cycle?

## SUMMARY OF KEY POINTS

In this Session, we have introduced branding, and covered the following key points:

■ Brands are of strategic importance, and they create and sustain a positive image in the mind of the customer.

■ Brands are used to differentiate between competing products, and strong brands offer many advantages to the organisation.

■ Types of branding include manufacturers' brands, own label brands, and product brands.

■ Brands can be developed through extension and stretching strategies.

## Improving and developing own learning

The following projects are designed to help you develop your knowledge and skills further by carrying out some research yourself. Feedback is not provided for this type of learning because there are no 'answers' to be found, but you may wish to discuss your findings with colleagues and fellow students.

---

**Project A**

Make notes about what branding is, and how it is used in your organisation. If it is not used, explain why it is inappropriate.

---

**Project B**

Identify two examples of each type of branding – manufacturer's, distributor's, and product brands.

---

**Project B**

Take three well-known brands (e.g. Tango, BMW and Levi's) and identify what differentiates them from their nearest competitors. Make notes of your findings and discuss them with colleagues or fellow students to obtain their views.

---

## Feedback to activities

### Activity 12.1

Brands such as the Body Shop have aligned themselves with a cause that curried favour with a target segment of the time. The brand, although still well-known, has lost market share to other competitors – the market has become more fragmented.

Virgin and Richard Branson used PR to gain their competitive advantage, whether it was good or bad press! Richard Branson has become a household name and his many business ventures seek to bring new products and services to established markets. Virgin Megastore was the first music store and filled a gap for those weekly, monthly and yearly buyers of music and associated products.

Each major brand of our time has used different mixes of communications to active cult status – each with a unique advantage expressed in their brand values.

### Activity 12.2

Perceptual mapping is an important tool in establishing gaps in the market related to customers' needs. Perceptual mapping can help clarify strategic differentiation and represent the important messages that need to be transmitted through the communications mix.

## Activity 12.3

Levi's have had some excellent advertising and promotional campaigns reinforcing the myths of the Wild West and the macho associations of the brand. In one's mind, we experience Levi's as rugged and tough with sexual overtones.

## Activity 12.4

Organisations spent huge sums of money on promoting new e-brands that had little consumer confidence, unsupported by a mix of communications and coherent marketing mix strategies. The Internet was an untried and untested medium for sales, and consumers have been hesitant in embracing this new opportunity and distribution medium. There was little understanding about the challenges web brands were facing and, in hindsight, organisations could have been more cautious about the introduction of new brands without a track record and consumer confidence.

## Activity 12.5

Coca-Cola extended its brand to a new flavour, which was a complete mistake, because consumers associate the taste with the brand. However, Diet Coke has been a success, as has Diet Pepsi. DHL and UPS have migrated their brands online and this has proved to be a complete success, allowing customers to track their parcel's progress online. The major lessons learnt are concerned with research and trialling the product before full launch, and making sure the same values are recognised in new market segments.

# Session 13

# Evaluating the outcomes of campaigns

## Introduction

This is the first of two Sessions that explore the evaluation of campaigns. In this Session we look at techniques used in evaluating the effectiveness of various promotional tools, and in the next Session we consider the impact of various external influences on campaign effectiveness.

---

### LEARNING OUTCOMES

At the end of this Session you will be able to:

- Understand pre-testing and post-testing of advertisements.
- Explain the role technology plays in the assessment and evaluation of advertising.
- Explain how advertising, sales promotion, public relations, sponsorship and personal selling can best be evaluated.

---

## Evaluating campaigns

Marketing communications activity can be expensive, and the responsible Marketing Manager must ensure he or she uses his/her budget in the most effective way. Testing is therefore an important part of the communications development process, both to assess in advance whether what is proposed is likely to achieve its aims – through **pre-testing** – and to evaluate afterwards whether it has done so – **post-testing**. Lessons learned can then be incorporated into future activity.

Pre-testing

Pre-testing comprises **qualitative** and **quantitative** techniques to gauge responses to communications. The techniques can be used both to measure and to improve effectiveness. Time and budget must be built into the marketer's campaign planning to allow for testing.

Testing can happen in several different ways:

Using **focus groups**, which may comprise users and non-users, is a common **qualitative technique**, allowing researchers to explore elements of the communication mix in semi-structured discussions. The researcher can learn about people's attitudes to brands and communications and, in particular, can undertake **concept testing** of promotional ideas at various stages of development. Artwork and/or **copy**, showing key elements of an advertising message, or storyboards illustrating a sequence of activities in a TV commercial, may be used. Feedback enables marketers to choose between options and to refine ideas. They will want to know, for example, if the message is clear, how readable the copy is, do the images enhance understanding, and do consumers feel positive about the product after viewing the communication.

Experimental techniques can also be used, though these can be expensive to set up. **Laboratory tests** give the researcher opportunities to control the variables which might impact the outcome of the research. Advertisements and package designs may be tested in this way, and technology may be used to record and measure reactions (see later this Session).

**Field tests** can be designed for point-of-sale material and packaging, using appropriate retail outlets in selected areas. The outcomes can be assessed by measurement of sales, customer interviews and observation. **Test marketing** can occur in other ways, such as sending slightly different direct marketing packs to a small sample of the target population to gauge which version is most effective, or trying out broadcast commercials in limited geographical areas.

**Surveys** conducted prior to a communications campaign give vital quantitative data for comparison with **post-testing** results.

## Post-testing

Measuring the effectiveness of a campaign after it has run allows the marketers to determine whether it met its objectives, and aids decision-making about future activities. What is measured in these post-tests will depend upon what objectives were set for the campaign.

Two common areas of post-testing advertisements are recognition and recall, often conducted through consumer surveys.

**Recognition tests:** interviewees are asked if they recognise an advertisement that is shown to them. Scores are allocated on the extent to which the respondent has noted the advertisement, and further questions may be asked to see how much of the content was absorbed.

**Recall tests:** in unaided recall tests, interviewees are asked to remember what advertisements they have seen or heard lately, without clues to jog their memory. In aided recall tests, names of products or brands are given and the interviewee is asked to identify which advertisements they remember, and what they remember.

Recognition and recall tests will assist understanding of campaign penetration and awareness, but do not necessarily indicate the extent to which people **liked** an advertisement. Research has shown a linkage between liking an advertisement and the subsequent level of purchase. Testing may also therefore seek to measure this aspect of response (see also Session 9).

## Tracking studies

The meaning of a piece of research data usually comes from its relationship to other data. At the very least this requires research to gauge attitudes before and after the campaign activity. This can be extended to **tracking studies**; regular **quantitative** surveys which track changes in consumers' perceptions, awareness, attitudes and so on over time. Major brands may conduct their own regular surveys. Alternatively, the questions may form part of omnibus or syndicated surveys.

## Financial analysis

As part of the evaluation process, organisations will want to assess financial aspects of any campaign. Marketing Managers must expect to be fully accountable for use of their budgets. Questions asked will include:

- How did actual expenditure compare with the plan?
- What quantifiable direct financial benefits are there? (For example, the aim may have been to generate sales)
- Can we measure other benefits in financial terms, e.g. cost per response?
- What financial lessons have we learned for future campaigns, for example did one form of media prove more valuable than another?

---

**Activity 13.1**

You are designing a new web site for your business.

Write a memo to the Marketing Director outlining a user research process to enable you to develop and maintain the site effectively.

Include suggestions for what you would want to find out at each stage.

---

## Changes in evaluation techniques due to developments in technology

As the part that technology plays in all our lives increases, so do its applications to the evaluation of communication activities.

### Observational techniques

These techniques are often used in laboratories to provide scientific evidence of consumer reactions to marketing communications. The facilities are expensive to set up and the researcher needs to be aware of what influence the artificial setting can have on respondents' reactions, so the evidence tends to be used alongside other sources of information.

**Eye cameras:** these record the individual's eye movements as they scan an advertisement. They can show which parts attract immediate attention, which parts they study most and which parts they skip over. The information is used to gauge and improve an advertisement's effectiveness. Eye cameras can also be used to measure pupil dilation and blink rate, both of which vary with excitement levels.

**Psycho-galvanometer:** this is like a lie detector, measuring perspiration rate on the skin. As the rate tends to increase with raised emotions, it can be used as a physiological measure of an individual's response to a stimulus such as a TV commercial.

**Tachistoscopes:** these devices expose the respondent to an advertisement, packaging, logo etc. for a limited time, maybe a fraction of a second. Responses then indicate how quickly the individual was able to take in key aspects of the subject matter.

Observation techniques can also be used in the field. Secret cameras linked to recording equipment can provide evidence of, for example, consumers' reactions to point-of-sale material.

### Data storage and analysis

Technology plays a vital role in the storing, sorting and analysing of research data. A consumer survey of recognition and recall may give rise to hundreds of completed questionnaires and thousands of answers to questions, all of which need to be sorted and interpreted to become meaningful.

Coding, prior to the use of the questionnaire, of quantitative data – for example simple "yes/no" answers, or responses on a **Likert Scale** – means that marked answers can be entered easily onto IT systems using optical recognition or direct entry keyboard software. Other responses will need to be coded before inputting.

Software programmes then analyse the data to meet the researcher's requirements, for example analysing responses by type of user or geographical distribution. The system can present the information in various ways and give supporting statistical information, such as the degree of significance of findings and their relationship to data from other sources.

These reports could form the basis of Key Performance Indicators for campaigns, departments, brands etc.

### Electronic Point-of-Sale (EPOS) Information

Marketers gather vast quantities of information about consumers from EPOS systems. Much of this information does not relate directly to communications, but it can supply valuable rapid quantitative feedback by, for example, indicating changed usage patterns following an advertising campaign, or recording usage of coupons included in a door-drop. Where this data can be linked to individuals, perhaps in conjunction with store-cards or via tracking of personalised direct marketing material, even more detailed information becomes available on usage by specific consumers and target segments.

### Internet

The use of online research methods is still relatively new, particularly in the UK, but the Internet does present opportunities to gather primary and secondary research data on a variety of subjects, including communications. Short web (or email) surveys can be a source of quantitative data, and qualitative information can come through focus groups and bulletin boards. Unprompted feedback on companies' sites can be a valuable source of comments on communication activity, which must be fed back to the relevant team.

Web-based research can be quick and cheap, but the principal challenges are in finding and reaching suitable individuals to take part, and identifying the extent to which web users' responses can be interpreted as those of a wider audience. It does, however, lend itself well to research on niche audiences who use particular sites.

Web sites themselves are, of course, part of the communications mix and a range of data can be collected on usage.

### Interactivity

Over time it has become possible for consumers to interact more easily with businesses. Technology has often become the medium for the communication (e.g. Internet, direct response TV, text messaging), the means of response (e.g. call centres, interactive digital TV, email) and, inevitably, the mechanism for gathering data on those responses, through IT systems, to evaluate the communication's effectiveness and drive future development.

---

**Activity 13.2**

You are a Brand Manager in the fast-moving consumer good sector. Name three technological sources of information you might use to help you evaluate the effectiveness of your brand's communications, and suggest two examples of information you could get from each source.

Is this information qualitative or quantitative?

---

# Case Study – British Glass Recycling Company

The need to protect our environment is of increasing concern to politicians, industrialists, environmentalists and a growing proportion of the public. The European Union has taken a proactive position and has, among other things, set targets for the recovery and recycling of waste materials, including glass. In the UK the Government has set a target that 50% of all glass packaging has to be recycled by the year 2000. This represents 900,000 tonnes of used glass per annum. Similar targets are in place throughout the European Union.

For the packaging industry, recycling offers numerous benefits such as savings on raw materials, energy and waste collection costs. It also cuts back on the use of landfill sites, helps conserve the environment and also creates employment. For those organisations actively involved there are opportunities for positive public relations messages.

The British Glass Recycling Company (BGRC) is a company set up in 1993 as a joint venture between Rockware Glass and United Glass to develop the UK national glass recycling programme. These companies are the two largest glass packaging manufacturers in the UK. BGRC receives waste glass from local authorities and private collectors (for example, retailers, restaurants and Clubs), offers them a guaranteed market and a fair price. However, there are problems associated with glass recycling in the UK, which explains to some extent why the national glass recycling rate is only 30%, one of the lowest rates in the EU.

First, there is a 'green cullet' problem. Cullet refers to waste glass of which there are three colour types: amber, clear and green, each of which has slightly different chemical compositions. Demand for glass packaging in the UK is for clear glass. As clear glass cannot be made of cullet which contains coloured glass and as the vast majority of waste glass is green, imported from other European countries in the form of wine and beer packaging, the green cullet problem represents a significant constraint on the UK reaching its recycling target. The UK glass industry also has a policy not to pay for glass that has not been colour separated.

The second issue concerns the public and their attitude toward recycling glass. Generally public support for glass recycling is positive partly as a result of the visual reminders provided by bottle banks (waste glass collection containers) sited around urban areas. These banks are constructed so that members of the public separate waste glass into their colour groups. However, some contamination can still occur, if only due to grease, dirt and bottle caps.

By the mid 1990s there were approximately 19,600 bottle banks in the UK, or 1 for every 2,850 people, one of the poorest ratios in comparison to other European countries. Of these banks, 73% are provided by local authorities, while the others are operated by private organisations who derive good revenue streams from the collection and sale of used glass. Public use of these sites is partly a function of the banks' proximity to residential areas and partly due to the attitude of the public to recycling. However, the siting of bottle banks is problematic because of the noise of breaking glass. The public want more convenient bottle banks but not outside their house or in their road.

Research indicates that 31% of AB women see recycling as a public duty whereas only 20%, of men share this view. Interestingly, it is the young and old who have a particular affinity with the recycling concept. It is quite apparent that middle aged men (72% of men aged 25 to 34), are the most ambivalent towards recycling. As it is this segment who are more likely to have a direct influence on children and their attitudes, this might be regarded as a weakness to the long-term development of glass recycling in the UK.

Whilst measures are being taken to encourage the greater use of coloured glass as a principal glass packaging material, efforts to improve the UK recycling rate for used glass need to be encouraged. Greater use of bottle banks needs to be stimulated and more bottle banks need to be provided. In addition, there needs to be greater awareness and conviction that recycling glass is a necessary, important and worthwhile activity.

If BGRC are to improve the rate of recycling in order that they generate a higher proportion of their raw materials from recycled glass, then they need to promote the concept more rigorously and change the attitudes of the public towards the recycling concept. The funds available for a communication programme are limited (under £500,000) so additional financial resources may need to be acquired, perhaps by attracting others to launch a joint campaign.

**Source:** *Marketing Communications Strategy Examination Paper*, June 1998.

**Questions**

1. Identify and explain the key factors in the environment that are impacting on the way BGRC will need to communicate their services.

2. Suggest appropriate communications strategies for BGRC's audiences.

3. Outline an appropriate communications mix for the organisation.

## SUMMARY OF KEY POINTS

In this Session, we have introduced methods of evaluating promotional activity, and covered the following key points:

■ Evaluation of campaigns goes back first to the measurable objectives that were put in place at the outset.

■ Pre- and post-testing can help ensure the effectiveness of advertising.

■ Technology has introduced new methods of evaluation – for example, EPOS systems can help track buying patterns following particular campaigns, and 'hits' on web pages can be logged online.

## Improving and developing own learning

The following projects are designed to help you develop your knowledge and skills further by carrying out some research yourself. Feedback is not provided for this type of learning because there are no 'answers' to be found, but you may wish to discuss your findings with colleagues and fellow students.

**Project A**

Talk to your Marketing Manager about ways in which campaigns are evaluated in your organisation.

Look at the results of pre- and post-tests and draw your own conclusions about the effectiveness of particular campaigns.

---

**Project B**

Talk to colleagues in your marketing department to find out whether recognition or recall tests are used to evaluate advertising in your organisation.

Look at the way that results of these tests are presented – what can be learnt to inform future advertising?

---

**Project C**

Talk to your marketing budget holder about ways in which campaigns are evaluated for cost effectiveness.

What measures are taken of the effectiveness of one tool over another?

Have any changes been made as a result of such measures?

---

## Feedback to activities

### Activity 13.1

**M E M O**

**To: Marketing Director**

From: A Marketer

Date: XXXX

**Company web site – user research**

You have asked me to put forward a user research process for developing our new company web site. I suggest that we have a three-stage process: firstly to identify the type of site users we want, secondly to test what we have built before we make it generally available, and thirdly to monitor usage post-launch to ensure it meets expectations and requirements.

It is important that the research identifies the extent to which the new site will meet the objectives we have set for it, e.g. is it to provide information only, or will we be selling online? These objectives need to stated clearly at the outset so that we can ask the right questions. If we are currently unclear about some of our objectives then we can ask questions during Stage 1 to clarify our thinking.

## Stage 1: **Focus groups**

These can be conducted online and/or off-line, and should comprise the type of people we want to use our site.

We should explore what attracts people to this type of site, what features would keep them there, preferred navigation methods, relative attractiveness of different types of call to action, design preferences, how would they use it, suggested links with other sites/within the site, views on competitor and non-competitor sites and user technology available.

## Stage 2: **User testing**

We should test with different user types: customers and non-customers, regular web users and unfamiliar users. At least some of the testing should be by respondents in their home/office, using password-protected access and an online questionnaire, to check compatibility with their normal equipment.

Design aspects: content, screen designs (colours, icons, layout etc.), speed of operation, ease of navigation, interactivity, helpfulness of search and help facilities and security features.

Attitudinal information: whether informative, interesting, entertaining or other relevant aspects, does it facilitate relationship building, will it help the user to meet the objectives we have set for the site and would they use it again?

## Stage 3: **Post-launch**

Monitor usage – visitor numbers to the site and to each page, duration and time of visits, navigation paths. Visitor profile – from registration details or cookies identifying returning visitors.

Track customer attitudes to the site through online and maybe off-line survey. Collect and analyse unprompted feedback.

Also, put in place measures against objectives set at outset.

I hope this meets your requirements, but please let me know if you have any queries. I look forward to your advice as to whether we can proceed with the research.

## Activity 13.2

Brand web site:

■ Unprompted responses to off-line communications (qualitative).

■ Number of site visits to on-pack web address (quantitative).

EPOS:

■ Comparison of usage rate of coupons published in two different women's magazines (quantitative).

■ Comparison of buying patterns for your brand when variants of POS material are tested in selected stores (quantitative).

Laboratory experimentation:

■ Tachistoscope tests to identify responses to variations in packaging design (quantitative).

■ Eye cameras – recording impact of different advertisement layouts for print media (quantitative).

# Session 14

# Evaluating the outcomes of campaigns – 2

## Introduction

This Session is the second looking at the evaluation of campaigns. In this Session we look at various influences on the outcomes of campaigns, in particular, competitor activity, resources available, the stage of the PLC and external environmental factors.

---

### LEARNING OUTCOMES

At the end of this Session you will be able to:

■ Explain the following influences on various promotional campaigns:

■ Competitive conditions.

■ Available resources.

■ Product Life Cycle stage.

■ External environmental factors.

---

## How external environmental factors have impacted on promotional campaigns

Context is everything in communications. Every exchange needs to be formulated with a view to the position of the buyer, the marketing organisation and the environment in which the communication is taking place. Sometimes change will be incremental, such as the rise of consumerism, or the growing usage of, and applications for, technology. On other occasions, change will be sudden and industries must react. The onset of foot and mouth disease in the UK in 2001 brought frantic PR and advertising efforts to try to persuade overseas tourists to visit the UK and UK citizens to take short breaks to use up the spare capacity. Then came September 11th, following which budget airlines slashed fares and promoted themselves heavily; meanwhile video and telephone conferencing organisations were able to add 'a safer way to do business' to their list of benefits and saw a huge rise in trade.

One major theme of the past few years has been consumers' growing interest in the impact of business activities beyond purely commercial transactions – the ethical and environmental dimension. The case study below look at how this interest sparked a revolution in attitudes to stakeholders at Shell, pushing PR, in its widest sense, to the top of the agenda.

## Case Study – Shell

Shell is one of the 10 largest UK companies. Although it has one of the best-known corporate logos, it has never really sought to develop its brand image beyond this. Marketing was not seen as central to the business, with a history of top management dominated by engineers and chemists. Then came 1995 and two incidents that forced Shell to completely change its stance.

First, Shell decided to decommission a floating storage tank – Brent Spar – by sinking it into the North Atlantic. The plan had government support but Greenpeace, the environmental activist group, objected vehemently, claiming there was 5,000 tons of oil on board (this later proved to be incorrect). Greenpeace gained massive support including backing from several EU ministers who called for a boycott of Shell. In Germany, Shell filling stations were firebombed and raked with gunfire. Images of protestors on Brent Spar being hosed with powerful water cannon reinforced public anger at this Goliath against David. Shell finally backed down, but its image was severely damaged.

A few months later came the death of Ken Saro-Wiwa in Nigeria. Shell had been operating in the region for decades, but local opposition had sprung up to its activities, especially concerning its attitude to the environment. Saro-Wiwa led the opposition but was arrested and tried by Nigerian officials on alleged murder charges. Shell was widely criticised for cosying up to the Nigerian government and failing to help Saro-Wiwa. During his hearing he said, "Shell is here on trial [too]". Saro-Wiwa was subsequently executed.

These incidents battered the public's trust in Shell that had been built up over decades. The brand was severely damaged and devalued. Following disappointing financial results, a completely new approach to marketing, corporate responsibility and public relations was adopted. For the first time Shell really started to find out about its customers – who they were and what mattered to them. Understanding and talking to its publics became top of the agenda with a policy of "constructive engagement" – open dialogue with critics. A series of nine Principles was adopted and enforced, reflecting Shell's responsibilities to customers, employees, business partners, shareholders and society in general. Policy was produced tackling issues such as sustainable development, employee rights and business integrity. Enhancing the brand was central to the plan, aiming for consistent global standards and associations of innovation and caring.

In all this, effective two-way communication was key, through dialogue, literature aimed at stakeholders, and internal material stressing the business's new ethos, including a Management Primer. The Internet has been used as a key communication tool, encouraging dialogue with stakeholders – some of it openly hostile – and providing a platform for accountability. Detailed environmental and social performance information is given, as well as comprehensive documents such as People, Planets and Profits – the Shell Report.

Shell is open about recognising that corporate social responsibility is an issue that can no longer be ignored, and that managing reputation is important. Not everyone is convinced about Shell's good intentions, but clearly the company has come a long way since 1995 and is demonstrating a willingness for openness and transparency that not every company aspires to.

**Source:** Compiled from secondary sources. List reproduced with kind permission of *Marketing Week* and *Consensus Research*.

---

**Activity 14.1**

What reasons might there have been to explain why understanding the needs and views of the general public may not have been central to Shell's agenda prior to the events of 1995?

What reasons may have made them change their mind?

---

# How competitive conditions have influenced promotional campaigns

All promotional campaigns aim to secure some kind of competitive advantage for the business or, at least, to counter a competitive disadvantage. This may be:

- directly, through extolling the virtues of the product or service, or

- indirectly, through sponsorship for example, which aims to enhance the brand's image and offers opportunities to link to other activities.

Tactics in competitive situations might include comparative advertising, pointedly comparing the advertiser's benefits with a rival. Or defensive promotions may be used in a direct attempt to blunt a competitor's simultaneous campaign. For example, in 2002 the supermarket Sainsbury's ran a free flights promotion, supported by heavy above- and below-the-line activity, just as Tesco started to offer and promote its newly-acquired Air Miles scheme. Sometimes comparative and defensive promotions may even coincide. In 2002 easyJet ran a print media campaign aimed at shareholders and senior executives. It pointed out that their company could be saving considerable sums if their employees used the low-cost carrier rather than travelling business class on mainstream airlines. The ads not only made a point about pricing against the competition, but were scheduled to run just as British Airways launched a campaign to entice passengers to them. (The BA campaign sought to convince business travellers of the benefits of face-to-face meetings. This was an attack on a different form of competition – from substitutes such as video-conferencing).

## Case Study – Seven Seas Cod Liver Oil

A non-advertising approach to competitive pressure was taken by Seven Seas, the brand leader in the cod liver oil market. In the late 1990s they realised they were losing ground to competitors; not only other brands on the shelves, but also from own label products and mail order. Existing heavy users (notably women 55+) were defecting heavily and there were fewer new users. Seven Seas had established this category, aimed at relieving joint pain and stiffness, but now it was being swamped by new entrants. Furthermore, research showed the market was being undermined in terms of its overall £ value and in terms of the value that users put on the benefits. Seven Seas decided to refresh the brand's image by reinforcing positive values that consumers were already familiar with. Images associations to be adopted included modernity and excitement, viewed in the context of the target audience.

One of the biggest challenges was how to reach this audience, as research had shown that traditional advertising methods were not always successful in shifting entrenched views amongst the target group or overcoming cynicism towards brand promotion. Through careful analysis of brand fit, audience assessment and opportunities for exploitability, broadcast sponsorship was decided upon. The selected programme was Channel 4's afternoon game show, *Countdown*.

The campaign aimed to raise awareness of Seven Seas' association with *Countdown*, to deliver the "relieves joint and stiffness message" and to drive sales of Seven Seas High Strength Cod Liver Oil. Established imagery was used alongside the opening, interval and closing programme credits: the Tin Man – a long-running brand image – and a gold and red colour scheme consistent with the product packaging. Interactivity was encouraged by setting a puzzle in the style of the programme.

Evaluation was carried out in several ways and was made easier by the decision not to run any simultaneous form of promotion. Spontaneous awareness of the Seven Seas brand, and of its cod liver oil specifically, soared. Analysis of recall data showed that people were remembering not only the brand, but where they had seen it and the Tin Man imagery. Very importantly, the "relieves stiffness" message was particularly well remembered. Both sales and market share also rose rapidly, reversing the previous trends in favour of competitors.

The campaign demonstrated that a non-traditional approach can offer greater value and salience when used well. Careful analysis and development was required to ensure an integrated fit between the audience and the vehicle (i.e. the sponsored programme), as well as the creative treatment.

**Source:** With thanks to Seven Seas and their agency, Advertising Principles, for permission to use their example.

---

**Activity 14.2**

Can you think of any other benefits that might have accrued to Seven Seas as a result of the campaign? (You may not have specific information about Seven Seas' circumstances, but think in general terms about what other benefits might have accrued).

---

## The impact of product life cycle stage on promotional campaigns

Promotional campaigns play differing but key roles during the stages of the product life cycle. In the introductory phase, emphasis will be on raising awareness, with advertising and PR often playing important roles in consumer markets. As sales grow, competition increases and the emphasis is on differentiating your product from everyone else's. The product eventually becomes established, reaching its 'mature' phase; brand-owners will want to prolong this phase by using communications to build loyalty. Getting this right is critical, and determining whether the product moves into decline, or maintains, or even increases, sales. New forms of the product may be developed and promotional activity will play an important role in bringing these to the attention of the public and other target groups. An example of a well-known brand that had peaked and moved into decline is the National Lottery, whose sales slumped as the brand became tired and the public became disillusioned. £72m is being poured into a relaunch, to be spent on radio and TV commercials, press campaigns, posters and an unprecedented mailing to 82% of UK households.

Promotional activity isn't just important to the life of a single product, but plays a role in developing product portfolios too, as the case below illustrates.

### Case Study – Terry's Chocolate Orange

Think of Terry's Chocolate Orange (TCO) and you may only think of a ball of 20 orange flavoured chocolate segments. But actually TCO is a range of products: the well-known ball established in the 1930s, a bar, and (today) mini-segments, individually twist-wrapped in a box. The challenge facing TCO in the late 1990s was that sales of the ball were declining, as they were for the bar too (from an already low level). It was important to stem the decline of these products and to lay the ground for the successful introduction of new variants, including the hoped-for mini-segments, but previous attempts at line and brand extensions had foundered. Overall the TCO portfolio was unbalanced with no growth products, the existing ones in decline and little prospect of successful introduction of variants.

A communications strategy was needed to resolve these problems. It needed to do two almost contradictory things at once: a. to raise the profile of the bar and any subsequent variations, giving them their own identities and b. to link all the TCO range so that there was a halo effect with each product benefiting from the advertising of the other.

Salience was vital: these brands, and the campaign, had to stand out in a crowded market whilst still being true to the brand's personality. To achieve this it was decided to focus on the use of chocolate as an indulgence. But instead of traditional soft-focus, dream-like images, the campaign would use humour and quirkiness, reflecting the bizarre fact that the ball is actually chocolate that looks like an orange! With a need for salience but with a low share of voice, the £5.75m budget was concentrated almost entirely on TV advertising in three bursts, with a minor spend on the trade press. Each advert depicted the comedian Dawn French using a different product (eventually including the newly launched mini-segments) in a different situation, always ending up hogging the chocolate. The aim was to communicate that it was OK to indulge in chocolate, and to also to demonstrate different types of occasion for usage. French was ideal for the part, with a real chocolate-eater's physique, but witty and charming at the same time.

Many evaluation measures were put in place (see Activity below) and overall the campaign was a great success. As well as having a direct, positive effect on sales, conclusions were:

■ Advertising can deliver an effect on the advertised variant, and have a wider halo effect.

■ These halo effects were greater for the weaker and newer variants in the portfolio.

■ Advertising had helped future new product development by providing a brand vehicle flexible enough to accommodate it.

**Source:** With thanks to the Institute of Practitioners in Advertising for permission to use information from this study.

**Activity 14.3**

What measures do you think were put in place to evaluate the effectiveness of the campaign?

## Organisational constraints on promotional campaigns

Organisational constraints of one sort or another are a necessary feature of every promotional campaign. Resourcing is the most obvious form of constraint, but think also about image. Organisations may have carefully and deliberately selected the kind of business they will or won't transact. The Co-op Bank, for example, now refuses to deal with companies involved with the development of GM crops, and this constraint forms part of its promotional proposition. Every brand, of course, has a particular set of characteristics that define it in consumers' minds. Great care must be taken not to damage existing branding, and only to develop it in a way that is consistent with consumers' understanding (unless, of course, the aim is to reposition altogether).

But let's return to resourcing. Human resourcing issues are behind the very structure of the marketing industry. The variety of agencies – DM (direct marketing), PR, advertising, e-marketing, research and much more – enables businesses to achieve efficiencies by outsourcing activities which may only be needed intermittently. Furthermore, it gives access to skills, knowledge, contacts and technology that the organisation would not usually be able to muster in-house. Most campaigns have some form of agency behind them, without which they could not have happened.

Financial constraints will feature in every form of promotion. Marketers are increasingly accountable and they must be able to demonstrate that they are using their financial resources to maximum effect.

Take two examples: publicity has the potential to create a massive return on investment. In a low budget campaign, the Birmingham radio station BRMB gained vast amounts of print and broadcast media coverage – locally, nationally and internationally – when it arranged the marriage of two listeners on a blind date. (The marriage failed, but BRMB more than achieved their objectives!) And new media has mushroomed partly because of the cost-savings it can produce. Two-way communications can be achieved, reaching large audiences if desired, at a fraction of the cost and in much less time, than traditional methods.

### The not-for-profit sector

All charities need to tread a fine line between spending on their cause and their fundraising (and administration) costs. The NSPCC has come in for criticism over its spending on the Full Stop campaign, standing accused of spending too little on helping children directly. But the charity has made clear it believes it has a major role as a campaigning organisation and uses its communication spend in a deliberate attempt to influence public debate. Meanwhile, charities are increasingly demanding about how they use media. Direct mail gives opportunities for creativity and can be effective in securing repeat donations in a sector where one-off giving is commonplace. In an award-winning campaign, Cats Protection almost doubled contributions though a mailing aimed at converting one-off donors. In 2002 the Red Cross is experimenting with interactive TV (iTV). The campaign aims to raise awareness and enables donors to set up a direct debit via their TVs, capturing the opportunity for impulse donations. Children in Need raised almost £500,000 last year through an iTV scheme.

One trend in the not-for profit sector has been towards obtaining benefits from commercial businesses. This provides value for both parties, raising funds and increasing awareness for the non-profit organisation (where this is appropriate). For example, the British Heart Foundation has created an association with Tetley Teabags, appearing on their packaging, and the National Osteoporosis Society logo is used on several high-calcium products. Tesco has been running its 'Computers for Schools' promotion since 1990 and other businesses have since launched similar schemes, such as Walkers Crisps' 'Free Books for Schools'. But these arrangements are not uncontroversial. The British Dental Association endorsed Ribena Toothkind but the latter's claims of protection against decay were subsequently found against in court. Other schemes have been criticised for bringing commercialism into the classroom.

---

**Activity 14.4**

What do you think the main benefits are for a commercial organisation developing a link to a charity?

---

# Case Study – NSPCC Campaign of the year

The charities market is highly competitive, with a large number of organisations trying to get their message across on a limited budget. Just prior to the launch of the NSPCC's FULL STOP campaign in March 1999, the annual Comic Relief Appeal took place. This was heavily televised for a two-week period and intensified the competition between charities to raise public awareness and gain support for their cause. Despite this, the NSPCC's campaign exceeded its target figure for new supporters by 70%.

'Together we can end cruelty to children', was the USP of the three-week FULL STOP campaign launched by the NSPCC in early Spring 1999. The charity believes that it was the biggest integrated campaign ever launched by the voluntary sector – and probably bigger than any commercial organisation had ever undertaken in such a concentrated time scale.

The campaign's objectives were four-fold:

- to raise awareness of the problem of cruelty to children.
- to communicate that the NSPCC had launched a campaign to end the problem.
- to generate support, and involvement in, the campaign.
- to create huge PR and media coverage.

The launch of FULL STOP was held in London, hosted by Cilla Black, and attended by Tony Blair, HRH Duke of York (Chairman of the appeal), Emma Bunton and a number of key business leaders. Throughout the campaign, ongoing support from celebrities, such as Madonna and Ewan McGregor, played a key part in raising public awareness of the cause.

"Increasing awareness was critical because a campaign like this was only ever going to succeed on the basis of mass support and involvement from individuals and organisations throughout the UK," explained Marion Rose, the charity's Head of Marketing. "What we wanted to achieve was partnership. The NSPCC was leading the initiative, but we wanted to encourage everyone to participate in the campaign."

"The timing was also significant. The NSPCC had been in business for nearly 100 years – the end of the century was the ideal time to look at what had been achieved and create a vision for the future."

The key involvement device used in the campaign – asking the public to sign a pledge promising to do something to help end cruelty to children – proved highly effective. A door drop of 23 million items reached every home in England, Wales and Northern Ireland, while a further mailing reached one million existing donors and 1.5 million leaflets were distributed face-to-face.

TV advertising ran on terrestrial and satellite channels, supported by press advertising in national newspapers and ethnic press. There were also a total of 8,242 poster sites used throughout the country.

## Passion and pain

The two-year planning process which took place prior to the launch of FULL STOP included extensive research. This had revealed that, although the public cared passionately about cruelty to children, they found it a difficult issue to deal with and often turned away from it because it was too painful to face.

The advertisements picked up on this theme, all featuring a number of children's icons – including Rupert the Bear, a teddy bear and Action Man – covering their eyes as a situation of abuse could be heard going on in the background.

Viewers were left to infer cruelty from what they saw or heard – a powerful, but not explicit approach.

One advertisement depicted a teenager's bedroom. A Rupert the Bear mug on the bedside table carried the words: 'One word of this to anyone and you're dead.'

A number of milestone events were arranged during the campaign period to keep its momentum going. These included a 'Call to Action' weekend, when campaigners went around the country setting up stalls in 1,500 shopping centres and public areas and encouraging people to sign the pledge.

"We did have the odd qualm about the possibility of getting a negative reaction to the campaign because the advertising was very strong," says Marion Rose. "However, it proved to be hugely motivating. We were overwhelmed by support – getting out on the streets and being visible made the campaign more real to people."

## Measuring effectiveness

The effectiveness of the campaign was measured by tracking both the response to it and the amount of PR generated – particularly vital to charities because of their limited resources. According to Marion Rose, the results showed that FULL STOP was the most ambitious and effective awareness campaign that any charity had ever run. "It met and succeeded all its targets," she claimed.

Television advertising reached an estimated 85% of the population at 7.1 OTS, while the posters were seen by around 55% of the public at 21 OTS. PR coverage exceeded all expectations. In addition to over 2,000 press articles, the campaign featured in 230 radio programmes and 71 TV programmes.

In addition to CIM/Marketing Week's 'Campaign of the Year' award, FULL STOP also won the 'Campaigning Poster of the Year' title, two Direct Marketing Awards, and a Gold Lion at Cannes '99.

## Evidence of success

The number of new supporters generated by the campaign was 70% above target, as the following figures demonstrate:

|  | Target | Actual |
| --- | --- | --- |
| Fund raisers | 83,000 | 100,000 |
| Donors | 75,000 | 103,000 |
| Campaigners | 43,000 | 141,000 |
| Total | 201,000 | 344,000 |

Interestingly, the huge database of new supporters created included a group of people – the young and single – who usually restrict their allegiance to political organisations and charities that campaign on the environment. According to the charity, prior to the campaign, its key supporters had been middle class, middle-aged women with older children.

While no other children's charity experienced a significant shift in spontaneous awareness, the NSPCC's rose from 19% pre-launch to 27% post-launch – an increase of 43%. The nearest competitor – Save the Children Fund – had less than half this level.

Calls to the NSPCC Helpline also increased by 280% over the launch period and related to more serious child protection concerns than usual.

### Brand benefits and future plans

Creating awareness is the cornerstone of everything the NSPCC does. The charity built on the success of its FULL STOP campaign as the Appeal continued to roll out over the 12-month period. Most of the successful milestone events – all of which focused on specific aspects of the campaign – were repeated.

In addition to a specially-designated Children's Day, concentrating on sexual abuse, a major above-the-line campaign was launched to raise awareness of the need to protect babies, who are recognised as being the most vulnerable to abuse and death through cruelty or neglect.

During the year-long campaign, new mothers also received an NSPCC birth pack and magazine called 'Get Ready', designed both to create a realistic picture of what parenthood is all about, as well as to offer tips on caring for children. Pushing home the importance of listening to children proved popular with schools, many of which demonstrated their support by running 'One Minute's Noise' events, which gave children the freedom to make as much noise as they could!

### The bottom line

Although profits are not applicable to the charity sector, this campaign provided highly effective support for the £250 million FULL STOP Appeal. Fund-raising was not the primary goal of this phase, yet over £1 million was raised over the launch period.

## Campaign details

Brand name: FULL STOP Campaign.
Campaign dates: March 16th to April 5th 1999.
Market category: Charity.
TV and Posters: Saatchi & Saatchi.
Direct Marketing: WWAV Rapp Collins.
Response and Fulfilment: The Computing Group.

## Selected quotes

'Creating awareness is the cornerstone of everything the NSPCC does.'

'FULL STOP was only ever going to succeed on the basis of mass support and involvement from individuals and organisations throughout the UK.'

'We were overwhelmed by support – getting out on the streets and being visible made the campaign more real to people.'

**Source:** *Marketing Business.*

---

## Questions

1.  Comment on the campaign objectives as they are stated in the Case Study.

2.  Use the facts in the Case Study to justify the expenditure of £250,000 on the campaign, to the NSPCC's donors.

3.  Prepare a table showing the NSPCC's target audiences, and the communications tools used to reach each of these groups.

---

## SUMMARY OF KEY POINTS

In this Session, we have introduced the impact of various factors on the effectiveness of campaigns and looked at some live examples of each influence.

## Improving and developing own learning

The following projects are designed to help you develop your knowledge and skills further by carrying out some research yourself. Feedback is not provided for this type of learning because there are no 'answers' to be found, but you may wish to discuss your findings with colleagues and fellow students.

---

### Project A

Search the Internet for other examples of 'small budget' or 'not for profit' campaigns. How have developments in technology 'levelled the playing field' in respect of various companies' promotional activity?

---

### Project B

Talk to colleagues in your marketing department about promotional responses that have been made to competitor activity.

What examples can you find? How effective were these activities?

Did any prompt unexpected counter-attacks?

---

### Project C

Look at the web site of the Advertising Standards Authority www.asa.org.uk and identify some instances where campaigns have been adjudicated against through the Authority.

Can any lessons be learned by your company from these adjudications?

---

## Feedback to activities

### Activity 14.1

The public's main contacts with Shell were through its petrol retailing operations, rather than its industrial businesses. Motor fuel is a largely non-discretionary purchase which people tend to make wherever its convenient – Shell had viewed simply getting the right sites (and, presumably, setting the right price) as the key factors in attracting custom. In any event, petrol retailing represented only a small part of the group's global energy business.

Some possible reasons why Shell changed their stance include:

■ Recognition that better understanding of customers can lead to higher profitability (especially in low margin petrol retailing).

■ Damage to value of the brand in measurable, balance sheet terms.

■ Increased public interest in corporate citizenship in the 1990s and beyond.

■ Awareness that the general public were not just buyers of motor fuel, but also investors, industrial buyers, employees etc. This could impact access to investment, new contracts, recruitment etc. (Many companies now insert contract clauses relating to the ethical behaviour of companies with which they do business).

■ Cost of management time, PR activity etc. in handling negative publicity.

■ Increased legislation/introduction of Codes of Practice on ethical/environmental issues.

■ Opportunity to differentiate in a market where differentiation is not easy (Shell has actually been accused of going too far in its corporate citizenship by some voices in the oil industry).

■ Concern about physical damage to properties and injuries to staff (and consequent knock-on costs – higher insurance premiums, lost revenue and profits etc.).

■ Fear of political alienation.

Web site: www.shell.com

## Activity 14.2

**It opened up new distribution channels:** Seven Seas had previously struggled in the Independent Pharmacies sector. However, users of these pharmacies were also the core target audience for Countdown, so this crossover, and the high visibility of the sponsorship, drove new sales through this channel.

**It drove sales of other Seven Seas products:** Although the focus was on the High Strength Cod Liver Oil, a knock-on effect was to push up sales in other areas too.

**It appeared to increase liking for the brand,** with unsolicited consumer comments on the value they got from the sponsorship and their consequent willingness to trial or continue purchase.

## Activity 14.3

Measures included:

- **Sales and market share** of TCO in total, and of each of the variants individually. Measures were by volume and value. Actual results showed an immediate reversal of the decline for ball and bar as soon as the ads started. The Mini-Segments launch was substantially more successful than previous launches.

- **Awareness of the advertising:** this was very much higher than for the confectionery average.

- **Appeal of the advertising:** Again, a very positive response, generating an **effective share of voice** much higher than the budget suggested.

- **Brand awareness:** again, very high.

- **Change in attitudes and image:** perceptions tested, with very positive results, included 'TCO is really delicious' and 'TCO – OK to indulge'. Recognition of wider usage occasions was also measured.

Where relevant, data was collected reflecting the pre- and post-advertising positions to enable comparison to be made. Quantitative data was collected for all the above, and this was supported by qualitative research. Regional data was also gathered.

Data was extrapolated to identify both the effect of the launch of Mini-Segments on sales of the other products, and also the 'halo effect', i.e. how sales of an advertised variant affected sales of the others in the portfolio.

Other evaluative measures included:

- Increase in distribution.
- Effect of extra sales in reducing unit production costs (by spreading fixed costs).
- Increase in profit – direct and indirect effects.

## Activity 14.4

You may be able to come up with several suggestions depending on the type of business, but the NSPCC encapsulates three main points:

- Cause-related marketing enhances brand image and highlights your company's ethics.
- Sponsorship – raises awareness of your company.
- Employee fund-raising [or involvement] – motivates staff and enhances internal relationships.

# Session 15

# Cross-border communications

## Introduction

This final Session looks at ways in which communications may need to be adjusted when communicating internationally. In particular, we look at the impact of culture and the availability of media, and how these factors impact on decisions about whether to adapt or standardise messages and campaigns.

---

### LEARNING OUTCOMES

At the end of this Session you will be able to:

■ Explain the need to understand how culture might affect marketing communications.

■ Explain how availability of media can influence marketing communications plans.

■ Understand the adaptation vs. standardisation of advertising messages.

■ Explain how advertising agencies have changed in order to meet the international communications requirements of their clients.

---

## The impact of national culture on marketing communications

As we will discuss further in later in this Session, it is not always a straightforward task to transfer promotional messages or executions between one country and another. Many factors influence this, for example political or technological considerations, but it is particularly important for marketers to recognise cultural differences. Receivers of messages are less likely to look favourably on a communication which has a context that is inappropriate to them, if indeed they bother to note the communication at all. Cultural differences also offer plenty of scope to trip marketers up, as it is easy to accept one of our own practices as the norm, overlooking its non-applicability to other people.

Culture is the accumulation of beliefs, attitudes of mind, values, customs and symbols that individuals learn within a society. Professor Geert Hofstede sought to define the key dimensions of culture, and we can consider how this might affect communications:

**Power-distance**, (i.e. how power is distributed). Where power-distance is high, authority is important. Conversely, a low score suggests willingness to challenge and reason. Communications in the former situation may be more directive, with strong recommendations, perhaps backed by the authority of an opinion-leader.

**Uncertainty avoidance**, i.e. whether order and security are preferred or whether people are happy with uncertainty. Where people prefer to avoid uncertainty, messages should be presented clearly and without ambiguity. The messages themselves may stress product features and benefits that suggest safety and security.

**Individualism-collectivism**, i.e. whether individual achievement is more important, or whether the family or other groups dominate the way of life. Communications in individualistic societies may stress the importance of the individual and 'looking after number one'. Collectivist cultures may find images of group decision-making or scenes depicting extended families more relevant.

**Masculinity-femininity**, i.e., are achievement and success considered to be most important, or should values of caring and quality of life be stressed? Dynamic goal orientation, status symbols and dedication to the workplace would be appropriate in masculine cultures. Understanding, intuition and caring for others and the environment might symbolise femininity.

Context is another important dimension to understanding of cultures. Context is about who conveys messages and how they are put across. In low context cultures, such as Germany, France or Scandinavia, messages are clearly spelt out, which could be taken as bluntness by some people. In high context situations, e.g. Japan or Arab countries, far more emphasis is put on symbolism, suggestion and non-verbal cues.

There are many other pitfalls to trap the unwary marketer. Shapes, symbols, colours and numbers can all mean different things in different cultures. For example, 13 is a negative number in Europe, Latin America and the Middle East, but it is 4 and 9 that have negative connotations in Japan. Blues are generally positive colours in European and Middle Eastern cultures, whereas in Latin America and India bright, positive colours are popular.

Body language can mean very different things to different peoples; depiction of kissing, which Britons might view as quite acceptable, may be considered outrageous in other cultures, while religious views may directly influence what can be said or shown.

Language can present all sorts of difficulties. Extensive research is needed before an acceptable international brand name cane be identified; and some promotional messages may simply not translate into certain languages. Even where there is no problem with writing messages, marketers need to be aware of literacy levels. This will affect not only the relative importance of word and images, but also the media used, for example newspapers and magazines versus out-door advertising.

Marketers, then, need to have a good understanding of national cultures if their communications are to make an impact with their target audience. This applies whether the communications are intended for that market only, or whether the aim is to use the same promotional material across several different cultures.

---

**Activity 15.1**

Choose a country other than your own and find out about features of its culture (you could get information from marketing text-books, country guide-books, personal knowledge, contacts and the Internet).

How might these features affect the country's communications?

---

## The availability of media for international marketing communications

The availability of media affects how international communications can be used in many ways. Issues include the extent of use of different media by target audiences, local restrictions on content and the different ways that media space or time can be purchased. Let us consider these individually.

### Use of media by target audiences

Different countries have varying levels of access to media by members of the public. Literacy rates, for example, will clearly influence the extent to which written media, particularly newspapers and magazines, are used and which segments of the population use them. If your audience has low literacy rates then outdoor or cinema advertising may be more appropriate to reach them. Television ownership rates could also be a significant factor, as could the extent of Internet usage for e-marketing.

Obviously, these issues have an impact on which media can be used in particular countries. Beyond this, they may impact how you would roll out a campaign that crosses several borders. A television commercial suitable for use in some countries may be inappropriate in others. You will need to find a way to communicate the same messages to different audiences without losing consistency.

A different angle on this relates to the diversity and fragmentation of media. The UK, US and many European countries have a very diverse media network with numerous broadcast media channels, and by looking on the shelves of any UK newsagent you will also see a vast range of special interest magazines and journals. While this presents great opportunities to reach particular segments, it also presents challenges if you want to reach wide audiences. It follows that it is important to understand the pattern of print and broadcast media availability in your target countries.

## Content restrictions

The rules regarding advertising vary hugely from country to country. Whatever sector you are in, and whatever country you propose to operate in, you need to be aware of what laws and regulations apply. This is a strong argument in favour of obtaining advice based on local knowledge, whether in-house or agency, before undertaking international campaigns.

There may be other content-related issues. Commercial TV stations do not exist in some countries; others may restrict when advertising can be shown. In some countries the media is state-controlled, or is heavily influenced by political or religious requirements; all this may affect both what you may be allowed to say and the credibility with which it is received.

## Media buying

Local practices for media-buying will need to be understood. Sometimes purchase can be made from the home country; while on other occasions media will need to bought locally, perhaps through agents. Local buying will require understanding of local business practices, which will include the extent of negotiability of rate-card figures.

Widespread international deregulation of media ownership has led to much cross-ownership of international media – think of Rupert Murdoch or the Italian Prime Minister Silvio Berlusconi. This has led to the advent of 'one-stop shopping'; the opportunity to buy media time and space across the globe by dealing with a single provider.

---

**Activity 15.2**

You have already identified potential markets for your product. Make a checklist of the main information you would want to find out about before undertaking print or broadcast media advertising in target countries.

---

## Adaptation and standardisation options for communications messages in an international context

When marketers want to expand outside their home territories, they are faced with a choice as to how to develop their communications. At one extreme comes standardisation: a homogenised promotional treatment is prepared in, and exported from, the home country to be used in all overseas markets. At the other extreme comes a wholly local approach, drawing on the skills and knowledge within each country where the advertisements are to be shown. In between lie other options, either a centrally created strategy, the execution of which is adapted for the needs of individual markets, or through mixing of centrally created material with additional promotions, specifically created for the target markets.

Each approach has its pros and cons, but let us focus on the standardised strategy, with communications prepared centrally – its pros and cons will tend to be the antithesis of the other approaches.

Standardisation can apply at many levels: there may be a move to standardise a brand name internationally – for example Unilever's Cif, which was previously known as Jif in the UK. Advertisements may be produced for showing in several countries, such as HSBC's 2002 campaign which aims to demonstrate its understanding of different international cultures. Sometimes names and packaging stay the same but the product varies. Alain Baxter thought he had become Britain's first Olympic medal-winning skier for decades in the Salt Lake City Games. But he was stripped of his medal after he found that the U.S. Vick's Sinex Inhaler, virtually identical in appearance to the UK product he was used to, contained a different formulation including a banned substance.

### Advantages of standardisation

What advantages does standardisation offer? Costs are an important factor. Creating a single set of promotional material presents considerable economies of scale, compared to producing separate material for each country. Economies can arise through, for example, having a single creative and production process and through large-scale media buying which may cross borders. Only minor changes may need to be made for local use, such as changing the voice-over or inserting a picture of a typical national. Overall, considerably less (expensive) management time is needed. Monitoring and controlling campaigns' effectiveness may also be easier, comparing the effect of like executions.

Creating a uniform brand image is another significant benefit. Though people across the world vary, buyers of a particular product are likely to share certain characteristics. Standardisation enables common messages and appeals to be created for all the audiences, wherever they are. This is also an important factor in reaching individuals whose exposure to the brand is international – though travel, Internet use or through other exposure to foreign cultures, e.g. from films or TV programmes. Overall, not only does standardisation ensure common messages, but it also prevents conflicting messages being created which might dilute global efforts and waste time and money in resolution.

## Disadvantages of standardisation

Production of a standardised message is a 'one size fits all' approach and this will often be inappropriate. Markets vary hugely: the form/product/brand may be in a different stage of its life-cycle in different markets, competitive conditions vary and there may already be local competitors with positioning that the standardised promotions are trying to secure. Cultural differences may mean that the way a product is used is not uniform, or that communications require different creative treatment. The availability of different media will vary, and countries may have diverse regulations about what can or can't be said or shown. A danger is that, with all these variables, the advertisements are reduced to the lowest common denominator and, as a result, become bland and uninteresting for everybody. Furthermore, not only may campaigns not engage target audiences but they may not engage staff in the local operation either. They may have little if any involvement in development of the material and, consequently, equally little enthusiasm for implementation of the campaign.

Is standardisation, adaptation or localisation the right approach? Each business must make up its own mind, but it is interesting to hear the views of Tom Long, president of the UK operation of one of the few truly global brands, Coca-Cola. To paraphrase his view on brands,[9] he believes they need to be built from the bottom-up, by connecting with individuals and addressing what matters to them. Every brand needs to find what interests, expectations, hopes etc. bind its target audiences together and focus on that, rather than seeing commonalities simply in terms of geographical areas. A global approach may be right, but only if that geographically diverse audience has particular points in common.

---

**Activity 15.3**

Your boss has asked for a summary of the different options available in relation to standardisation and adaptation of international advertisements.

Set out the options in a memo, with a brief explanation and a couple of bullet point pros and cons for each.

---

## How advertising agencies have developed to meet international communications requirements of clients

Increased international trade has brought a need for grater understanding of international markets and easier access to them. Global brands have wanted to extend and cement their penetration, while smaller operations have wanted to take advantage of international trading and economic groupings, such as the EU (European Union), ASEAN (the Association of South East Asian Nations) and NAFTA (the North American Free Trade Agreement), to expand their markets. At the same time, improved communication and transport opportunities have effectively shrunk the globe.

This has meant that the services that organisations have traditionally required from agencies in home markets – research, creative, planning, production, media, PR, promotions and new media management – have also become needed in relation to their overseas operations. Other services, such as translation, may also be required. Agencies have addressed these opportunities in several ways.

### Multinational agencies

Multinational agencies have developed, sometimes through organic growth, i.e. setting up their own operations away from home territories, or through acquisition of established overseas businesses. The latter incurs acquisition costs but means the agency is starting with local expertise and established contacts. Sometimes growth has been client-driven, with agencies expanding in synchronisation with the growth of their major accounts. Multinationals' size means that they can meet the resource requirements of major international clients, for example large-scale budget handling, breadth of expertise, or diversity of knowledge and experience. However, conflicts of interest are a potential problem with multinationals. Their size, and the tendency for large clients to have operations in a range of market sectors, means that conflicts can arise. This needs to be a criterion for clients to consider when choosing an agency.

### Networks

Networks are a means for geographically separate agencies to work together, and provide a way for independent operators to group together to fight off the threat of the multi-nationals. Resources are available in the home market, and access to overseas agency services can be offered via partner businesses. ELAN, the European Local Advertising network, is one example. Care needs to be taken to ensure that businesses in the network have the services, skills and knowledge appropriate to the clients' needs. Control and accountability are also issues that need to be considered by clients, with responsibilities that are clearly defined; this is likely to be more straightforward when dealing with a single multi-national.

Decisions about how work is apportioned will need to be made. Sometimes one agency, usually the domestic one, will act as lead agency, undertaking strategic planning and creatives for example, but with implementation – say, any adaptation, and media buying – undertaken locally.

## Independent local agencies

Another way into international markets is through a direct approach to an agency, based in and specialising in the target country. This presents obvious, though not insurmountable, challenges to clients in tracking down a suitable agency and maintaining adequate communications during the relationship. The decision will partly depend on the client company's structure, e.g. whether it has a base in the overseas territory. If more than one country is involved, the client will also need to take into account whether it has the resources available to manage a series of individual relationships.

Whatever type of agency a client chooses, relationships should play a key part in selection, as they will directly affect the success of the venture. As with any agency selection, the client-agency relationship is critical. However, in addition, the client must be satisfied that the relationships between domestic and overseas agencies (where there is a need for both, whether as part of a network or as two elements of a multi-national) are co-operative and effective.

# Case Study – Harley-Davidson

Harley-Davidson began manufacturing motorcycles in the USA at the turn of the century. Virtually from the beginning they had a unique design with a powerful, robust engine. Thus from the outset, Harley had created a style that would become a familiar part of their heritage today.

Steadily, through the first 50 years or so of the company's history, they destroyed domestic competition until, in the early 1960's, they dominated the US market. Then, in the early 1960's, the Honda Motor Company of Japan entered the US market. Initially no one, including Harley-Davidson, paid any attention to the tiny motorcycles that Honda imported. They were not taken seriously and appeared to pose no threat to Harley's seemingly impregnable position. But the Honda initiative sparked a motorcycle craze, and Honda, having established the beachhead with small motorcycles, then started importing larger motorcycles. In less than 10 years, financial problems forced Harley-Davidson into a take-over by A.M.F., an American conglomerate with no motorcycle heritage. However, by the end of the 1970's, after 10 years of ownership, A.M.F.'s interest in Harley-Davidson waned. For Harley-Davidson the picture looked bleak. Japanese competition (for Yamaha, Kawasaki and Suzuki had now entered the US market) accounted for 70% of what was previously Harley-Davidson's key market segment – the super heavyweight motorcycle (defined as cycles with over 700cc capacity). Then in the early 1980's, Harley-Davidson's management managed to buy the company back from A.M.F. and so began the first stage of recovery.

Throughout the 1980's the company focused on improving quality, cutting costs, and monitored closely the relationship between the product and the customer. By 1993, the position had changed with Harley-Davidson once again dominating the super heavy motorcycle market sector and proving that the Japanese onslaught could be halted.

| 1993 Market Share (USA) | |
|---|---|
| Harley-Davidson | 63% |
| Honda | 26% |
| Others | 11% |

## Harley-Davidson's strategy

Harley-Davidson has focused on its key market sector – the heavyweight motorcycle market. Unlike the Japanese, who concentrated on a global standardisation strategy to get economies of scale, Harley concentrated on highly differentiated sub niches. Based on individual customer needs, Harley produced a range of tailor made models based on a few basic types, appealing to the older, educated, executive type customer in the upper income bracket, prepared to pay a high price uniqueness.

Harley's market research suggested that its customers did not see "other motorcycles" as its competition – but products like conservatories, swimming pools and luxury cruises. When buying a Harley-Davidson, price was not a factor. Its competitive advantage was "nostalgia" based on the dream and legendary mystique of owning an American classic. Customers did not buy a motorcycle, but the dream of "escaping from business" and the "freedom of the open road".

## International expansion

Harley-Davidson has been a long time exporter of its products. Curiously one of the earliest overseas countries to import Harleys was Japan, capitalising on American occupation following World War II. However, faced with a deteriorating domestic market position, Harley-Davidson virtually abandoned the overseas market. With its recovery in the USA and the retrieval of its position of dominance, coupled with a saturation of demand, the company has in recent years once again focused its attention on overseas markets. With a very limited overseas marketing budget, Harley has seen exports rise steadily and today sales in overseas markets account for around 30% of turnover, caused by the steady growth of the 'executive' sectors in the world market with rising capital income and increased leisure and recreational activities.

The company has recently established a 3-year goal of overseas sales accounting for 50% of its turnover, with a strong ambition to be represented in the European Union, and South East Asia, including Japan.

Harley-Davidson is a uniquely American company. The heritage, the product, the production facility, the marketing and the dealership network are all handled from corporate headquarters in Milwaukee, USA. It has very little overseas experience. All it knows – via unsolicited enquiries and its emerging very small-scale international distributor network is that there is a demand. What is not known is the nature of the customer, the degree of competition, state of the development of the market and the role and contribution of marketing.

**Source:** *Adapted from International Marketing Strategy Examination Paper,* June 1998

## Questions

1. Advise Harley-Davidson of the key issues they should consider when planning communications with overseas markets.

2. Recommend either a standardisation or adaptation approach for the marketing communications to overseas markets, justifying your recommendation.

3. Harley-Davidson has decided to use an Agency to help with their overseas communications. Advise them of the issues they need to consider when selecting an Agency.

## SUMMARY OF KEY POINTS

In this Session, we have introduced marketing communications in an international context, and covered the following key points:

■ Many more organisations are now looking to extend their markets internationally, and there are considerations to be made when communicating in international markets.

■ Two of the main factors that impact on the need to change promotions are national culture and the availability of media in other countries.

■ The main strategies are referred to as standardisation or adaptation.

■ Advertising agencies have had to adapt to keep pace with trends towards globalisation and internationalisation.

## Improving and developing own learning

The following projects are designed to help you develop your knowledge and skills further by carrying out some research yourself. Feedback is not provided for this type of learning because there are no 'answers' to be found, but you may wish to discuss your findings with colleagues and fellow students.

---

### Project A

Does you organisation trade internationally? If so, talk to colleagues in your marketing department about whether communications are standardised or adapted.

Why is this?

---

### Project B

Choose one country, ideally one that your organisation markets to, and contrast the cultures of your home country and the selected country. What are the main differences?

If your organisation does market to this country, how has promotion been adapted to deal with the differences in culture?

---

### Project C

Find out more about the structure of international agencies. Speak to your own agency(ies), if you have one/them, and find out about its/their international operations. Questions to ask include:

- Where do they have bases, or partner operations?
- What services are available overseas?
- How do they structure international campaigns, e.g. assignment of responsibilities (this may vary significantly between campaigns – what criteria determine the modus operandi?)
- What communications methods do they use between offices?
- What type of clients do they have, e.g. businesses whose main office is in the same country, or satellite operations of business with Head Offices abroad?

If you do not have direct access to any international agencies, try to get similar information from the Internet. A marketing directory will give you names of agencies, but here are some suggestions – winners of the award for "Top 10 Coverage of Major Markets Outside the UK" in the 2001 Marketing Week Agency Reputation Survey.

J Walter Thompson
McCann-Erickson
Saatchi and Saatchi
Abbot Mead Vickers.BBDO
BMP DDB
Ogilvy and Mather
TBWA/London
Carat
Publicis
Rainey Kelly Campbell Roalfe/Y&R

*List reproduced with kind permission of Marketing Week and Consensus Research.*

## Feedback to activities

### Activity 15.1

Using Hofstede's dimensions, France has:

■ relatively high power-distance.

■ relatively high individualism.

■ high uncertainty avoidance.

■ below-average masculinity.

The culture is low-context. Great pride is taken in the French language and culture.

Bosses have a lot of power and decisions will often have to be referred upwards. Care is taken in understanding the logic of proposals and piecing together a convincing chain of arguments, rather than being 'sold' on arguments using interpersonal skills.

Communications should recognise the French culture and language- – or, at least, certainly not slight them. Trying Britain's self-deprecating humour may not work at all. Sources of power and influence should be considered – managers, unions, local councils officials and, if possible, direct or implied endorsement would be valuable. The low-context culture suggests that messages can be delivered effectively in a straight way. This supports the preference for logical step-by-step thinking and the liking for high uncertainty avoidance by making messages clear and unambiguous.

## Activity 15.2

### Media availability

- Extent of TV/radio ownership and profile of owners.
- Viewing/listening figures – by channels/stations, audience profiles. Viewing/listening patterns.
- Print media – range, circulation and reader profile.
- Technical requirements, e.g. film format or artwork size, also lead times.

### Rules and regulations

Rules concerning sector.
Rules concerning international advertisers.
Other general rules on advertising, e.g. statements that can/can't be made.

### Media buying

Who from?
Who by?
Rates and negotiability.

### Other

Local agents or other source(s) of advice to guide you through the above.

You would also want to check out the proposed content to ensure it did not breach cultural, political or religious taboos.

**Activity 15.3**

# M E M O

**To: Marketing Director**

From: A student

**Re: Options for Standardisation and Adaptation of International Advertisements**

I refer to your request for a summary of the options available. I am pleased to set out below four options which, in ascending order, move from a wholly centralised approach to a wholly localised one.

## 1. Standardised approach

Advertisements are developed, produced and controlled centrally, i.e. in the 'home' country.

+ Consistent world-wide messages.
+ Significant cost savings.

– May not be appropriate for all markets.
– Local 'buy-in' may be limited.

## 2. Standardised approach supplemented by local material

Standardised material is produced as before, with additional locally produced material.

+ Main world-wide messages communicated consistently.
+ Allows for needs of differing markets.

– Additional costs and management time (compared to standardised approach).
– Danger that messages may conflict.

## 3. Standardised strategy but adapted and executed locally

Principles and guidelines produced centrally but production is undertaken locally, adapted to the specific market.

+ Messages consistent with both Head Office and local requirements.
+ More involvement/buy-in from local team (compared to standardised approach).

– Limited opportunities for local creativity.
– Additional costs and management time (compared to standardised approach).

## 4. Localised development and production

Power to develop, produce and control advertisements is devolved to local offices.

+ All advertisements suited to particular circumstances of local markets.
+ Maximises local creativity.

− Lack of consistency of brand-building messages, imagery etc. between regions/countries.
− Most expensive option.

I would be happy to develop and add to these notes whenever it is convenient for you.


Signed _____


Date _____

# Glossary

# Glossary

**Above the line** – advertising for which a payment is made and for which a commission is paid to the advertising agency.

**Account management** – the process by which an agency or supplier manages the needs of a client.

**ACORN** – a classification of residential neighbourhoods: a database which divides up the entire population of the UK in terms of housing in which they live.

**Acquisition** – one company acquiring control of another by purchase of a majority shareholding.

**Added value** – the increase in worth of a product or service as a result of a particular activity. In the context of marketing this might be packaging or branding.

**Advertising** – promotion of a product, service or message by an identified sponsor using paid for media.

**AIDA** – Attention, Interest, Desire, Action: a model describing the process that advertising or promotion is intended to initiate in the mind of a prospective customer.

**Alliance** – an agreement of two or more organisations to cooperate to pursue a defined strategy or activity.

**Ansoff matrix** – Model relating marketing strategy to general strategic direction. It maps product/market strategies.

**Asset-based marketing** – an approach to developing strategy and conducting marketing activities in which opportunities in the organisation's environment are found to match its assets and capabilities rather than the other way round.

**Attack strategies** – see offensive strategies.

**Balance sheet** – one of the three parts of a financial statement showing the assets, liabilities and shareholders' funds of the company at a point in time, usually the end of the period on which the report is being made.

**Balanced scorecard** – a technique allowing a company to monitor and manage performance against defined objectives. Measurements typically cover financial performance, customer value, internal business process, innovation performance and employee performance.

**BCG Matrix** – a model used for product portfolio analysis based on relative market share and market growth.

**Below-the-line** – non-media advertising or promotion when no commission has been paid to the advertising agency.

**Benchmarking** – the process of comparing performance of a specific activity with that of a similar activity performed in one or more organisations, usually with the aim of making improvements to the process.

**Brand** – the set of physical attributes of a product or service, together with the beliefs and expectations surrounding it.

**Brand equity** – the 'value' of the name and image of a brand in terms of its assets and liabilities. It is essentially a measure of the additional cash the organisation can generate through its brand.

**Brand extension** – extending the use of a brand to other products in the same market.

**Brand stretching** – taking a brand into a new, unrelated market.

**Brand valuation** – the process of determining the financial value of brand for the purposes of accounting for it on the balance sheet.

**Break-even analysis** – A technique used in decisions about cost, volumes and pricing of products and services. The break-even point is the point at which revenues based on a given price result in neither a profit nor a loss.

**Budget** – a plan in monetary terms of activities for a future period. Each department, function or unit in an organisation will usually have a budget against which its performance is measured. There are various forms of budget in organisations.

**Business plan** – a strategic document showing cash flow, forecasts and direction of a company.

**Business strategy** – the means by which a business works towards achieving its stated aims.

**Business-to-business (B2B)** – relating to the sale of a product for any use other than personal consumption.

**Business-to-consumer (B2C)** – relating to the sale of a product for personal consumption.

**Buying behaviour** – the process that buyers go through when deciding whether or not to purchase goods or services.

**Capabilities** – a collective term for the assets and competencies of an organisation.

**Cashflow statement** – One of the three parts of a financial statement for a company, showing the main inflows and outflows of cash over a period.

**Centralisation** – the tendency in an organisation for information to flow towards its centre or head and for the majority of decisions to be taken by top management.

**Channels** – the methods used by a company to communicate and interact with its customers.

**Comparative advertising** – advertising which compares a company's product with that of competing brands.

**Competencies** – the skills that are contained within an organisation. Core competencies provide the foundation for competitive advantage.

**Competitive advantage** – see sustainable competitive advantage.

**Competitive intelligence** – information of value to an organisation about its competitors and their activities that may be used in decision-making.

**Competitor analysis** – the process of analysing information about existing or potential competitors to inform decisions about future actions of an organisation in its markets.

**Confusion marketing** – controversial strategy of deliberately confusing the customer.

**Consumer** – individual who buys and uses a product or service.

**Consumer behaviour** – the buying habits and patterns of consumers in the acquisition and usage of products and services.

**Context analysis** – an analysis of the context in which communications will be formulated. It is similar to a 'situational analysis', but strongly focused on the communications aspects – customer, business, internal, and external factors.

**Control** – the process of ensuring that actions taken to achieve a strategy or plan conform to the requirements or standards laid down.

**Corporate identity** – the character a company seeks to establish for itself in the mind of the public. The cues by which stakeholders can recognise and identify the organisation.

**Corporate image** – the image held by the different audiences of an organisation. An organisation cannot change its image, but can change its identity.

**Corporate personality** – an element of corporate identity, corporate personality is created by the culture, values and beliefs held by the organisation.

**Corporate reputation** – a complex mix of characteristics such as ethos, identity and image built over time that go to make up a company's public personality.

**Cost leadership** – one of Porter's three generic strategies in which the organisation takes on a wide market and attempts to achieve lower costs than its competitors.

**Critical success factors** – those aspects of the business or process which must result in order for objectives to be achieved; factors that are critical to success.

**Culture** – a shared set of values, beliefs and traditions that influence prevailing behaviour within a country or organisation.

**Customer** – a person or company who purchases goods or services.

**Customer analysis** – the process of collating and analysing information about customers in a market in order to identify opportunities for a particular organisation.

**Customer loyalty** – feelings or attitudes that incline a customer to return to a company, shop or outlet to purchase there again.

**Customer Relationship Management (CRM)** – the coherent management of contacts and interactions with customers.

**Customer satisfaction** – the provision of goods or services which fulfil the customer's expectations in terms of quality and service, in relation to price paid.

**DAGMAR Defining Advertising Goals for Measured Advertising Response** – a model for planning advertising in such a way that its success can be quantitatively monitored.

**Database marketing** – whereby customer information stored in an electronic database is utilised for targeting marketing activities.

**Data Protection Act** – a law which makes organisations responsible for protecting the privacy of personal data.

**Decision Making Unit (DMU)** – the team of people in an organisation or family group who make the final buying decision.

**Defensive strategies** – competitive strategies analogous to military strategies that an organisation may adopt to defend itself from attack by other players in the market. They include position defence, flank defence, pre-emptive defence and counter-attack.

**Delphi technique** – A forecasting technique in which the view or estimate for the future is compiled from inputs by a number of individuals, usually experts in their field, working independently of each, usually in successive rounds.

**Demographic data** – information describing and segmenting a population in terms of age, sex, income and so on which can be used to target marketing campaigns.

**Differentiation** – ensuring that products and services have a unique element to allow them to stand out from the rest. Specifically one of Porter's three generic strategies in which the organisation takes on a wide market and exploits perceived uniqueness.

**Direct marketing** – all activities that make it possible to offer goods or services or to transmit other messages to a segment of the population by post, telephone, e-mail or other direct means.

**Direct response advertising** – advertising incorporating a contact method such as a phone number or enquiry form with the intention of encouraging the recipient to respond directly to the advertiser.

**Direct Product Profitability (DPP)** – The technique of using contribution to make decisions about price and monitoring performance of the organisation's assets, such as channels and production or retail space.

**Discounted Cash Flow (DCF)** – a method, used in making investment decisions, for calculating the present value of capital expenditure and future revenues for a project based on a discount rate.

**Discount rate** – the rate used in DCF, IRR and payback method to discount future values to calculate the present value of an investment. It is either the interest rate or cost of capital.

**Distribution (Place)** – the process of getting the goods from the manufacturer or supplier to the user.

**Diversification** – an increase in the variety of goods and services produced by an organisation. Diversification may be related to current goods and services, or unrelated.

**E-commerce** – business conducted electronically.

**E-marketing** – marketing conducted electronically.

**Employee Relationship Management (ERM)** – an approach based on CRM in which an organisation recognises and treats its employees as 'customers' and uses marketing techniques to communicate and maintain loyalty.

**Environmental analysis** – the process of collating and analysing information about the environment an organisation operates in, usually as an early step in the strategic management or planning cycle.

**Environmental scanning** – the process of monitoring and evaluating the organisation's environment on a continuous and routine basis to detect events that may have significance for the organisation and the way it operates.

**Ethical marketing** – marketing that takes account of the moral aspects of decisions.

**Export marketing** – the marketing of goods or services to overseas customers.

**External analysis** – study of the external marketing environment.

**Field marketing** – extending an organisation's marketing in the field through merchandising, product launches, training of retail staff, etc.

**Financial statements** – statements made by a company that presents a 'true and fair view' of its financial position at the end of a period, usually one year. They consist of a profit and loss statement, balance sheet and cash flow statement.

**Five forces model** – an analytic model developed by Michael E. Porter which analyses the competitive environment and industry structure.

**FMCG** – Fast Moving Consumer Goods such as packages food and toiletries.

**Focus** – one of Porter's three generic strategies in which the organisation focuses on one segment or a narrow part of the market and exploits either perceived uniqueness or low costs.

**Forecasting** – estimation of the probability and scope of future events and performance. A forecast is usually used as the basis for a budget.

**Franchising** – the selling of a licence by the owner (franchisor) to a third party (franchisee) permitting the sale of a product or service for a specified period.

**Gap analysis** – the process of identifying the gap over a period of time between an organisation's objectives and the projected results of its current or potential objectives. The gap is then filled by one or more strategies or courses of action.

**Generic strategies** – the term used to describe Porter's three competitive strategies available to organisations to develop and maintain advantage (differentiation, cost leadership and focus). Failure to develop a clear strategy will usually result in an organisation becoming 'stuck in the middle'.

**Geo-demographics** – a method of analysis combining geographic and demographic variables.

**Grey market (silver market)** – term used to define a population over a certain age (usually 65).

**Industrial marketing (or business to business marketing)** – the marketing of industrial products.

**Innovation** – development of new products, services or ways of working (processes).

**Innovation audit** – the process, conducted usually as part of the internal analysis, of investigating and evaluating an organisation's innovations capabilities and performance.

**Internal analysis** – the study of a company's internal marketing resources in order to assess strengths, weaknesses and opportunities.

**Internal customers** – employees within an organisation viewed as 'consumers' of a product or service provided by another part of the organisation.

**Internal marketing** – the process of eliciting support for a company and its activities among its own employees in order to encourage them to promote its goals.

**International marketing** – the conduct and co-ordination of marketing activities in more than one country.

**Investment decisions** – the decisions made in organisations by senior managers on investments in assets and capabilities of the organisation, based on the calculation of net present value of capital expenditures and revenues.

**Joint venture** – a business entity or partnership formed by two or more parties for a specific purpose.

**Jury technique** – a forecasting technique in which a group of people, usually experts in their field, working together make a forecast.

**Key account management** – account management as applied to a company's most valuable customers.

**Knowledge management** – the collection, organisation and distribution of information in a form that lends itself to practical application. Knowledge management often relies on information technology to facilitate the storage and retrieval of information.

**Logo** – a graphic usually consisting of a symbol and or group of letters that identifies a company or brand.

**Macro-environment** – the external factors which affect companies' planning and performance, and are beyond its control. (SLEPT).

**Margin** – a generic term used to express profit as a percentage of sales. Gross margin is gross profit as a percentage of sales, net margin is net profit as a percentage of sales.

**Market development** – the process of growing sales by offering existing products (or new versions of them) to new customer groups.

**Market orientation** – a business culture whereby customers' needs and wants determine corporate direction.

**Market penetration** – the attempt to grow ones business by obtaining a larger market share in an existing market.

**Market research** – the gathering and analysis of data relating to markets to inform decision making.

**Market segmentation** – the division of the market place into distinct sub-groups or segments, each characterised by particular tastes and requiring a specific marketing mix.

**Market share** – a business' sales of a given product or set of products to a given set of customers expressed as a percentage of total sales of all such products to such customers in a market or segment.

**Marketing audit** – scrutiny of an organisation's existing marketing system to ascertain its strengths and weaknesses.

**Marketing communications (Promotion)** – all methods used by a firm to communicate with its customers and stakeholders.

**Marketing information** – any information used or required to support marketing decisions.

**Marketing mix** – the combination of marketing inputs that affect customer motivation and behaviour (7 Ps – Product, Price, Promotion, Place, People, Process and Physical Evidence).

**Marketing planning** – the selection and scheduling of activities to support the company's chosen marketing strategy or goals.

**Marketing research** – the gathering and analysis of data relating to marketing to inform decision making (includes product research, place research, pricing research, etc).

**Marketing strategy** – the broad methods chosen to achieve marketing objectives.

**McKinsey Seven S's of management (7S Model)** – a framework for considering business strategy with reference to seven interrelated aspects of the organisation: Systems, Structure, Strategy, Style, Staff, Skills and Shared values.

**Merger** – the formation of one company from two existing companies.

**Micro-environment** – the immediate context of an organisation's operations, including such elements as customers, competitors, channels to markets and suppliers.

**Mission statement** – a summary of an organisation's business philosophy, purpose and direction.

**Model** – simplified representation of a process, designed to aid in understanding.

**Net Present Value (NPV)** – the value in today's terms of expenditures and revenues associated with a specific set of activities or project over a period of time, discounted at a specific rate. The main method for arriving at a NPV for a project is discounted cash flow.

**New Product Development (NPD)** – the creation of new products from evaluation of proposals through to launch.

**Niche marketing** – the marketing of a product to a small and well-defined segment of the market place.

**Norms** – commonly understood rules, often defined culturally rather than formally, that provide guidelines for personal behaviour.

**Objectives** – an organisation's defined and measurable aims or goals for a given period. Objectives are usually defined at corporate, business or marketing level.

**Offensive strategies** – competitive strategies analogous to military strategies that an organisation may adopt to attack other players in the market. They include frontal attack, flank attack, encirclement and bypass attack.

**Packaging** – material used to protect and promote goods.

**Personal selling** – one-to-one communication between seller and prospective purchaser.

**PIMS** – Profit Impact of Marketing Strategies. A US database supplying data such as environment, strategy, competition and internal data.

**Planning** – the process of determining and defining the future actions over a specified period for an organisation. Formal planning results in a written plan that usually requires the approval of head office.

**Portfolio (and portfolio analysis)** – the set of products or services which a company decides to develop and market. Portfolio analysis is the process of comparing the contents of the portfolio to see which products and services are the most promising and deserving of further investment and those which should be discontinued.

**Porter** – Michael Porter known for his work in competitive strategy who developed a number of well-known models, such as Five Forces model, value chain and strategic groups model, used for analysing the competitive environment of an organisation.

**Positioning** – the creation of an image for a product or service in the minds of customers, both specifically to that item and in relation to competitive offerings.

**Pricing decisions** – decisions to determine the price at which products or services will be sold. There are a number of methods available to determine price taking into account the relevant costs.

**Product life cycle** – a model describing the progress of a product from the inception of the idea via the main people of sales, to its decline.

**Profit** – the amount that is left out of revenues at the end of a period once all the relevant costs have been deducted. Profit is measured at a number of levels including gross profit (after direct costs), operating profit (after all operating expenses) and retained earnings (after interest, tax and dividends).

**Profit and Loss (P&L) account** – one of the three parts of the financial statement for a company showing the revenues and costs over the period being reported.

**Profile strategy** – the marketing communications strategy devised to influence all relevant stakeholders, and concerned with the reputation of the organisation.

**Project management** – the use of various management techniques to plan and control a set of activities designed to achieve a specific goal, often undertaken as a non-routine activity.

**Promotional mix** – the components of an individual campaign which are likely to include advertising, personal selling, public relations, direct marketing, packaging and sales promotion.

**Public Relations (PR)** – the planned and sustained communication to promote mutual understanding between an organisation and its stakeholders.

**Pull promotion** – addresses the customer directly with a view to getting them to demand the product and hence 'pull' it down through the distribution chain.

**Push promotion** – relies on the next link in the distribution chain, e.g. wholesaler, to 'push' out products to the customer.

**Qualitative research** – information that cannot be measured or expressed in numeric terms. It is useful to the marketer as it often explores people's feelings and opinions.

**Quantitative research** – information that can be measured in numeric terms and analysed statistically.

**Ratio analysis** – the use of financial ratios, usually as part of a wider analysis of an organisation and its current situation, to ascertain its performance and financial health. The analysis usually involves the use of profitability, liquidity, solvency, utilisation and investment ratios.

**Reference group** – a group with which the customer identifies in some way and whose opinions and experiences influence the customer's behaviour.

**Relationship marketing** – the strategy of establishing a relationship with a customer which continues well beyond the first purchase.

**Sales forecast** – a forecast of the sales revenues expected for a future period. It is significant in that it determines the level of activity for the organisation for that period and as such forms the basis for the other forecasts of costs generated by organisations. Considerable emphasis is therefore placed on its accuracy.

**Sampling** – the use of a statistically representative subset as a proxy for an entire population, for example in order to facilitate quantitative market research.

**Scenario planning** – a technique used in planning to identify the possible future scenarios for an organisation which can then be quantified and modelled and a view taken on the probability of occurrence of each. This technique is particularly useful to organisations facing high uncertainty.

**Segmentation** – the process of dividing customers in a market up into discrete groups, each group being unique and having identifiable and similar needs.

**Sensitivity analysis** – the modelling and assessment of the potential risks facing an organisation in a specific situation using the question 'what if?'. It is commonly used in planning at the forecasting stage, setting budgets and making investment decisions to take into account different circumstances and risks.

**Share of voice** – a method of determining financial resources to be invested in advertising. The concept suggests that within any market, the total of all money spent on advertising can be analysed in the context of the proportion each organisation or brand has made to the total. The advertiser spending the most has the highest 'share of voice' (SOV)

**Skimming** – setting the original price high in the early stages of the product life cycle to get as much profit as possible before prices are driven down by increasing competition.

**SLEPT** – a framework for viewing the macro-environment – Socio-cultural, Legal, Economic, Political and Technical factors.

**SMART** – a mnemonic referring to the need for objectives to be Specific, Measurable, Aspirational, Relevant and Timebound. (Note: Variations exist in the specific terms used.)

**Sponsorship** – specialised form of promotion where a company will help fund an event or support a business venture in return for publicity.

**Stakeholder** – an individual or group that affects or is affected by the organisation and its operations.

**Strategic drift** – the gradual shift of an organisation's responses away from what the market needs which, if uncorrected, may lead to the organisation becoming uncompetitive and its strategy wearing out.

**Strategic groups model** – a model, developed by Porter, in which competitors in an industry are grouped according to similarities of the way they compete.

**Strategic Business Unit (SBU)** – a part of an organisation, irrespective of its size, that is a complete business with its own customers and strategies and contains all the necessary functions to operate independently. In organisations, SBUs may take the form of divisions, departments, operating companies

**Strategy** – the goals (vision, purpose, aims or objectives) and the means for achieving them. Originally applied to armies, the term was accepted into business use in the mid 20th century.

**Strategy formulation** – the process of determining the goals, identifying and evaluating options, and specifying actions. It may be part of planning or independent of it.

**Strong and weak theories of advertising** – Strong theory suggests that consumers are influenced by advertising, and weak theory suggests that they are pushed more by habit than by promotional messages.

**Structure** – the way a group is organised such as reporting line, lines of authority, specification of roles (commonly shown on the organisational structure chart).

**Sustainable competitive advantage** – the advantage that an organisation can gain and sustain over its competitors, usually by offering higher customer value through the products, proposition or benefits it offers.

**SWOT analysis** – analysis to determine strengths, weaknesses, opportunities and threats; often used to summarise other parts of a detailed analysis.

**Targeting** – the use of market segmentation to select and address a key group of potential purchasers.

**Trend extrapolation** – the use of historical data to identify trends and extrapolate them forwards as the basis for a forecast.

**Unique Selling Proposition (USP)** – that benefit that a product or service can deliver to customers that is not offered by any competitor.

**Unit contribution** – see contribution.

**Value chain** – the primary and support activities undertaken in a firm to add value to materials and other inputs which it sells to customers.

**Variance** – the difference between a planned or budgeted activity and the actual cost or result. A variance may be positive (or favourable) or negative (or adverse). Variance analysis is used to assess performance and identify when corrective action is required.

**Virtual organisations** – organisations that deliver products and services but which have few of the physical features usually associated with organisations.

**Vision** – the long-term aims and aspirations of the organisation for itself.

**Word-of-mouth** – The spreading of information through human interaction alone.

# Appendix 1

# Feedback to Case Studies

## Session 1

**1. Summarise Dutton Engineering's current situation from a communications perspective.**

- Need to shift strategically to generate new business and change culture.
- Need to look at new segments, and so research their perceptions, attitudes, etc. before building communications plans.
- Need to make positioning decisions.
- Need to consider the most appropriate mix and ensure that all communications are integrated.
- Need to consider planning and resourcing issues, as well as mechanisms to measure and monitor effectiveness.

**2. Identify the communications tools currently used by the company, and suggest how these might be changed to communicate with all audiences.**

Only the following are used currently:

- Word of mouth
- Limited PR
- Basic web site
- Exhibitions
- Some telemarketing

Need to integrate all communications activity and consider:

Profile strategy – PR, web site, consistent sales material.
Pull strategy – trade press, personal selling, web site.

## Session 2

**1. Explain what supermarkets hope to gain by stocking Fair Trade products.**

- A reinforcement of brand values.
- Perception of customers and potential customers as socially responsible.
- A degree of competitive advantage in terms of customers with high ethical values.
- Customers may associate socially responsible approach with reputation, and organisation may enjoy enhanced loyalty.

2. **Recommend an appropriate communications mix for a supermarket deciding to communicate their stance on ethical trading.**

   A balance has to be achieved here – there is a danger that too much emphasis will have a negative impact. 'Look how good we are!'

   PR, the corporate web site and the Annual Report & Accounts, plus internal communications would be most appropriate.

3. **Explain why marketing communications in themselves are sometimes considered unethical. How can organisations measure whether they are acting unethically through their communications?**

   - They can be viewed as encouraging society to be materialistic, and setting aspirations beyond the reach of the general public (which might lead to crime).

   - There are several 'tests' put forward to assess how ethical planned marketing communications are. Laczniak & Murphy put forward some useful 'rules' – for example – 'Think about the outcomes of the decision and how appropriate it is for those impacted upon', and 'Only act as you would find acceptable'

## Session 3

1. **Dutton Engineering are now trying to attract new customers rather than merely maintain relationships with existing clients. How might their communications need to be adapted to handle these differences?**

   Need to integrate all communications activity and consider:

   Profile strategy – PR, web site, consistent sales material.
   In particular, they need to consider the 'change' issues involved internally, and ensure that all staff are 'on board' with the new culture. What happens inside the organisation has a direct impact on what is communicated externally.
   Pull strategy – trade press, personal selling, web site.

2. **The Managing Director is concerned that, if an expensive communications campaign is launched to attract new customers, you may not be able to establish where any new business is coming from. What element of the communication model might cause this problem?**

   This would be the result of a problem with the feedback mechanism within the communications model. If clear objectives are set for each part of the communications campaign, and feedback mechanisms allow monitoring of where business is coming from, then this problem should be overcome.

3. **The Case Study mentions that much of Dutton's existing communication is via 'word-of-mouth'. How might this element be used to attract new customers? Use the communication theory in this Session to explain.**

Word-of-mouth communication comes from individuals who have had a good (or a bad) experience of a product or an organisation. It comes from the 'source' of the message, and individuals who are respected as 'knowledge centres' about a particular topic, as well as people in a potential customer's reference group, will have credibility with its audience.

Dutton need to ensure that experiences are positive, and capitalise on the word of mouth communication that is supportive. For example, with permission, they can use existing customers' comments in some of their promotional material.

# Session 4

1. **Apollo operates in a business-to-business environment. Explain how the organisational buying process might impact on communications from them and their distributors.**

   ■ There with increased competition, they need to communicate with their channel members more quickly and efficiently.

   ■ There Currently, they only communicate via their distributors.

   ■ B2B buying usually involves a DMU – mass communication cannot guarantee that decision makers are reached, therefore mix tools need to be selected carefully.

   ■ Decisions are often made based on logical factors rather than emotional factors.

   ■ Specifications are drawn up for both product and supplier – profile and pull strategy therefore appropriate.

2. **How is Apollo's internal culture likely to impact on their marketing communications?**

   ■ Strong relationships with distributors, and strong reliance on them to communicate internationally.

   ■ Difficult to control and ensure consistent message.

   ■ Danger of alienating/breaking down these relationships if use of Internet is perceived as disintermediation.

   ■ Need to build a strong brand image for company and products.

# Session 5

1. **Undertake a context analysis for Woodstock Furniture, drawing out the key issues from this analysis.**

   - Business context – the organisation has a new mission and strategic direction. The new marketing plan has growth objectives through a market penetration strategy of 15% per annum. Marketing communications issue here is to reposition Woodstock.

   - Customer context – customers currently perceive Woodstock to be a manufacturer and installer of bathroom and kitchen furniture, and they wish this to be changed to a perception of craftsmanship and design and construction of customised furniture. Many customers are celebrities who value privacy – this could be a perceived risk to the affluent market they target, and they need to communicate that Woodstock is trustworthy and reliable. Other forms of perceived risk include social – how will the finished product be seen by their social set, and financial – in this case, the new premium price is probably more fitting with the target market. The purchase is high involvement, and customers need much reassurance about its suitability.

   - Internal context – Woodstock's employees are loyal and identify with the customised approach. However, some change is necessary internally, and staff will need to be kept 'on board' in the light of these changes. There are financial constraints that will impact on the extent of any communications campaign run.

   - Stakeholder context – Woodstock is looking to form alliances with firms operating in the same market, and also build relationships with architects and developers, who may commission their services. Communications will play a role in building these relationships – personal selling/networking being a useful tool in this respect.

   - External context – There is little in the Case Study about the organisation's external environment, apart from the competitive situation in which they find themselves.

2. **Identify the key stakeholder groups that Woodstock Furniture should communicate with, and recommend the messages that might be communicated to each.**

   - Architects – need to communicate the new positioning, and trustworthiness of business, in order to try to build relationships and generate further business.

   - Media – use of PR to build brand awareness and assist with repositioning.

3. **Outline the stages of the communications planning process as they relate to Woodstock Furniture.**

The marketing communications planning process includes the following stages:

- Introduction.
- Contextual analysis.
- Promotional objectives.
- Positioning.
- Promotional strategies – pull, push and profile, as well as branding, in Woodstock's case.
- Promotional mix and schedule (with budget).
- Evaluation and control mechanisms.

## Session 6

1. **From the information in the Case Study, describe two potential segments for Weetabix.**

Family with babies and young children, C1C2D – attractive because of added value offerings and flexibility of use – for whole family.

New minibix – Family with teenagers, BC1C2 – attractive because of health characteristics and added ingredient (for variety).

2. **Suggest attributes of the cereals mentioned in the Case Study that might be used to construct perceptual maps for the market.**

Nutritional value, flavour, preparation method and time taken, 'fun'.

3. **From the information in the Case Study describe a potential target segment for the new Nutrigrain bar.**

There could be many potential segments for the new bar. One suggestion might be:

Healthy eaters, in a hurry, no time for breakfast, working – 20-35 age group using public transport to travel to work.

# Session 7

1. **Explain why objectives are needed as part of the planning process, differentiating between corporate, marketing and promotional objectives.**

   Objectives state what is to be achieved through a plan, and give clear direction for the organisation, department or individual.

   Corporate objectives give the organisation direction, and reflect the mission and the 'business we are in'.

   Marketing objectives show what marketing will achieve to help achieve the corporate objectives.

   Marketing communications objectives relate to the context in which the brand exists now, and where it needs to be in the future. They are relevant to marketing objectives and contribute to the achievement of these objectives. They will be expressed in terms of raising awareness, improving or changing perception or attitudes, etc.

2. **Suggest marketing objectives for each of Kellogg's, Weetabix, and Cereal Partners Ltd, based on information in the Case Study.**

   Kellogg's – to maintain market share at current level during the financial year 2003/2004.

   Weetabix – to increase sales volume of core product by xx% in the year commencing 1st April 2003.

   Cereal Partners – to achieve 2% growth in market share over the year commencing 1st July 2003.

3. **Based on the marketing objectives you have developed in (1), suggest one promotional objective for one product from each company.**

   Kellogg's:
   To remind target audience of health benefits associated with Cornflakes on an ongoing basis.

   Weetabix:
   To persuade a further 5% of target market to buy Weetabix 48 packs over the campaign period.
   (Note: Campaign using added value of sales promotion – free jar of coffee with pack.)

   Cereal Partner's:
   To increase prompted awareness of Fruitful among target group of young adults by the end of financial year commencing 1st July 2003.

## Session 8

1. **Basing your answer on the information in the Case Study, suggest a pull strategy and associated promotional mix for the launch of the repositioned 'Bonio'.**

Sales promotions as described in Case Study, together with new packaging design to attract attention. Direct mailing to database of customers known to be past or present users.

2. **Basing your answer on the information in the Case Study, suggest a push strategy and associated promotional mix for the launch of the repositioned 'Bonio'.**

Personal selling to encourage retailers to stock and display new packaging in a prominent position, and to communicate the USP – new formula, proven to fight plaque and tartar. Also to communicate the sales promotions which will be offered through the pull strategy, convincing retailers that there will be demand.

Also target vets to recommend because of 'health' characteristics, and to help create PR through their opinion former status.

3. **Basing your answer on the information in the Case Study, suggest a profile strategy and associated promotional mix for the launch of the repositioned 'Bonio'.**

Emphasis on the 'Bonio' and the 'proven to fight plaque and tartar' message – giving the fact that Friskies 'care' about the dog's health.

PR, and new packaging design.

## Session 9

1. **Evaluate the marketing communications strategy of each of the main brand manufacturers, commenting on the role of advertising.**

|  | Kellogg's | Weetabix | Cereal Partners |
|---|---|---|---|
| Target market | Parents | Family | Children |
| Branding | Family | Corporate | Multibranding |
| Strategy | Mainly pull + push & profile | Mainly pull & profile | Mainly pull |
| SOV | >SOM | <SOM | >SOM |
| Core message | Health | Added value | Positioned for children – fun proposition |

2. **Suggest how Weetabix Ltd might use marketing communications to counter the new promotional strategy announced by Kellogg's.**

Kellogg's are using a price/discounting strategy, whereas Weetabix uses an added value strategy.

Weetabix have stated they want to avoid a price war, and so options are:
Maintain the status quo.
Differentiate and reposition the brand.
Build their corporate brand.

I would suggest they use marketing communications to help differentiate their offering, and reposition their brand.  In order to achieve a competitive advantage Weetabix need to develop their brand values, through both profile and pull strategy.

Advertising could play a large part here, and Weetabix have an opportunity to increase their share of voice to compete with Kellogg's, following their announcement that they are increasing their advertising budget.

# Session 10

1. **Identify and justify a communication strategy for AP Engineering for the next year.**

Profile strategy needed – followed by pull.
Key reasons:

■ **change in business strategy** needs to obtain buy-in of existing staff.

■ **acquisitions** – need to bring staff of other organisations on board, and develop an integrated culture.

■ profile strategy will help communicate a **consistent message** to **internal and external** audiences.

2. **Which tools of the promotional mix might best be used to implement this strategy? Why?**

Remembering that the key strategy is '**profile**', and to **internal as well as external** audiences, this would suggest:

■ **PR**
■ **Conferences and training for internal audience**
■ **Corporate advertising** (rather than pull – advertising of services)
■ **Exhibitions**

These can be justified through links to your answer to Q.1

3.  **List the issues that AP might consider before implementing an integrated marketing communications policy.**

    The key word in this part of the question **is implementation**. Ideally, you need to link back to the **objectives** to be achieved, and list **resource issues** relevant to the scenario. For example, will a senior representative from management be available to 'champion' the campaign? How should events be scheduled? How will budget be allocated? How will events be co-ordinated? How will the plan be monitored and evaluated?

# Session 11

1.  **Explain the main ways of setting promotional budgets, making a recommendation for the company in the Case Study.**

    | Method | Description |
    |---|---|
    | Arbitrary | Budget decisions made by senior person, but with no real consideration of context or strategy. Figure may be plucked out of the air. |
    | Affordable or "All-we-can-afford". | The organisation's non-communications fixed and variable costs, plus an allowance for profit, are deducted from revenues. What is left is what the business can afford to spend on communications. |
    | Inertia | Rather than re-calculate, this year's figure is simply the same as last year's. |
    | Media multiplier | As for inertia, but an allowance is made for increases in media costs. |
    | Percentage of sales. | Comms. budget is calculated as a percentage of value of sales – either historical or forecast.<br>% may be based on company or industry norm, or be arbitrary. |
    | Competitor comparison (and Competitor Parity) | Comparison is made against individual competitors/ the industry as a whole, often in terms of the ratio of communications (usually advertising) spending to sales. Your organisation can identify how it compares with industry/ category averages and specific competitor information to benchmark how much you should be spending to achieve particular market share targets.<br>Using Competitor Parity your budget equals that of competitor(s). |

| Method | Description |
|--------|-------------|
| Profit maximisation | Keep on spending on comms. until the point where extra spending equals extra revenue, i.e. there in no more profit generated by comms spend. |
| Objective and task | A bottom-up approach which reviews each promotional objective, and identifies the tasks, and associated budget, to achieve each one. |

Strategically, the organisation should be considering share of voice in looking to promote a brand rather than a car. However, of the above methods, I would recommend the objective and task method, spreading the budget across the pull, push and profile strategies.

2. **Examine the key strategic factors that need to be considered when determining the level of financial resources to be allocated to the launch campaign.**

   The key factors for consideration include:

   ■ Context analysis.

   ■ Target market.

   ■ Corporate, marketing and promotional objectives.

   ■ Competitor activity.

   ■ Financial resources available.

   ■ Split across pull, push and profile strategies.

# Session 12

1. **The Case Study mentions that previously your organisation has sold cars and not a brand. What would be the difference in promotional strategy if this was to change?**

   A brand creates a strong, positive impression in the mind of the customer. Cars rely on logical (rather than emotional) and informational messages, supported by image style messages.

   Advertising is used in promoting car brands (pull), and direct mailings may also be used to target existing customers who may be thinking of changing their car, seeking to retain their business by raising their awareness of the new model.

2. **Decide upon a promotional strategy for your company in support of the launch of the Zen. You should argue the benefits for your strategic approach.**

   Pull and push strategies will be needed for the launch. To build a corporate identity will take considerable time, and a profile strategy will need to be built in the future, but would not help with the launch of this new model.

3. **Which promotional tools are said to be most appropriate at the beginning of the product life cycle?**

   At the introductory stage of the PLC, sales are low, and direct competition is also low. The focus of promotional activity is on raising awareness, and providing information.

   Suitable tools will include:

   ■ Advertising and PR as part of the pull strategy.

   ■ PR, sales promotion and personal selling as part of the push strategy.

# Session 13

1. **Identify and explain the key factors in the environment that are impacting on the way BGRC will need to communicate their services.**

   EU targets had recently been set for recycling of glass.
   UK government pressures to encourage more people to recycle.

2. **Suggest appropriate communications strategies for BGRC's audiences.**

   Pull strategy necessary to provide information to the public about the need to recycle, and to persuade them to use BGRC.

   Push strategy to encourage traders to provide facilities on their premises, so that it is easier to recycle.

3. **Outline an appropriate communications mix for the organisation.**

   **Push strategy**
   Trade press advertising, and direct mailings to audiences such as local authorities and major supermarkets, to encourage the provision of facilities.

   **Pull strategy**
   Targeted outdoor and point of sale literature, to provide reminders to the public both where they buy glass and where they can recycle it.
   Government lobbying to encourage informational ads to the public.

# Session 14

1. **Comment on the campaign objectives as they are stated in the Case Study.**

   Key points here are that the objectives as stated in the text of the Case Study do not lend themselves to measurement – i.e. they are not SMART. Words such as 'huge' are not suitable in objectives, particularly where expenditure will need to be justified to stakeholder groups and a discerning donating public. However, later in the Case Study it becomes evident that targets have been set, and evidence of success is given in a comparison of number of new supporters targeted and generated is given.

   It is also clear that the campaign was pre- and post-tested.

2. **Use the facts in the Case Study to justify the expenditure of £250,000 on the campaign, to NSPCC's donors.**

   Whilst the budget for this campaign seems high for an organisation whose main aim is to generate funds for the protection of children. However, the figures shown in the Case Study speak for themselves:

   ■ Awareness – raised from 19% to 27%.

   ■ New supporters up by 70% over target.

   Despite not being a direct objective of the campaign, £1,000,000 of funds were generated over the launch period of this campaign.

3. **Prepare a table showing the NSPCC's target audiences, and the communications tools used to reach each of these groups.**

| Audience | Communications tools |
|---|---|
| General public | 'Pledge', door drop, advertising, Call to Action events, Posters |
| Donors | Mailing, advertising, plus the impact of general public activity |
| Collectors | PR |
| Businesses | PR |
| Campaigners | As 'general public' |
| New mothers | Pack & magazine |
| Schools | Events |

# Session 15

1.  **Advise Harley-Davidson of the key issues they should consider when planning communications with overseas markets.**

    The key issues for consideration are:

    Culture – beliefs, values and attitudes, affecting lifestyles. The propositions used to promote the bike in the USA may not suit the equivalent target market overseas.

    Media availability – they may not be able to use an identical mix, because of lack of availability or suitability of media overseas. Technology differs in the stage of its development, and this will also impact.

2.  **Recommend either a standardisation or adaptation approach for the marketing communications to overseas markets, justifying your recommendation.**

    This may differ from area to area, but I would recommend a standardised approach for Europe, as culture will be similar within the target group.

3.  **Harley-Davidson has decided to use an Agency to help with their overseas communications. Advise them of the issues they need to consider when selecting an Agency.**

    Many agencies have expanded to meet the needs of their key clients, so Harley-Davidson may find an Agency with its Head Office in the USA, and offices in most countries/regions that it wishes to target. This is an ideal scenario.

    If this is not possible, they will have to choose between an Agency in the home market, that understands them and their product and target customer group, or an Agency overseas in the local market that understands more of the culture, language and media availability, but is more difficult to control.

# Appendix 2

# Syllabus

# Integrated marketing communications

## Aims and Objectives

■ To develop an understanding of the formulation and implementation of integrated marketing communication plans and associated activities.

■ To enable you to manage marketing communications within a variety of different contexts.

■ To encourage you to recognise, appreciate and contribute to the totality of an organisation's system of communications with both internal and external audiences; to help you to be aware of the processes, issues and vocabulary associated with integrated marketing communications so that you can make an effective contribution within your working environment.

## Learning Outcomes

By the end of this module, you should be able to:

■ Determine the context in which marketing (and corporate) communications are to be implemented in order to improve effectiveness and efficiency, understand the key strategic communication issues arising from the contextual analysis and prepare (integrated) marketing communications plans.

■ Determine promotional objectives, explain positioning and develop perceptual maps and suggest ways in which offerings can be positioned in different markets.

■ Formulate marketing communications strategies with particular regard to consumers, business-to-business markets, members of the marketing channel and wider stakeholder audiences such as employees, financial markets, environmental groups, competitors and local communities.

■ Determine specific communication activities based upon knowledge of the key characteristics of the target audience and the influence of product positioning.

■ Determine appropriate levels of marketing communications expenditure/ appropriation.

■ Be aware of the impact and contribution technology makes to marketing communications.

■ Appreciate the issues associated with cross-border marketing communications.

■ Advise on the impact corporate communications can have on both internal and external audiences and their role in the development of integrated marketing communications.

## Indicative Content and Weighting

### 1.1 Strategic Marketing Communications (20%)

1.1.1 A definition and appreciation of the scope and dimensions of marketing and corporate communications.

1.1.2 A contextual analysis understanding and justification for marketing and corporate communication strategies.

1.1.3 The strategic significance and impact of integrated marketing communications.

1.1.4 Identify key (strategic) communication issues that might influence an organisation's marketing communications.

1.1.5 The appreciation and recognition of the importance of ethical and technological influences on promotional activities and to be aware of the social responsibilities organisations have towards the way they communicate with their target audience.

### 1.2 Developing a Theoretical Understanding of Marketing Communications (20%)

1.2.1 Understanding the key drivers associated with information processing and buyer decision-making processes.

1.2.2 Communication issues for internal and external audiences.

1.2.3 The role of personal influences on the communication process.

### 1.3 Managing the Marketing Communications Process (40%)

1.3.1 The determination and appreciation of the prevailing and future contextual conditions as a means of deriving and developing promotional strategies and plans.

1.3.2 The target marketing process as a means of identifying significant promotional opportunities.

1.3.3 Determining promotional objectives and selecting positioning opportunities.

1.3.4 Identify, select and formulate integrated promotional strategies ensuring reference is made to:

i) Push, pull and profile strategies.

ii) Any existing or proposed branding activities.

iii) The Internet and e-commerce activities relating to both consumer-to-business and business-to-business markets.

1.3.5 Selecting appropriate promotional mixes.

1.3.6 Determining message styles and key media goals.

1.3.7 Deciding upon the level and allocation of the promotional spend.

1.3.8 Managing internal and external resources necessary for successful promotional activities.

1.3.9 Managing and developing product and corporate brands.

1.3.10 Evaluating the outcomes of promotional activities.

## 1.4 Evaluation of Different Types of Marketing Communication Campaigns (10%)

1.4.1 Knowledge and understanding of different campaigns from different contexts (incl. FMCG, business to business, services and public sectors, and not-for-profit organisations.

1.4.2 Consideration of the competitive conditions, available resources, stage in the product life cycle and any political, economic, social or technological factors that might be identified as influencing the development of a campaign.

## 1.5 Cross-Border Marketing Communications (10%)

1.5.1 Cultural, social and media influences.

1.5.2 Organisational type and communication approaches.

1.5.3 The Adaption/Standardisation debate.

1.5.4 Agency structure and support.

**Note:** The words "promotional" and "marketing communications" are used interchangeably.

# Appendix 3

## Specimen examination paper

The Chartered
Institute of Marketing

# Postgraduate Diploma in Marketing

## Integrated Marketing Communications

**9.51:** **Integrated Marketing Communications**

**Time:** **14.00-17.00**

**Date:** **4th December, 2001**

3 Hours Duration

This examination is in two sections.

**PART A** – Is compulsory and worth 40% of total marks.

**PART B** – Has **SIX** questions, select **THREE**. Each answer will be worth 20% of the total marks.

**DO NOT** repeat the question in your answer, but show clearly the number of the question attempted on the appropriate pages of the answer book.

Rough workings should be included in the answer book and ruled through after use.

© The Chartered Institute of Marketing

# Postgraduate Diploma in Marketing

## 9.51:    Integrated Marketing Communications

## PART A

### AP Engineering

AP Engineering (AP) is a privately owned civil engineering company, employing approximately 4,200 people in the Asia Pacific region. The company designs and manages the building of major civil engineering projects in a variety of vertical market sectors.

The company wins contracts by bidding for client-specified projects and offering the best (perceived) value for money. The problem with this approach is that the appointed civil engineering company has limited input to the original requirement/ specification and, as soon as the project is completed, its involvement is normally terminated. Perhaps even more importantly, the margins earned on such projects are notoriously slim, so in order to grow the business, higher margins need to be generated.

Following a review of the business, AP's new strategy is based upon a total engineering service, one which centres on client needs and their total project requirements, rather than the previous engineering/product focus. In other words, the company now adopts a relationship marketing approach. The emphasis is upon providing added value by shifting the offering both upstream and downstream. Therefore, AP Engineering now provides three connected offerings.

a.    The front-end work, which involves undertaking the planning and risk analysis work for its clients.

b.    The core work, which is about the design and build aspect of the project.

c.    The tail-end work, which is essentially Facilities Management.

Among the many advantages this strategic approach presents, there are two significant benefits. The first lies in the substantially higher margins that the front- and tail-end work attracts. The second concerns the reduced 'resource' wastage by being able to help accurately define the client problem at the earliest possible stage in the project life cycle.

In order to develop and implement this strategy, AP has had to evolve a new skills mix, namely Asset Management and Facilities Management skills. AP chose to purchase a number of small consultancies and formed alliances with other targeted companies specialising in these particular skill areas.

Whilst this might sound reasonably straightforward, AP has had to address further issues concerning the development of a suitable commercial culture for the established employees and those new to the enlarged organisation. The company now views each project as a commercial activity and all employees must adopt increased levels of commercial awareness (e.g. project risk assessment, the importance of working within budget and invoicing on time). In addition, the employees of the newly acquired organisations have to be incorporated into the values and corporate philosophy of the new company culture. A further issue concerns the way the company presents itself to clients and other key stakeholders.

The organisation is deliberately seeking to develop closer client relationships based upon trust and empathy. It has done this by improving understanding of its clients' business, by getting involved right from the start of a new project, by completing projects on time and within budget, and by a willingness to share sensitive information. It also helps that the AP Engineering brand is highly visible and has developed a credible reputation based upon clients' perceived value.

The level of communication frequency between client and AP Engineering varies across the life of a project. There is a great deal of communication at the outset of a project as the brief is determined by all parties. As the project moves to the design phase, the level of communication tends to fall. However, projects often run tight on their deadlines; hence interorganisational, and even intraorganisational communication levels intensify in an attempt to resolve on-site problems as quickly as possible.

The company realises that personal contact is the most significant communication tool used in the development and maintenance of client relationships but the company is undecided about its communication strategy, and has asked you, in your capacity as Marketing Communications Consultant, for your advice.

## PART A

### Question 1.

As a Marketing Communications Consultant, advise AP with regard to the following questions:

a.      Identify a communication strategy that AP should pursue in the next year.

**(5 marks)**

b.      What is the justification for your strategy?

**(10 marks)**

c.      Which tools of the promotional mix might best be used to implement this strategy? Why?

**(10 marks)**

d.      What might be the core message that needs to be delivered over the next year?

**(5 marks)**

e.      Make a list of the issues that AP might consider before implementing an integrated marketing communications policy.

**(10 marks)**
**(40 marks in total)**

## PART B – Answer THREE Questions Only

### Question 2.

An office furniture manufacturing company is about to launch a new range of products.

a.  Explain what is meant by a push communication strategy and contrast this with a pull communication strategy.

**(10 marks)**

b.  Briefly outline the main characteristics of the marketing communications mix used to reach members of the marketing channel.

**(10 marks)**
**(20 marks in total)**

### Question 3.

As Brand Manager with a telecommunications company, and as part of a management of change process, you have been invited to explain the positioning concept to colleagues in the finance department.

Prepare notes which:

a.  Explain what positioning means.

**(8 marks)**

b.  Evaluate the importance of the concept, illustrating your points with examples from a sector of your choice.

**(12 marks)**
**(20 marks in total)**

### Question 4.

As the owner and manager of a company that rents holiday apartments to members of the public:

a.  Explain the advantages of using Internet-based communications.

**(10 marks)**

b.  Evaluate the role of offline communications when pursuing an online branding strategy.

**(10 marks)**
**(20 marks in total)**

## Question 5.

Appraise the role and significance of marketing communications for organisations operating in international business to business markets. Use examples to illustrate your points.

**(20 marks)**

## Question 6.

You are the Marketing Manager for a charity and the concept of perceived risk has been brought to your attention. Identify the main types of perceived risk and evaluate the influence of marketing communications on the management of risks, as they might affect your organisation.

**(20 marks)**

## Question 7.

You are reviewing the communication policies of large retail organisations (e.g. supermarkets) in a country of your choice. Using examples to illustrate your answer:

a.     Discuss the advantages of using an above-the-line branding strategy.

**(10 marks)**

b.     Compare this strategy with one that focuses on sales promotions.

**(10 marks)**
**(20 marks in total)**

# Appendix 4

# Feedback to the examination paper

The following do not represent full specimen answers to the Examination Paper, but look at:

■ the rationale for the question – what the examiner is looking for.

■ the best way to structure your answer.

■ the key points that you should have included, and expanded upon.

■ how marks for the question might have been allocated.

■ the main syllabus area that is being assessed.

Note that many of the key points are represented here in the form of bullet point lists. All of these points should be expanded in your answer, unless the examiner **specifically** asks for a bullet point list.

You should also remember that this paper is all about communications and you should make your answers coherent and professional in terms of presentation.

The timings given for each part of each question allow a little time for reading the case study, planning your answers, and choosing which questions you will answer. Remember to follow the instructions on the paper.

## Part A

## Question 1.

The Case Study for this paper looks at a **privately owned engineering company**, and asks you for **advice about marketing communications strategy** for the company. Each section of the question looks for a different topic to be covered – the **identification and justification** of a **strategy** for the **next year**, recommendation of **appropriate promotional mix tools**, a **core message**, and a list of **considerations before implementation** of the strategy.

The important thing to remember about approaching the mini-case question is that you must apply the **concepts** that the examiner is looking for to the **context** and situation described in the case and/or the question. With every question that is broken up into sections, you also need to consider how marks are spread across the various parts of the question, as this should dictate how much time you allocate to each part.

a. In this first part of the question, the Examiner is looking for you to suggest a **profile strategy** for AP Engineering in the next year. (You might also suggest a **pull strategy, after** the profile has been established.) It asks you to **identify a communication strategy**, and as only 5 marks are allocated you would not need to much more than to identify the correct strategy and express it briefly, but in the **context** of the Case Study.

There are 5 marks for this part of the question, so you should spend approximately 5-6 minutes answering it.

*Syllabus – 1.3.4*

b. This next part of the question asks you to **justify your recommendation** in a. This involves some understanding and interpretation of the scenario in the Case Study, and might include the following key points:

■ **change in business strategy** needs to obtain buy-in of existing staff.

■ **acquisitions** – need to bring staff of other organisations on board, and develop an integrated culture.

■ profile strategy will help communicate a **consistent message** to **internal and external** audiences.

There are 10 marks for this part of the question, so you should spend approximately 15 minutes answering it.

*Syllabus – 1.1.2 & 1.1.4*

c. This part of the question asks you to select the most appropriate promotional tools for the scenario, and linked back to the previous answers. Remembering that the key strategy is '**profile**', and to **internal as well as external** audiences, this would suggest:

■ **PR**

■ **Conferences and training for internal audience**

■ **Corporate advertising** (rather than pull – advertising of services)

■ **Exhibitions**

These can be justified through links to your answer to part b.

There are 10 marks for this part of the question, so you should spend approximately 15 minutes answering it.

*Syllabus – 1.3.5*

d. Again, there are only 5 marks for this part, so do not spend too much time. It asks for **'core' message**, so should be a corporate message about the new organisation.

There are 5 marks for this part of the question, so you should spend approximately 5-6 minutes answering it.

*Syllabus – 1.3.6*

e. The key word in this part of the question is **implementation**. Ideally, you need to link back to the **objectives** to be achieved, and list **resource issues** relevant to the scenario. For example, will a senior representative from management be available to 'champion' the campaign? How should events be scheduled? How will budget be allocated? How will events be co-ordinated? How will the plan be monitored and evaluated?

There are 10 marks for this part of the question, so you should spend approximately 15 minutes answering it.

*Syllabus – 1.3.8*

## Question 2.

This question concerns an **office furnishing manufacturing company**, and a **new product range launch**. This sets the scene in a **business to business** context, and asks specifically about the **channel** to market.

a. The first part of this question asks you to contrast a **push** communication strategy with a **pull** strategy.

You should explain the **difference between the two strategies**, using **examples** to demonstrate your understanding.

Key points:

| Push | Pull |
|---|---|
| Targets members of distribution channel. | Targets end users of product. |
| Emphasis on building relationships – trust and commitment. | Raises awareness of products and 'pulls' customers to suppliers. |
| Personal selling helps to personalise message. | Advertising in trade press might be used. |
| With office furnishings, audience might be office furniture distributors/retailers. | Audience might be buyers/ purchasing managers of businesses. |

There are 10 marks for this part of the question, so you should spend approximately 15 minutes answering it.

*Syllabus – 1.3.4*

b. This part of the question asks you to look at the **promotional tools** which are most appropriate for reaching **members of the marketing channel**.

**Personal selling** helps to **personalise message**. You should then go on to explain why this appropriate for this audience – **demonstrate** new product range, **provide technical information**, post purchase **training, relationship building including building trust.**

There are 10 marks for this part of the question, so you should spend approximately 15 minutes answering it.

*Syllabus – 1.3.5*

## Question 3.

There are several key words setting the context of this question – **Brand Manager, telecommunications company (so service), management of change, positioning**, and, your **audience**, colleagues in the finance department.

a. The first part of the question looks for you to **define positioning**, and how it fits with segmentation and targeting. You would then need to explain various **positioning strategies**, and the **benefits** positioning offers, linked to the **context** of the question.

There are 8 marks for this part of the question, so you should spend approximately 12 minutes answering it.

*Syllabus – 1.3.3*

b. This section of the question gives you the option to use an **example of your choice**. It has a higher proportion of the marks, and you should therefore split your time accordingly.

The question asks you to **evaluate the importance** of the concept of positioning. Your discussion around this should be illustrated with **examples** to demonstrate your understanding. Key points include –

- ■ **Differentiates** from the competition.
- ■ Offers potential to achieve **competitive advantage**.
- ■ Helps deal with '**noise**' from other brands.
- ■ Can be 'managed' to achieve a new 'position' in buyers' minds – **repositioning** – although this is not easy, as it involves **changing attitudes**.

There are 12 marks for this part of the question, so you should spend approximately 16 minutes answering it.

*Syllabus – 1.4.1*

# Question 4.

a.

The context of this question is again very clear – **owner/manager** of company **letting holiday apartments to members of the public**.

■ **Write in role.**

■ Link the **benefits and advantages of Internet based communications** to the letting of holiday apartments.

■ Benefits might include:
  ■ **Interactivity.**
  ■ **Reduced costs.**
  ■ **Speed.**
  ■ **Booking online.**
  ■ **Competitive advantage.**
  ■ **Improved service.**

There are 10 marks for this part of the question, so you should spend approximately 15 minutes answering it.

*Syllabus – 1.3.4*

b.

■ **Write in role.**

■ Link the **role of offline communications** to the use of **Internet communications** in letting of holiday apartments.

■ Uses might include:
  ■ **To help build on line brand.**
  ■ **To bring traffic to the site.**
  ■ **To provide information.**
  ■ **To give consistency of message.**
  ■ **To remind customers and get them to return to the site.**

There are 10 marks for this part of the question, so you should spend approximately 15 minutes answering it.

*Syllabus – 1.3.5*

## Question 5.

This question brings together **many aspects** of Integrated Marketing Communications, and it is important to respond to all of these:

- **The role of marketing communications.**
- **In business to business markets.**
- **Communicating across borders.**
- **Use examples.**

Key points to expand upon, using examples, include:

- **DRIP factors – role of communications.**
- **Role in B2B markets specifically, and characteristics of these markets.**
- **Choice of promotional mix tools.**
- **International issues – standardisation/adaptation and culture and media availability.**

There are 20 marks for this question, so you should spend approximately 30 minutes answering it.

*Syllabus – 1.5*

## Question 6.

As Question 5., this question brings together a **number of key issues**, all of which should be responded to. The key issues in the this question are:

- **Context is not for profit – specifically a charity.**
- **Communications issue is perceived risk.**
- **Question asks how communications can be used to respond to perceived risks.**

Key points to cover include:

- **Explanation of perceived risk and link to not for profit.**
- **Types of risk – performance, physical, financial, social, ego, time.**
- **How marketing communications can be used in each case – using charity as the example.**

There are 20 marks for this question, so you should spend approximately 30 minutes answering it.

*Syllabus – 1.2.1 & 1.4.1*

# Question 7.

a. This final question assesses your knowledge and understanding of communication policies in **large retail organisations** – **supermarkets** specifically.

The first part asks about the **advantages** of **above-the-line branding** strategy. Key points include:

■ **Define above the line.**

■ **Explain branding.**

■ **Advantages of above the line** – **impact, effectiveness of mass communication, low relative costs, particularly in this context.**

■ **Role of above the line in establishing and maintaining positive brand associations.**

■ **Use examples linked to supermarket.**

There are 10 marks for this part of the question, so you should spend approximately 15 minutes answering it.

*Syllabus – 1.3.4*

b. This second part of the question links back to the first. It asks you to **compare above the line** (in part a) to **sales promotion** – a **below the line strategy**. Key points to cover include:

■ **Definition of below the line.**

■ **Assessment of whether sales promotion can be used to build a brand. Traditional view – no – as could do the opposite. However, developments in technology now allow it to be used in this way – key points – must help build through a consistent association.**

■ **Use examples linked to supermarket.**

There are 10 marks for this part of the question, so you should spend approximately 15 minutes answering it.

*Syllabus – 1.3.5*

# Appendix 5

# Assessment guidance

**The method used for assessment of candidates at Diploma level is Examination.**

The Chartered Institute of Marketing has traditionally used professional, externally set examinations as the means of assessment for the Certificate, Advanced Certificate and Postgraduate Diploma in Marketing.

The information in this appendix will:

■ Provide hints and tips to help you prepare for the examination.

■ Manage your time effectively in preparing for assessment.

## Examinations

Each subject differs slightly from the others, and the style of question will differ between module examinations. All are closed book examinations apart from Analysis and Decision (see below).

For all Diploma examinations, the examination paper consists of two sections:

### Part A – Mini-case, scenario or article

This section has a mini-case, scenario or article with compulsory questions. You are required to make marketing or sales decisions based on the information provided. You will gain credit for the decisions and recommendations you make on the basis of the analysis itself. This is a compulsory section of the paper designed to evaluate your practical marketing skills.

### Part B – Examination questions

You will have a choice from a number of questions, and when answering those you select, ensure you understand the context of the question. Rough plans for each answer are strongly recommended.

The examination for **Analysis and Decision** takes the form of a Case Study. This is mailed out 4 weeks before the examination and posted on the CIM student web site (www.cimvirtualinstitute.com) at the same time. Analysis and preparation should be completed during these four weeks. The questions asked in the examination will require strategic marketing decisions and actions. The question paper will also include additional unseen information about the Case Study. The traditional form of the examination is an open book examination. However,

CIM is piloting a 'closed book' form, which centres can elect to undertake by registering with CIM. Further details can be found in the Companion for the Analysis & Decision module or obtained from CIM.

## CIM code of conduct for examinations

If being assessed by examination you will receive examination entry details, which will include a leaflet entitled "Rules for Examinations". You should read these carefully, as you will be penalised by CIM if you are in breach of any of these rules.

Most of the rules are common sense. For example, for closed book examinations you are not allowed to take notes or scrap paper into the examination room, and you must use the examination paper supplied to make rough notes and plans for your answer.

If you are taking the Analysis and Decision examination, ensure that you do take your notes in with you, together with a copy of the Case Study.

## Hints and tips

There are a number of places you can access information to help you prepare for your examination, if you are being assessed by this method. Your tutor will give you good advice, and exam hints and tips can also be found on the CIM student web site (www.cimvirtualinstitute.com).

Some fundamental points are listed below.

■ Read the question carefully, and think about what is being asked before tackling the answer. The examiners are looking for knowledge, application and context. Refer back to the question to help you put your answer in the appropriate context. Do not just regurgitate theory.

■ Consider the presentation style of your answer. For example, if you are asked to write a report, then use a report format with number headings and not an essay style.

■ Structure – plan your answer to make it easy for the examiner to see the main points you are making.

■ Timing – spread your time in proportion to the marks allocated, and ensure that all required questions are answered.

■ Relevant examples – the examiners expect relevant theory to be illustrated by practical examples. These can be drawn from your own experience, reading of current journals and newspapers, or just your own observations. You could visit "Hot Topics" on the CIM student web site to see discussions of topical marketing issues and practice.

## Managing your time

What is effective time management? It is using wisely one of your most precious resources, TIME, to achieve your key goals. You need to be aware of how you spend your time each day. Set priorities, so you know what's important to you, and what isn't. You need to establish goals for your study, work and family life, and plan how to meet those goals. Through developing these habits you will be better able to achieve the things that are important to you.

When study becomes one of your key goals you may find that, temporarily, something has to be sacrificed in favour of time needed for reading, writing notes, writing up assignments, preparing for group assessment, etc. It will help to "get people on your side". Tell people that you are studying and ask for their support – these include direct family, close friends and colleagues at work.

Time can just slip through your fingers if you don't manage it, and that's wasteful! When you are trying to balance the needs of family, social life, working life and study, there is a temptation to leave assignments until the deadline is nearly upon you. Don't give in to this temptation! Many students complain about the heavy workload towards the end of the course, when, in fact, they have had several months to work on assignments, and they have created this heavy workload themselves.

Knowing how to manage your time wisely can help you:

- Reduce pressure when you're faced with deadlines or a heavy schedule.
- Be more in control of your life by making better decisions about how to use your time.
- Feel better about yourself because you're using your full potential to achieve.
- Have more energy for things you want or need to accomplish.
- Succeed more easily because you know what you want to do and what you need to do to achieve it.

## Finally...

Remember to continue to apply your new skills within your job. Study and learning that is not applied just wastes your time, effort and money! Good luck with your studies!

# Index

See also the Glossary on page 235.

You may find referring back to the Learning Outcomes and the Summary of Key Points at the beginning and end of each Session will aid effective use of the Index.

Only where subjects are relevantly discussed or defined are they indexed.